The aim of this study is to show that the Evangelists consciously set out to distinguish Jesus' time from their own. Professor Lemcio thus highlights the literary skill of the Evangelists, and draws attention to the sophisticated relationship between idiom and time which the gospels exhibit. He argues that the gospels are not essentially or primarily expansions of Christian oral proclamation represented elsewhere in the New Testament. Kerygmatic expressions of "faith" found outside of the gospels were *not* projected back on to the narrative: the Evangelists do not write with such explicit self-consciousness.

SOCIETY FOR NEW TESTAMENT STUDIES

MONOGRAPH SERIES

General Editor: G. N. Stanton

68

THE PAST OF JESUS IN THE GOSPELS

The past of Jesus
in the gospels

EUGENE E. LEMCIO

Professor of New Testament
Seattle Pacific University
Seattle, Washington

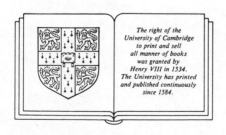

The right of the
University of Cambridge
to print and sell
all manner of books
was granted by
Henry VIII in 1534.
The University has printed
and published continuously
since 1584.

CAMBRIDGE UNIVERSITY PRESS

CAMBRIDGE
NEW YORK   PORT CHESTER
MELBOURNE   SYDNEY

Published by the Press Syndicate of the University of Cambridge
The Pitt Building, Trumpington Street, Cambridge CB2 1RP
40 West 20th Street, New York, NY 10011, USA
10 Stamford Road, Oakleigh, Melbourne 3166, Australia

© Cambridge University Press 1991

First published 1991

Printed in Great Britain at
the University Press, Cambridge

British Library cataloguing in publication data
Lemcio, Eugene E. *1942–*
The past of Jesus in the Gospels.
1. Bible. N.T. Gospels – Critical studies
I. Title II. Series
226.06

Library of Congress cataloguing in publication data
Lemcio, Eugene E.
The past of Jesus in the gospels / Eugene E. Lemcio.
    p. cm.
Includes bibliographical references.
ISBN 0 521 40113 5
1. Bible. N.T. Gospels – Criticism, interpretation, etc.
2. Kerygma. 3. Jesus Christ – Historicity. 4. Jesus Christ –
Biography – Sources. 5. Jesus Christ – History of doctrines – Early
church, ca. 30-600. I. Title.
BS2555.2.L385 1990
226'.066–dc20   90-40228   CIP

ISBN 0 521 40113 5 hardback

To The Reverend Professor C. F. D. Moule,

Fellow of Clare College,
Emeritus Lady Margaret's Professor of Divinity
in the University of Cambridge,
F.B.A., C.B.E., D.D. (St. Andrews and Cambridge)
mentor, example, and friend of two decades

CONTENTS

ACKNOWLEDGMENTS

Two research grants from Seattle Pacific University enabled me to produce earlier drafts of the chapters on Matthew and Luke. But it was a generous research fellowship from Tyndale House that enabled our family of four to return to Cambridge and live there for five months during the Easter and Summer Terms of 1987. This leave would not have been possible except for the creative administration of Drs. David Dickerson, Larry Shelton, and my colleagues in the School of Religion that allowed for a "research load reassignment". Another grant, this time from the Faculty Research Committee, funded travel to Cambridge for two weeks during my sabbatical in the autumn of 1989 for final checking and editing. Dr. Bruce Winter, Warden at Tyndale House, made it possible for me to take up residence under the auspices of the original fellowship. His enthusiasm and encouragement merit my heartiest thanks.

To my wife, Miriam, is due gratitude for converting the initial rough manuscripts into a typescript. Acting Dean Dr. Robert Drovdahl generously allowed me the use of equipment in the School of Religion and the expertise of our assistants. Marcy DeMarco, Nancy Dinger, Beth Haight, Charla Kemp, and Dr. Carl Roseveare patiently and cheerfully initially "processed" these words onto the computer disks that made revision and printing so much easier.

Subsequently, it was my colleague, Dr. Les Steele, who helped me to make the painful transition from the age of the quill to the brink of modernity in the use of computer technology. My friend and student Carla Wall read the entire manuscript, saving me from several kinds of errors, and made astute observations throughout. In the final stages, it was Rikk Watts of Tyndale House whose generosity, cheerfulness, and wizardry caused the work to be produced in its penultimate form. The equipment, services, and people there have few equals. And the entire enterprise would not have been possible apart from the editor of the Monograph Series, Professor Graham

Stanton, whose patient and unfailing help is impossible to praise adequately.

Finally, I should like to thank the Syndics of the Cambridge University Press for giving written permission to publish substantial portions of chapter 2 which appeared as "The intention of the evangelist, Mark" in *NTS*, 32 (1986), 187–206. "The unifying kerygma of the New Testament", was originally published in two parts: *JSNT*, 33 (1988), 3–17 and 38 (1990), 3–11. I am indebted to the Sheffield University Press for giving written permission to combine them as the appendix.

ABBREVIATIONS

AB	Anchor Bible
ASNU	*Acta seminarii neotestamentici upsaliensis*
BETL	*Bibliotheca ephemeridum theologicarum lovaniensium*
BTB	*Biblical Theology Bulletin*
CBA	Catholic Biblical Association
EvT	*Evangelische Theologie*
HBT	*Horizons in Biblical Theology*
HTK	*Herders Theologischer Kommentar*
ICC	International Critical Commentary
Int	*Interpretation*
IVP	Inter-Varsity Press
JAAR	*Journal of the American Academy of Religion*
JBL	*Journal of Biblical Literature*
JETS	*Journal of the Evangelical Theological Society*
JSNT	*Journal for the Study of the New Testament*
JSNTSS	Journal for the Study of the New Testament Supplement Series
JSOT	*Journal for the Study of the Old Testament*
JTC	*Journal for Theology and the Church*
JTS	*Journal of Theological Studies*
LCL	Loeb Classical Library
NCBC	New Century Bible Commentary
NICNT	New International Commentary on the New Testament
NIGTC	New International Greek Testament Commentary
NTS	*New Testament Studies*
RGG	*Religion in Geschichte und Gegenwart*
SBLDS	Society of Biblical Literature Dissertation Series
SBLMS	Society of Biblical Literature Monograph Series

SBLRBS	Society of Biblical Literature Resources for Biblical Study
SBLSBS	Society of Biblical Literature Sources for Biblical Study
SBT	Studies in Biblical Theology
SCM	Student Christian Movement
SE	*Studia Evangelica*
SNTS	Society for New Testament Studies
SNTSMS	Society for New Testament Studies Monograph Series
SPCK	Society for the Promotion of Christian Knowledge
TC	*Traditio Christiana*
TDNT	*Theological Dictionary of the New Testament*
TST	Toronto Studies in Theology
TU	*Texte und Untersuchungen*
TynBul	*Tyndale Bulletin*
ZNW	*Zeitschrift für die neutestamentliche Wissenschaft*
ZTK	*Zeitschrift für Theologie und Kirche*

1

INTRODUCTION: FAITH, KERYGMA, GOSPELS

It would not be melodramatic to say that gospel study has entered a period of heady upheaval. The reigning though tenuous consensus among redaction critics has been dissolving without a newer one to take its place. Methods tried and true have been found wanting by a new generation of critics. The promise of redaction criticism to treat the gospels as wholes has finally been fulfilled by the appropriation of insights outside of biblical studies *per se*, from literary criticism. In the wake, some intriguing crossovers have occurred. At least one leading critic in the maturity of his career has moved from one discipline to the other.

An opportunist, observing this profusion of many and diverse techniques, might be tempted to ignore standard approaches. Of course a completely idiosyncratic method ought to be viewed with suspicion. But given the "state of the art," a reasoned fruitful approach sensitive to the gospels themselves and open to debate with opponents should not be turned aside. Such is the apologia offered for what follows. In this chapter, I shall state the thesis of the entire work, describe the method which confirms it, and then anticipate how both might fare among the various "schools" of criticism that dominate academic study of the gospels. However, I shall not merely report what potential objections might be. They will be analyzed and evaluated according to the "logic" and procedure characteristic of each. Of course, such engagement will not end here. In the chapters that follow, I shall attempt to provide further evidence and argument, gospel-by-gospel, beginning with Mark, the fountainhead of the written tradition.

Thesis

I intend to show that the Evangelists, to an extent heretofore unrecognized, produced narratives distinguishing Jesus' time from their own. This effort transcended merely putting verbs in past tenses and

1

dividing the account into pre- and post-resurrection periods. Rather, they took care that terminology appropriate to the Christian era does not appear beforehand. Vocabulary characteristic prior to Easter falls by the wayside afterwards. Words common to both bear a different nuance in each. Idiom suits the time. And these are not routine or incidental expressions. They reveal what Jesus the protagonist and the Evangelists as narrators believe about the gospel, the Christ, the messianic task, the nature of salvation, etc.

This much is apparent from the study of internal evidence. Evidence outside of the gospels provides something of a control and enables one to know how to interpret the significance of these results. The gospels are not essentially or primarily expansions of Christian oral proclamation represented elsewhere in the New Testament. Kerygmatic expressions of "faith" found outside of the gospels were *not* projected back onto the narrative. None of the Evangelists writes with such explicit self-consciousness. Furthermore, expectations for idiomatic and linguistic verisimilitude in Greco-Roman historical and biographical writing *were* met and often exceeded by the Evangelists. Such data may prove useful in separate efforts to reconstruct the course of Jesus' life. And the literary critic can employ them to describe more fully the literary art of the narrators. Attempts to inhibit these two enterprises by calling them impossible, irrelevant, or illegitimate cannot be justified.

Method

In the confusing state of affairs alluded to above and evaluated recently by Robert Morgan,[1] some scholars are quite ready to rank the gifts bequeathed by generations of critics according to "a more excellent way." For example, in a welcome revision of Stephen Neill's much admired survey of NT research, Tom Wright has all but called for a reversing of steps in the critical process:

> I would ... propose that work on the Gospels should be undertaken in the reverse order to that which is usually imagined to be normal or correct. Historical criticism, along the lines begun by the Third Quest, and literary criticism, taking the Gospels in the first instance as wholes and using all the tools currently available [including comparative religions], are the primary disciplines. Form-criticism and Source-criticism are essentially secondary, as can be seen by

their tacit, and thoroughly-warranted, neglect by modern students of history and literature.[2]

However, neglect by non-specialists cannot itself be a reason. Rather, the very possibility of form criticism can be called into question if the logic of a thoroughgoing redaction criticism is pressed. Wright is on surer ground when he observes, "If the evangelists' work of redaction was as heavy as some would claim, our chances of recovering early forms, let alone sources, are at the mercy of so much speculation and so many unverifiable hypotheses that we are in a bad state indeed. How can we advance?"[3] Although one might wish to wait for a "super-method" that would embrace and integrate all legitimate ones, the presses continue to roll.

Without presuming a definitive answer to so important a query, I suggest that the way forward lies in beginning with the firmest data available, i.e. working from the best- to the lesser-known to the unknown: literary criticism, redaction criticism, comparative religions (Judaism, hellenism), historical criticism (life-of-Jesus research). Despite the caveats leveled later against certain versions of redaction criticism, I have not rejected either the premises or practices of the method *in toto*. Rather, I want to claim a place to stand between two disciplines. Because I affirm the redaction-critical commitment to treat the gospels as intentional compositions with purpose and plan, I have conducted the analysis at the literary level (i.e. the redactional product) without resorting to the past of Jesus or to the "present" of the Evangelists' communities. The literary investigation can and should be conducted before either of these historical operations is done. Each will be enhanced and enriched as a result.[4]

Yet I will not perform a full-scale literary-critical analysis. My goal is more specific. It fits more nearly with the attempt to determine voice(s) and tone(s).[5] However, in this case it will be various levels of theological tonality expressed throughout the gospel narratives. In practice, terms will always be examined within the range of meanings supplied by various historical contexts. But the ultimate objective will be to ascertain meanings *from within the text*. Their shades and gradations will depend upon the point being made by the narrator either directly or through the characters in the story.[6] Such is the burden of this monograph. A more specific account of the procedure is now in order.

My approach takes its cue from two studies conducted by C. F. D. Moule (the second is summarized in ch. 2). In "The Christology of

Acts," he investigated the use of ὁ κύριος in Luke's writings and discovered that the Third Evangelist rarely allows the *dramatis personae* of the gospel to employ this title in the fully confessional sense that became so common after Easter. Moule then suggested that the Evangelists might not be as guilty of reading other post-resurrection convictions into the narrative as is often alleged.[7] To confirm his suspicion required other examinations along broader fronts. Otherwise, it might be deemed idiosyncratic or exceptional. In other words, did Luke and his colleagues show the same restraint with other christologies that refer to Jesus' status? And what about the nature of the messianic task? Might the same be found with soteriology and mission, too?

Even though I have been able to answer these questions affirmatively, I do not go further and posit historicity. That requires a separate step. All that emerges is a profound reluctance on the part of the gospel writers to recount the story of Jesus in their own terms. Strictly speaking, one has achieved only a fuller understanding of the narrators' representation of the past. However, their commitment to preserve its content and idiom give one confidence to pursue the historical task. Historians, accustomed to analyzing unpromising and prejudicial data anyway, may find the effort in the case of the gospels more rewarding.

In conducting the search for evidence, I appealed to the most obvious expressions of each Evangelist's beliefs. A necessary but often overlooked step examines the hardest surface information before proceeding to the softer strata below. One should read the lines ahead of the spaces between them. Consequently, I turned first to the resurrection appearances. (In the case of Mark, of course, there was none to investigate; but his title proved useful.) Here was vocabulary by which to determine both the precise "Easter faith" of each Evangelist and the extent to which it was or was not imposed on the preceding narrative.

Often, the gospel writer's point of view appears in obvious editorial comments on the scene: "The Lord chose seventy others" (Luke 10:1). Here one can test the use of ὁ κύριος as Moule did. Matthew's concept of Scripture's fulfillment in Jesus belongs to the editorial framework of the narrative. Mark 1:1 is also such an instance: "the beginning of the gospel about Jesus Christ [God's Son]."

The next places to detect post-Easter beliefs were those instances where Jesus (usually in private and to the disciples) speaks of the future − either near or remote − but after his death. Examples are:

"Many will come in my name" (Mark 13:6), and "Whoever receives one of these little ones in my name" (Mark 9:37). Occasionally such future reference points appear in introductions (the birth narratives of Matt. 1–2, Luke 1–2). Preludes sometimes parallel postludes. Once again, the vocabulary here can be used to determine how much, if any, has been injected into the narrative.

On a different level, perhaps the subtlest task of all (and therefore the most contestable) is the search for clues provided by teaching given before the resurrection to various audiences. Especially distinctive are the public and private phases of Jesus' ministry. While one cannot claim in advance that the latter usually reflects an Evangelist's convictions, nevertheless the very fact that some topics are reserved for more restricted consumption makes one curious. Why were certain things not said to the crowds?

Once these data were gathered (including allied vocabulary, cognates, and ideas that naturally clustered together), I examined them according to various (alleged) sources, oral or written. Could the distinctions observed be maintained in the regions of text demarcated as triple tradition, Q, M, and L? Such an approach enabled the test to be conducted on a *number* of fronts using *several* key categories. Thus, even if half had to be ruled out as inappropriate or insufficient, then the case might still be capable of standing on three legs rather than six.

This appeal primarily to internal evidence need not otherwise be justified. However, the pressure from some redaction critics to view the results in such a way as to deny an historical or literary reading required attention to external data. This represents the most promising way of breaking the impasse between those who make opposing assertions. Consequently, I ranged beyond the gospels but within the NT to determine whether or not they may be regarded as written expansions of the oral Christian proclamation. The appendix provides the evidence and arguments against the connection.

Finally, the results of study based upon internal evidence were compared with literature outside of the NT altogether: biographical and historical writing in the ancient world. The aim was not to make a case for the gospels as history or biography. Instead, the task was more specific: to see how the Evangelists' attention to preserving earlier and other idiom squares with ancient efforts to do so. If they compared favorably, then here was another criterion by which to evaluate the claims of some redaction critics that such data might only be accounted for as expressions of rival Christian points of view.

Possible responses and antithesis

The thesis of page 1 will be congenial among two of three groups in critical circles. To those who have become convinced on other grounds that the gospels provide four portraits of Jesus that are in essence historically reliable, the statements above and data below will be corroborative,[8] since they appear to suggest that his very *manner* of speaking has been preserved.

The next group, literary critics concerned with the "story" or "narrative world" of the texts rather than the "real world" of Jesus, might say (they have not as yet), "These features belong to a fine story. A good yarn about the past needs to convey a remoteness of time and place through language. Such attention to detail makes for the best kind of historical fiction."[9] While I am unable by training to contribute to the development of literary critical theory or its application to the gospels, I may succeed in supplying grist for the mill. The phenomena summarized in the thesis statement may contribute to a more precise analysis of characterization, story, plot, voice, tone, and tension. Their appropriation will have to be accomplished by those who are expert enough in both fields to do them justice. It is not the job for an amateur who must also beware that, as in all fields of specialization (especially those which are being applied to others), debates rage amongst advocates along a broad spectrum.[10] And those proficient as "omniscient observers" will have to determine how the "Jesus of literature/narrative" fits among the "Jesus of history" and the "Christ of faith."

Among scholars who call themselves redaction critics, two different responses are possible. The most positive will come from those who on methodological grounds restrict their analyses to the *product(s)* of redaction. For them (they are sometimes called "composition critics"), attempts to discover the *process(es)* of redaction lack sufficient methodological control and rely on circular reasoning of an unacceptably high order. Like the literary critics, their primary datum is the final form of the text.[11] My conclusions will serve to elucidate further the theological interests which led the Evangelists to write as they did. Moreover, there are redaction critics who have not closed the door on historical research even though they maintain that theological interests have determined the adoption, adaptation, and arrangement of dominical traditions. Neither their presuppositions nor their conclusions rule out the possibility or the importance of discovering all that one can about Jesus. Although not many works have appeared which show precisely how the historical and redactional enterprises complement each other, some scholars find themselves at least open to the task.[12] Therefore, critics in this camp should not be adverse to my thesis as it attempts to articulate how the gospel writers represented Jesus' past in their narratives.

However, my claim will not go down well with exponents of what might be called classical redaction criticism. Scholars of this persuasion may object that my analysis makes the gospels out to be historical or biographical works when in fact they are unique as written kerygma and unlike anything ever written, ancient or modern. The distinctions which I have displayed do not delineate two different periods of time, before and after the resurrection. Rather, they reveal with even greater precision post-Easter conflicts among Christians holding different views about christology, salvation, faith, the gospel, discipleship, etc. Each Evangelist sought to resolve the tension or win the battle for the right side by making Jesus speak for him and his party while the disciples and others espouse inadequate or erroneous points of view.[13] The drama that unfolds on papyrus or parchment thus veils the polemical historical circumstances out of which the gospels emerged. Hence, redaction critics may attempt to enlist my results (minus the temporal claims which could be eliminated) in their cause: to illuminate further the *readers'* or *communities'* world rather than the "story world" of the text or the "real world" of Jesus.

Rejoinders

Obviously, since the last of these responses militates against my thesis, it will require the fullest rejoinder. (Although I shall interact with the issues throughout the book, it is necessary to treat them together at the outset in order to display the logic behind particular claims that might otherwise be missed.) As a point of departure, I quote in full the opening paragraphs of an essay by Günther Bornkamm which has been credited with launching redaction criticism:

> It has increasingly become an accepted result of New Testament inquiry and a principle of all Synoptic exegesis that the Gospels must be understood and interpreted in terms of *kerygma* and not as biographies of Jesus of Nazareth, that they do not fall into any category of the history of ancient literature, but that in content and form as a whole and in matters of detail they are determined and shaped on the basis

of faith in Jesus Christ. We owe the methodical establishing of this knowledge above all to form-critical research into the Gospels. This work put an end to the fiction which had for so long ruled critical investigation, that it would eventually be possible to distill from the Gospels a so-called life of Jesus, free from and untouched by any kind of 'over-painting' through the faith of the Church. Faith in Jesus Christ, the Crucified and Resurrected, is by no means a later stratum of the tradition, but its very foundation, and the place from which it sprang and grew and from which alone it is intelligible. From this faith in Jesus, the Crucified and Exalted, both characteristics of the primitive Christian tradition can be understood — the obvious pains taken to preserve the tradition about Jesus conscientiously and faithfully but at the same time the peculiar freedom with which this tradition is presented in detail. The evangelists do not hark back to some kind of church archives when they pass on the words and deeds of Jesus, but they draw them from the kerygma of the Church and serve this kerygma. Because Jesus is not a figure of the past and thus no museum piece, there can be no "archives" for the primitive Christian tradition about him, in which he is kept. This insight into the nature of the tradition about Jesus is confirmed in detail again and again.[14]

In this classic summary of form-critical convictions (which influence Bornkamm's and others' redaction-critical analysis), several central issues require special attention.

(1) *The gospels are products of faith in the crucified and risen Jesus.* A somewhat fuller way of putting this is that the gospel tradition both oral and written was preserved, altered, organized, and understood from the perspective of such a faith. At one level, there is little to quarrel about. However, unless "faith" in this statement is carefully defined and made gospel-specific, discussion will be subject to uncontrolled speculation and mere assertion. One can begin by eliminating the understanding of "faith" as "point of view." The gospels have an angle of vision, a bias, a *Tendenz*. But this quality is hardly distinctive since all literature, even chronicle, is ultimately written "according to."

The more existential meaning of faith does not qualify either. Rudolf Bultmann has observed that faith as that which effects a "relation to the person of Christ" emerged with the thought of Paul (Gal. 2:20) and John.[15] It was foreign to the thinking of the earliest church, both Palestinian and Gentile.[16] And one finds it lacking in the synoptic gospels also. The Evangelists do not make relation to the person of Christ the express motive or goal of their literary efforts. Within the narratives themselves, such language is absent. No one from the crowd offers or is invited to believe in Jesus. Furthermore, never is the response of the disciples either before or after the resurrection cast in these terms.[17] Jesus never charges them to elicit faith in him from the nations. They are to repent (Luke 24:47), be baptized, and obey Jesus' teaching (Matt. 28:19−20). Even John's Gospel (considered more fully below) conforms to this pattern in crucial places. If anything, Jesus seeks to relate his hearers *to God*, an achievement sometimes occurring through intermediaries *in addition* to Jesus: a child (Mark 9:37, Luke 9:48) and disciples (Matt. 10:40, John 13:20). However, here the language is that of receiving (δέχεσθαι) rather than believing. At Mark 9:37 Jesus even removes himself from the process (cf. John 12:44).

Belief that (in the sense of "assent to the message that"[18]) God raised the Jesus who had been crucified (Rom. 10:9−10) reflects the earliest expression of Christian faith, both Palestinian and Gentile.[19] Rather than being the mode of interpersonal, subjective communion with Christ, it means "only a relation to God on the basis of God's deed in Christ"[20] Divine action, not christocentric interaction, is the focus. And it is that which one can infer from the gospels. Although they do not say so, the Evangelists are obviously *convinced* that God raised Jesus from the dead. Of course, they believe a good deal more at this level: that he anointed Jesus with the Spirit and authorized his teaching with mighty works. However, the synoptists avoid appealing directly to the reader/hearer in order to elicit a corresponding conviction. Furthermore, no one within the narratives voluntarily or in response to Jesus' call believes that God will raise him from the dead. Nor does Jesus after that very event commission his disciples to call for such a response from the nations.

The synoptic mode seems to be broken or ignored by John. Believing in his person appears to be demanded frequently by Jesus himself before and after Easter. Yet, other Johannine expressions convey the sense of intimate communion more fully: "eating" and "drinking" his flesh and blood (ch. 6), "abiding" (ch. 15), and "knowing" (17:3). "Believing in," as Bultmann notes, may be shorthand for "belief in God's saving deed in Christ."[21] Such a meaning occurs in the Fourth Gospel in more than one notable crux. The Evangelist wants to get his readers "to come to believe [or, "to go on believing," the textual variant not affecting the point] that Jesus is the Christ, the Son of God" (20:31). This is primarily cognitive and "static." But at 17:21, Jesus prays that the world may believe *that God has sent him.* This focus on divine action (the sending) also occurs in two other significant passages (analyzed more fully later): 5:24 and 12:44. In the latter instance, Jesus removes himself as the subject of faith (as he removed himself as the subject of "receiving" in Mark 9:37). John wants his readers to accept as true his report that Jesus, as God's Son, best represents his interests and reveals his will.[22]

The importance of belaboring this point lies in demonstrating how considerably these definitions affect one's attitude to the tradition, oral and written. If faith means the mode of dwelling in the risen Christ, then those traditions will have served to promote such a relation between him and the readers/listeners. The gospels will have made possible a two-way conversation between the living Lord (through the words of the earthly Jesus) and the original recipients (voiced by disciples, Jewish authorities, the crowds). Communication of this sort is immediate and direct. There is no need for plot or story, before or after. Then and now become indistinguishable.

On this view, it is much easier to distance the gospels from historical or biographical writings, ancient and modern. Since Jesus lives in a way that Socrates no longer does, he will speak in a manner that Socrates cannot. The philosopher may utter timeless truths from the past. But Jesus conveys a relevant word to a particular situation in the present. The words of the former, because they are timeless, can be preserved intact for subsequent generations and contexts; they need merely to be adopted. But revelation *ad hoc* requires adaptation to later and other generations. Consequently, the oral and written traditions about Jesus, on this view, are bound to function more didactically.

However, if by faith we mean convictions about God's (reported) action in Jesus (raising him from the dead), then the point, conveyed in proto-narrative, comes across indirectly, "mediately," and more "objectively." The literature will function less didactically, story being the medium rather than what amounts to a form of address. What the risen Jesus "says" to me in any subsequent moment will be heard through an account of what he formerly "said." The mode is more subtle. Every statement will not necessarily speak with equal clarity. Some items might be quite obscure or even seem irrelevant at first hearing. Of course, the risks of such an estimate are obvious. Faith can become too cognitive and abstract, its dynamic, vital character lost to the past and frozen in a text. But the gains are considerable, too, because one is free to explore ancient and modern literature for clues about the ways in which narrative works. The author of Hebrews knows that the blood of Jesus "speaks a better word than the blood of Abel" (12:24). But he also insists that "by faith he, though dead, still speaks" (11:4).

(2) There is an analogous claim, the corollary, as it were, of the one about faith: *the gospels are to be understood in terms of kerygma, not of biography or history, ancient and modern.* Once again, it will make all the difference in the world what one means by "kerygma" and whether it will suit the gospels. Christians proclaimed what they believed. And the gospel tradition, oral and written, served this purpose, too.

But did Christians at first proclaim the *person* of Christ? One could get this impression by uncritically citing Bultmann's famous slogan without considering the context:

> As the synoptic tradition shows, the earliest Church resumed the message of Jesus and through its preaching passed it on. But Jesus was more than that to the Church: he was also the Messiah; hence that Church also proclaimed him, himself — and that is the essential thing to see. He who formerly had been the *bearer* of the message [about the dawning of God's Rule] was drawn into it and became its essential *content. The proclaimer became the proclaimed* ...[23]

From this statement alone, one could answer the opening question affirmatively. Yet immediately thereafter, Bultmann goes on to say,

> but the central question is: In what sense?
> It is clear ... that when Jesus was proclaimed as Messiah, it was *as the coming Messiah*, in other words, as Son of Man. Not his *return* as Messiah, but his *coming* as Messiah was expected.[24]

This view *"keeps quite within the frame of Jewish eschatological expectation."*[25] Consequently,

> neither the picture of the future is thereby basically remolded as yet, nor is man's relation to God understood anew. For the latter is *not yet* founded upon one's relation to the *person*

of Jesus [my italics], but is externally mediated, if he is nothing more than the Judge and Salvation-bringer whom Judaism also expected.[26]

I have quoted Bultmann at length so that his point (developed over sixty pages but often missed) will be understood. He did not mean that the early church had proclaimed the person of Jesus in the sense that it promised intimate communion with him. Rather, Jesus' message, which had focused on the imminent act of God, acquired in the Palestinian and pre-Pauline Gentile churches' kerygma a decisive christological component: God had acted decisively in raising him from the dead. This proclamation corresponds with the most widespread kerygmatic formula in the NT.[27]

But can the gospels be regarded as working in the service of this or another kerygma? Is it true to say that they are expanded, written versions of the orally proclaimed message? Amazingly, all four are silent on the matter. Not one author claims his work to be kerygma or gospel. The closest one comes is Mark 1:1. However, it is far from clear that 'Αρχὴ τοῦ εὐαγγελίου 'Ιησοῦ Χριστοῦ is the title of the entire document.[28] Even if it could be shown conclusively that the words were meant to embrace the whole, one would still not know whether to include the narrative in the gospel or to regard it as its prolegomenon. Matthew does not clarify matters at all. His work is βίβλος γενέσεως (1:1). Although critics contest the meaning and significance of the expression,[29] it is clear that Matthew, who had appropriated so much of Mark's form and structure, did not use εὐαγγέλιον to describe his work. Luke, who is the first to be "aware of the literary genre of his work and of the relationship of his work to previous similar writings"[30] calls it a διήγησις (1:1−4). John (in whose gospel the words εὐαγγέλιον/εὐαγγελίζεσθαι and κήρυγμα/κηρύσσειν fail to appear) refers to his opus as a βιβλίον (20:30; cf. 21:25). Indeed, Helmut Koester has shown that the use of εὐαγγέλιον "as a technical designation for a written document by Marcion ... appears as a revolutionary novelty."[31] Prior to this time (first and early second century), "εὐαγγέλιον is always and every-where" understood as the proclamation of God's salvation in Christ or the coming of the kingdom.[32]

When one moves from the gospels *per se* to the kerygmata that they report, the following dramatic phenomena emerge. Table 1 displays the results which are subsequently expounded more fully in the text according to the method described above (JB = John the

Baptist, J = Jesus, D = Disciples, italicized material indicates *differences* between pre- and post-Easter narratives):

Table 1

Kerygma and gospel	
Pre-Easter	Post-Easter

MATTHEW

		Pre-Easter	Post-Easter
	JB	*proclaim KH drawn near*	
	J	*proclaim KH drawn near*	
	D	*proclaim KH drawn near* [*Israel only*]	
	J	*this gospel of the KG will be proclaimed* *wherever this gospel is proclaimed*	

make disciples [*all nations*] ⟨ baptize / teach

MARK

| | JB | proclaiming baptism of repentance for release from sins proclaimed coming of Stronger One, baptism with HS | |
| | J | *proclaiming* gospel of *God* Kingdom of God drawn near necessity that gospel *be proclaimed universally* wherever gospel *proclaimed* | beg. gospel about *Jesus Christ* [*Son of God*] |

LUKE

| | JB | proclaim *baptism of* repentance for release from sins | J | repentance to be proclaimed *in his name* for release from sins |
| | J | *preach good news to the poor* proclaim release *to captives* proclaim *Year of Lord's favor* | | |

JOHN

| | | *hears* *my word* believes *him* who sent me has eternal life | *believe that* *Jesus is the Christ, the Son of God* believing *in his name* have life |

First, a close inspection, gospel by gospel, reveals these features. In Matthew there is nothing distinctive in the messages proclaimed by John the Baptizer (3:2), Jesus (4:17), and the disciples (10:5): ἤγγικεν ἡ βασιλεία τοῦ θεοῦ. How striking that this should not be extended in the "Great Commission" and that making disciples, never enjoined upon them previously, should become their sole task to the end of the age. In other words, there is nothing explicitly "kerygmatic" about the mission, even though Jesus, anticipating the situation after his death, speaks of the gospel's being proclaimed widely (24:14 [of the kingdom], 26:13).[33] The scope of their role differs dramatically, too: only to Israel and expressly not to the Samaritans or Gentiles (10:5−6; cf. v. 23 and 15:24), but now to all of the nations (28:19). So far as the response required is concerned, there is variation as well: repentance at the preaching of John and Jesus (3:2, 4:17) but the observance of Jesus' commands, taught by the disciples (28:20), who never themselves teach before Easter (only Mark reports that the disciples ever gave instruction: 6:30). Finally, the theocentricity of the former message (the Kingdom of Heaven) gives way to the christocentricity of the subsequent task.

Although there are no post-resurrection accounts in the best manuscripts of his gospel, Mark as narrator reveals his Easter conviction at 1:1 where he introduces the work as "the beginning of the Gospel of/about Jesus Christ [the Son of God]." The εὐαγγέλιον is sufficiently christocentric, even without υἱὸς θεοῦ. Yet, when he summarizes the kerygma that Jesus preached, it is "the Gospel of God" (1:14), whose rule had drawn near (v. 15). Mark resembles Matthew in this regard and also in the response required of the listener: repent. But the Second Evangelist adds, "and believe in the Good News." Believing in Jesus is never called for. Mark also recorded the kerygma of John the Baptizer who had earlier proclaimed a "baptism of repentance for the release of sins." His preaching, unlike that of Jesus, contained a christological and pneumatological dimension: the coming of a Stronger One who would baptize with the Holy Spirit (1:8−9). Before and after, protagonist, *dramatis personae*, and narrator are kept distinct.

The Easter kerygma of Luke is clearly set forth in chapter 24. With minds opened by the risen Jesus to understand the Scriptures about the Messiah's suffering and resurrection, the disciples are to herald repentance in his name for release of sins to all the nations (vv. 45−47). Before the resurrection, John had proclaimed a similar message to Israel alone (although he declared that ethnic heritage by itself brought no advantage): a baptism of repentance for the release of sins (3:3). Specific behaviors, equivalent to such conversion were to follow (vv. 11–14). In the wake of this declaration, the crowds wondered about John's messianic potential (v. 15), so there is a christology implied and perhaps inherent in such News. But he himself was not linked to the proffered forgiveness in the way that Jesus' *name* was after Easter. However, it is the εὐαγγέλιον and κήρυγμα of Jesus, showcased early on by Luke alone, that bears the most striking difference from that of chapter 24. It may be observed in one of the rare claims of scriptural fulfillment attributed to Jesus. In the language of Isa. 61, his anointing by the Spirit (only implied: thereby made Messiah) was for the purpose of announcing Good News to the poor, proclaiming release to captives (not release from sins), and heralding the year of the Lord's (i.e., God's) favor (4:18–19). The focus is upon Israel whose response should have been the *honor* (δεκτός, v. 24) shown by Gentiles to Elijah and Elisha (vv. 25–27). Thus, the Easter kerygma in its content, scope, and response has not "painted-over" (to use Bornkamm's phrase) the dominical kerygma. Among the synoptics, the integrity of the narratives before and after has not been compromised.

But what of the Fourth Gospel? As in other respects, John will be John regarding the key terms which I have been examining. As noted, neither εὐαγγέλιον nor κήρυγμα (nor their cognates) is ever employed. So, strictly speaking, there is no way to determine his kerygma or gospel. However, if one looks for statements bearing the constants of the message (God's saving action and the response expected), it will be possible to detect equivalent expressions. Two such examples occur at the Evangelist's statement of purpose and in a declaration of Jesus that sums up his entire mission. At 20:31, John's aim is to engender conviction of Jesus' status as God's Messiah and Son and to persuade readers that reliance on his name brings life. Here, for the first time in the gospel tradition the language of "faith" (really, "believing") describes one's response to the message. *Individually*, these themes occur in profusion in the pre-Easter narrative, quite unlike what we saw in the synoptics. Nevertheless, there are some striking divergences at pivotal moments that conform to the pattern observed among them. Jesus, at 5:24, declares that God is the focus of faith that leads to eternal life. The christocentricity of the epilogue contrasts with the theocentricity of the earlier narrative. Different, too, is the nature of the response. One hears Jesus' word rather than believing in his status or name. This distinction is made even more sharp at 12:44. After eleven chapters containing calls for belief in him (v. 37), Jesus suddenly cries out, "the one who believes in me does *not* believe in me but in the One who sent me." Here the response is the same as in 20:31; but the objects are different. In this stunning denial, Jesus underscores the radical theocentricity of his message which a careful reading of the text will discover. John's Gospel is not about the revelation of the Word, but of God.

Second, when these same data are examined from a more panoramic perspective, the following phenomena come into view. Among the synoptic gospels, the pre-Easter kerygma preached by Jesus *never* matches the post-resurrection kerygma that he enjoins on the disciples. Not one of the Evangelists merges Jesus' era with the church's or overlays the former with the latter. Not one of the post-Easter kerygmata matches. Few of the pre-resurrection kerygmata correspond to one another. John the Baptist's differs in Matthew and Luke. Jesus' differs in Matthew (cf. Mark's "Gospel of God"), Luke, and John. Furthermore, neither Jesus himself, nor any christological title, nor his death and resurrection (though reported by all four and central to kerygmatic statements elsewhere in the NT) are ever the explicit objects of kerygma or gospel before Easter or afterwards. This is striking, indeed, for one constantly hears that the Jesus tradition was from the beginning shot through with the church's kerygmatic estimates about him. Yet nothing from the Easter accounts of the gospels warrants the wholesale practice of reading into the titles that do appear in the pre-resurrection narratives meanings found outside of the gospels in examples of early Christian preaching. Insisting upon this point does not allow one to deny that Christian nuances have ever been supplied in such a fashion. Rather, one should be advised, with this kind of evidence, to proceed cautiously, evaluating each instance on its own merits without prejudice, and looking for meanings appropriate to the narrative setting. Furthermore, the reported kerygmata on both sides of resurrection day are not proclamations of *Jesus' status*: he is Lord or Christ. Nor are they invitations to enter into relation with him by faith. Rather, Jesus and his followers herald *divine action*. They recite its imminence or accomplishment, producing a proto-narrative. Finally, the gospels merely report the kerygmata that the Baptizer, Jesus, and his followers proclaimed. They do not take the form or content of any single one; nor do the Evangelists provide a rigid *Gestalt* for them.

Yet the fact that all four display a similar "form" has long suggested that it originated in the sort of early Christian preaching illustrated in the sermons of Acts, especially in Peter's address to Cornelius and his household (ch. 10). Whatever the answer to the continuing debate about the origin and influence of its form and content, this much can be affirmed: while both the Gospel and Peter's message bear a tripartite form and retain the distinctive idiom of each, the differences in content deny the presence of heavy-handed redactional activity. Once again, a chart will summarize the phenomena at a glance (italics pointing to *differences*) before they are expounded (see table 2).

The similarities lie mainly in the general structure and perspective. In neither case is the overall message called "kerygma" or "gospel".[34] Likewise, three kerygmata are nevertheless differentiated: John's (10:37); God's, announced through Jesus (v. 36); and the Apostolic witnesses' (v. 42). Furthermore, the idiom of each remains intact; Luke does not confuse pre- and post-Easter

Table 2

	Kerygma and gospel	
	Luke	Acts 10
J	proclaiming baptism	baptism which John proclaimed
B	*for release from sins*	
	Spirit of the Lord anointed	*God*
J	me	through Jesus
E	to announce Good News	announced Good News (of) *peace*
S	*to poor*	*to sons of Israel*
U	*to proclaim release to captives*	
S	*to proclaim Year of Lord's favor*	
	repentance to be proclaimed	to proclaim
C		*this is the One Designated by God*
H		*to be Judge of living and dead*
U		*to receive*
R	*for* release from sins	release from sins
C	*in* his name	*through* his name
H	to *all the nations*	to *everyone who believes*

"dialects." Both gospel and Acts make Jesus' earthly career significant (although it belongs to common knowledge according to Peter, v. 37). And both make God the causative agent throughout (vv. 34, 38, 40, 42).

But the differences are more telling. In Acts 10, John's baptism is not credited with issuing in release of sins. *God* announces the gospel of peace through Jesus, whereas in Luke's Gospel, the Spirit anoints him to publish Good News (without a specific object). Jesus' proclamation of release to captives and announcing the Year of the Lord's favor has no parallel in Acts 10. Finally, the content of the Apostolic proclamation differs, too. In Luke 24, it is "merely" repentance for the release of sins in Jesus' name. But in Acts 10, the substance of the proclamation is more heavily christological (though with clear theological overtones) and in a manner unexampled in Luke's Gospel: God has designated this Jesus (about whom the audience had had previous knowledge) Judge of the living and the dead (v. 42). And believing rather than repentance becomes the means of receiving release from sins. (As many have observed, in neither work does there emerge a clearly developed view about the efficacy of Jesus' death.) Given so much that has been written about Luke's extensive redactional activity in both the gospel and Acts, it is remarkable to find so little of his handiwork in so fundamental an issue as the kerygma. Where is the sign of his cunning?

Thus, in both gospel and Acts (including the first Christian sermon preached by Peter at Pentecost in ch. 2), there is an uncontrived scheme of presenting the Jesus story without rigidly imposing a standardized redactional overlay upon the contents. Both contain gospels/kerygmata without themselves claiming to be such (much like many thoughtful Christians who say that the Bible "contains" the Word of God without itself being the Word of God). By the middle of the second century, however, the association between oral and written gospel had become complete.

Yet some redaction critics would say that my analysis of *di*verse kerygmata and various responses to them simply reflects *ad*verse points of view. Put in the language of statements (1) and (2), they claim that:

(3) *The gospels are the result of* competing *kerygmata and* rival *responses* (only some of which were "faith"). As with positions (1) and (2), this one relies upon a series of interdependent sub-points and proceeds according to a certain "logic" which, though rarely stated much less defended, needs to be exposed before accurate analysis and evaluation can occur.

(a) From the outset, Christians believed and proclaimed different things about the crucified and risen Jesus.[35] The Living Lord "spoke" in many and various ways to his people. And, of course, each distinctive kerygma contained an appropriately distinctive christology, theology, soteriology, mission concept, etc.

(b) Christians relied on distinctive traditions to articulate those beliefs and aid in their proclamations (or else they gave diverse significance to the same traditions). Collections of miracle stories and exorcisms supported the view of Jesus as end-time salvation bringer or hellenistic divine man. Catenae of wisdom logia showed Jesus as the Rabbi like Moses, etc.[36]

(c) Although many of these diverse convictions co-existed, others produced strife. Consequently, respective traditions became embroiled in the fray.[37] The powerlessness of the Son of Man in the Passion Narrative (PN) could not happily share the stage with the cycles of stories glorifying the powerful Galilean Miracle Worker.

(d) Thus, the Evangelists did not compose in serenity and leisure. Instead, they sought to ameliorate conflict or were themselves engaged in it as champions of one view over another. They attempted to bring order to this chaos. The written tradition provides verbal tableaux of the struggle.[38]

(e) Consequently, wherever tensions appear in the gospels between Jesus and his disciples or opponents, here is where different Christian points of view met head on. The Evangelists made Jesus espouse the correct view, thus silencing inadequate or erroneous ones (and their supporters).[39]

(f) These features make the narratives even farther removed from biographical or historical writing, ancient or modern, than was previously thought. If anything, the documents provide the data for reconstructing the history and "biography" of four congregations splintered by disputatious, factious Christians in the second half of the first century. Although critics may not succeed in assigning a particular *chronos* or *topos*, it may be possible to describe an *ethos* within which such tumult occurred. There can be little doubt that such theological layering is so deep and the reasons for writing so sociologically particular, that one does not even have grounds for regarding the gospels as historical fiction. Looking for analogs in ancient literature is futile from the beginning.

Despite the almost axiomatic status that this scenario enjoys in many critical circles, it lacks substantiation at several points, any one of which could bring the edifice down were it to be unsound, so interlocked are the girders and stones of the structure.

(a) This way of putting the matter exceeds all of the incontrovertible evidence available. There are simply no data in the earliest period of *fundamental* diversity in kerygma and the response called for. The conviction and proclamation that God raised Jesus from the dead cut across several traditions, spheres of influence, and genres of expression. Of course, variations on these themes did occur among the component parts of the "outline".[40]

(b) Once again, a dearth of real data vitiates this claim. It rests upon a traditio-historical *assertion* that clusters of tradition imply a kerygma with attendant "doctrines" and that these traditional units expressed the *totality* of what was believed by those who preserved them. But not a thread of argument based upon a shred of evidence has ever been offered in support of this far-reaching and widely assumed postulate. Its advocates build upon Martin Kähler's questionable analogy that "In every drop of the bedewed meadow the light from the sun is reflected; likewise in *each little story the full person* of our Lord encounters us" (my italics).[41] But are complex linguistic expressions of theological convictions like optical phenomena? At least Kähler did not divorce the dew of the stories from the sun of the PN. All of the written tradition looks with "that constant anticipation of the double end [i.e., crucifixion and resurrection] as the real goal of his journey."[42] But Bornkamm has taken Kähler's statement even further, dissolving the connection that he had forged with the PN: "These story scenes give his story *not only when pieced together, but each one in itself* contains the person *and history* of Jesus in their entirety" (my italics).[43] One can, without further ado, regard such analogies for *unwritten and independent oral* tradition with suspicion.

(c) This point holds only if (b) is true and if clear testimony for conflicting traditions can be found in the gospels. The tendency to look for incompatible points of view supported by inimical types of tradition stems from the legacy of William Wrede who himself shared Kähler's belief that the gospels were dogmatic documents.[44] He convinced a school of critics that Mark's Gospel was a theological (now "kerygmatic") work, not historical in the least, itself containing traces of two, earlier, *conflicting* theologies about the origins of Jesus' messiahship. The earliest Christians proclaimed that God had made Jesus Lord and Christ at the resurrection (Acts 2:36, 13:33; Rom. 1:3−4). Subsequently, other believers insisted that Jesus had claimed to be Messiah during his lifetime (Mark 8:29−30).[45] But Wrede could only sustain this point by violating his own principle of interpretation: not to leave the terrain of the text and to evaluate it on its own terms in its own spirit.[46] So, although Acts 2:36 etc. may well reflect the earliest Christian convictions about the origins of Jesus' messiahship, *there is none of it in Mark or in any of the other gospels.* Without doubt, one can find examples of controversies elsewhere in the NT where the heart of the gospel is at stake, for example between Paul and the "superapostles" in 2 Corinthians (10–12) and the promoters of the ἕτερον εὐαγγέλιον in Gal. 1.6–9. But such polemics lack documentation in the gospels despite recent efforts to find some.[47] It cannot be demonstrated that certain traditions (e.g. miracle stories) were in themselves incompatible with others (e.g. the PN).

(d) One can rely on this only if (c) stands fast. It shows indebtedness to Wrede's theory that Mark sought to resolve the tension by supplying a third, reconciling position: Jesus had been the Messiah during his life; but he urged his disciples to keep this information secret until the resurrection (Mark 9:9). Therefore, the first gospel to be written about Jesus actually records the earliest history of church dogmatics in three stages, Mark's being the last. And the other gospels continue the story of Christianity rather than the story about the Christ.[48] Subsequently, Wrede's sympathizers, while agreeing with his premise that Mark sought to reconcile rival post-Easter convictions, nevertheless differed sharply in their estimate of what those issues were.[49] Eventually, some suggested that the battle had been joined on several fronts simultaneously. The differences in what one proclaimed as gospel would affect a host of other interdependent subjects.[50] However, since Wrede failed to "practice what he preached" by first reconstructing the history of the church's kerygmata and then finding them in the gospel, his conclusions ought to be viewed with suspicion by those who wish to pursue his noble literary-theological ideal in a more thoroughgoing way.

(e) Unless the "logic" of previous steps holds, this point becomes vulnerable too. Furthermore, its advocates lay themselves open to the charge that they have replaced one historical, even historicist, procedure with another,[51] the only difference being that the subject has changed. In the wake of this shift, the redaction-critical objective of treating the gospels as documents with literary integrity has been lost sight of. The possibility of regarding the tension within the narrative *as a function of narrative* seems to have been ignored in the goal of identifying the needs of those who first received the message.

Of course, I do not regard the task as illegitimate in itself. All literature reflects a two-level interest, one being the desire to address the present and future generations. But one makes discriminations in part by the manner in which the author makes his or her point. The extremes range from the sublimely subtle from which the readers/hearers leave wondering "What was that all about?" to the supremely didactic where one is virtually bludgeoned with the moral. An extension of this "hard sell" is allegory, a category into which redaction-critical exposition of this sort sometimes falls. Of course, the modern interpreter does not assume responsibility for it; he "credits" that to the Evangelists' account. For Norman Perrin, Peter is not the historical or narrative Peter at Caesarea Philippi. Rather, he represents or stands for Christians whose outlook on Jesus is inimical to Jesus' (i.e. Mark).[52] Such is the direction of Bornkamm's Storm-Stilling analysis. As the oldest exegete of Mark's narrative, Matthew was "the first to interpret the journey of the disciples with Jesus in the storm and the stilling of the storm with reference to discipleship, and that means with reference to *the little ship of the Church*" (my italics).[53] It will not do to appeal to "this usual and altogether legitimate exegesis from the time of the early Church,"[54] for why then should one patronize St. Augustine and all other interpreters until A. Jülicher for pronouncing that the Jew who fell among thieves in the Parable of the Good Samaritan was none other than Adam?

Wherein lies the answer? It would be presumptuous to offer anything that even sounded remotely definitive. But one can insist upon distinguishing between what the narrative says, how the point is being conveyed (i.e., how it "works"), and what sort of situation the narrative speaks to. While I would never claim that nothing of the latter can be known, I doubt on methodological grounds that the gospels ought to be used as the exclusive or primary data for the effort. The texts exist as texts. As the hardest evidence available, they should be known as intimately as legitimate methods will allow.

However, some redaction critics might respond that the Jesus of literature is as irrelevant to gospels' study as is the Jesus of history (i.e. the Jesus discovered by the literary critic as the Jesus reconstructed by the historian). One must take into account the kerygmatic character of these documents. Otherwise, mere literary criticism in the twentieth century will miss the significance of their form and function as surely as historical criticism did in the nineteenth. Yet, this objection will stand only if "kerygmatic" is defined by criteria which are either abstract or foreign to the gospels themselves.

(f) Ironically, one could argue that redaction critics who have taken this approach nevertheless sold their literary-theological birthright for a mess of historical porridge. A natural rejoinder might be, "Yes, the literary objective had to be sacrificed. But the loss was worth the gain: a more precise knowledge of Christianity in the latter part of the first century." I have already protested about using the gospels as the *means* towards this end. But what about the *results*? And have they really made recourse to contemporaneous Greco-Roman literature moot?

First, setting the scene is important. All four communities and two traditions (synoptic and Johannine) were wracked with dissension caused either by interlopers from without or malcontents from within. Christians were engaged in a veritable "Thirty Years' War" (*ca.* A.D. 70–100), dispute spreading like wildfire wherever sayings by and narratives about Jesus became collected. Nothing was taken for granted. Each point lay open for challenge. Parties vied for every inch of ground. No word or nuance that had any potential doctrinal significance was overlooked. Were the results of my analysis above to be enlisted, then no less than eight kerygmata would have to be acknowledged (ten with John the Baptist's). Here, however, a new element would have to be considered. Instead of Jesus (read "Evangelist") engaged in controversy with misguided disciples and religious opponents (read "errant Christians"), it is a house divided against itself: one Jesus kerygma versus another Jesus kerygma. In Matthew, the Kingdom Party (for Jews only) regarded the disciple wing that welcomed Gentiles as dangerous innovators. According to Luke, the faction promising release from sins to all had outgrown the activistic, lower class, and Jewish Jubilee sect. The Front for the Integrity of God in Mark and John tried to hold its own against the inroads made by the Cadre for Christocentric Inclusionism.

Second, one needs to ask if this account (not exaggerated if one combines all that has been said about all four gospels) exceeds "the constraints of history."[55] Do the claims for such a high level of particularity fit what we know (or do not know)? Mark's readers were acquainted with Alexander, Rufus, and their father (15:21). So, there is a "local" character to the first gospel written. And Luke writes for "Theophilus" – somewhere. The suggestions of church tradition do not help. Because a gospel was written *at* a particular location (Rome, Antioch, Ephesus, etc.) does not mean that it was composed *for* Rome, etc.

More comprehensive questions need asking, if not answering. What does one mean by a community? Is it a local congregation? If so, how would a document like Mark, written anonymously to such an unnamed group, achieve the kind of authority that led Matthew and Luke to appropriate 90 and 50 percent (respectively) of its content and to adopt its basic outline? Does not the widespread reception that the gospels enjoyed lead one to think regionally and beyond? In other words, what if (to borrow from John Wesley) "the world was their parish"? Might each of the Evangelists have attempted to interpret Jesus' significance for the church universal? If not the world, or the church throughout the οἰκουμένη, then perhaps a significant ethos or era was in view. In the closest analogy to the multiple and diverse gospel tradition available, 1–2 Chronicles (redacted finally after the Exile) reinterpreted 1–2 Samuel and 1–2 Kings for all of Jewry. These observations and queries suggest that the war-torn spectre offered by the critic of this persuasion lacks the sort of internal and external corroboration to enjoy anything like probability. Though historicist in mood, it is unhistorical in result. Therefore, one should not be detracted by claims persistently made that:

(4) *the gospels must not be understood and interpreted as biographies of Jesus and they cannot be classified under any category of the history of ancient literature.* So far, the argument by Bornkamm and others has been: the gospels as kerygma are unlike histories or biographies in kind, so do not read them as such. Now the claim is: do not read the gospels as histories or biographies because they do not compare with anything of that genre in Greco-Roman literature. The first of these is a qualitative claim allegedly based upon the internal evidence of the NT, a position however that I maintain lacks gospel-specificity. The second is a formal judgment which relies upon comparisons with external data but which in the light of recent investigation needs to be revised radically.

If the issue is focused enough, it will not be necessary to rehearse the history of research on the subject. My limited intent is to determine whether the idiomatic differentiation of which the thesis speaks (1) was a value of ancient authors and to discover (2) how well they and the Evangelists measured up to the ideal. Fortunately the recent work of David Aune, an acknowledged expert in the field, may represent something of a breakthrough leading to a possible consensus. Against an earlier tendency to find the gospels wanting by selecting one type of Greco-Roman biography or by positing an abstract pure type prescribed by ancient rhetorical theory,[56] he claims that "ancient biography is a complex genre consisting of many sub-types."[57] Furthermore, "it never attained a fixed form but continued to develop from ancient to modern times."[58] This assessment includes historical writings: "neither history nor biography was constricted by static canons."[59] After illustrating these points. Aune concludes:

> An analysis of the constituent literary features of the Gospels situates them comfortably within the parameters of ancient biographical conventions in form and function. They constitute a *sub-type* of Greco-Roman biography primarily determined by *content*, reflecting Judeo-Christian assumptions. The Gospels (and other types of early Christian literature) have connections with *both* Jewish and Greco-Roman literary traditions. Hellenistic Jewish and early Christian literature invariably exhibit various degrees of syncretism. *Adaptation*, not wholesale borrowing, was the rule.[60]

Having provided the broader setting of the question, I should like to sharpen the focus more narrowly to matters of idiom. Of efforts to represent past persons and events, Aune says,

> In epic, tragedy, comedy, and Herodotean history, characterization does *not include linguistic individualization*; direct speech uniformly reflects *the author's style* [my italics in both clauses]. Thucydides, writing of recent or contemporary events proposes to give a reliable account of what the original speakers needed to say in order to accomplish their objectives with particular audiences in particular situations. There is little doubt, however, that he did not fully carry out his intentions. *The language of the speeches is uniformly Thucydidean* [my italics].[61]

Subsequent historians and biographers practiced their craft within the ideals and shortcomings of their mentors. According to Aune, failure to meet the standard might be attributed to at least three causes: (1) a lack of sources and information, (2) an inability to use historical imagination, or (3) a desire to provide moral guidance, regarding "the past as normative for present conduct." Thus,

> Hellenistic history and biography, no less than the Gospels, tended to *merge* the past with the present. If the Gospels and Acts deserve the (exaggerated) designation "theology in

narrative form,'' then Greco-Roman history and biography fully merit the label "ideology in narrative form." Functionally, the differences are minimal.[62] Past and present merge in the Gospel narratives because the Evangelists regarded the story of Jesus as an example for Christian faith. Christian values and beliefs were personified, and history legitimated, in the person of Jesus of Nazareth. This coheres with the significance that ancient Greek and Roman communities attached to their founders.[63]

Such fully two-level intent is not always given equal attention in the kind of redaction-critical interpretation examined in this chapter. Its scholars have often concentrated on the second, blurring the distinctions between them.[64] Even Aune, who acknowledges that many attempts to discern the reader's level have been trivial and contradictory,[65] nevertheless himself fails to see the nuances of texts which I discussed above and elaborate upon more fully later:

> While one cannot assume that each Gospel story exactly mirrors the situation of the Evangelist's community, each Evangelist wrote on *two levels*. One level was the "historical" presentation of the story of Jesus, while the other involved superimposing concerns and circumstances of the author's own day upon the narrative (occasionally with tell-tale anachronisms). The proclamation of Jesus in Mark 1:14f., for example, is a mixture of Jesus' own terms ("Kingdom of God") and those of the early church ("believe", "gospel").[66]

This example, as demonstrated above, is incorrect. It is more accurate to say that, although the Evangelists employed characteristic vocabulary, they did not obliterate language appropriate to the narrative setting. In the chapters that follow, I shall attempt to demonstrate that, measured against the ideal, the synoptic gospels (especially) succeeded more often than they failed. And even John, idiosyncracies and proclivities notwithstanding, maintains an analogous scrupulosity. They spoke to the present in the idioms of the past. Of course, I am not claiming, "idiomatic, therefore historical." Establishing that requires a related but separate step, as Aune himself cautions:

> If one argued that speeches reflecting the historian's style are not authentic, the speeches of Thucydides would fail the test (dubious), but if one argued that speeches exhibiting stylistic

variety are authentic, the speeches of Herodotus could be judged historical (equally dubious). Luke's speeches [and one could add, gospel] stand between these two extremes, and no historical judgment is possible based on stylistic criteria alone.[67]

What then should be made of these observations regarding the gospels' differences *from* the kerygma and their similarities *to* certain kinds of hellenistic biography? What does one gain from the fact that expressions of "faith" were *not* projected back onto the narrative in a thoroughgoing manner and that Greco-Roman ideals for verisimilitude *were* met? First, the study above (and hereafter) tends to support C. F. D. Moule's claim that "the Synoptic Gospels (not St. John) were written not primarily to convey the Christian message independently and self-containedly, but to supplement the preaching of it with historical explanations."[68] They were "meant to be only ancillary to the preaching."[69] The "Evangelists' main purpose was explanation rather than 'preaching'."[70]

Second, such an estimate frees one to examine the gospels within their Greco-Roman literary milieu, enabling similarities and differences in form, content, and function to be determined with greater precision. Frank Martin puts the matter succinctly:

> Luke was well aware of the Hellenistic milieu of his audience as his double allusions to Jewish and to Hellenistic motifs have shown us. We may legitimately infer from this sensitivity to the motifs and aspirations of the Hellenistic world of his day that he knew and was influenced by the type of Biographies known and esteemed in his milieu. Yet his expressed purpose remains distinctive. He writes to provide assurance concerning the fundamentals of the faith.[71]

Philip Shuler makes the same point about the First Evangelist, although the last lines of his remarks seem rather obscure:

> In the encomium biography, Matthew either consciously or unconsciously appropriated a ubiquitous literary type sufficiently flexible to carry out his designs of faith and emulation and to project his kerygmatic assertions within the cult (church) to be used for worship and didactic functions.[72]

In the introduction to a work full of examples of multiple genres from Jewish and Hellenistic works, both diminutive and extensive, Martin concludes thus:

I believe that the distinctive purpose of the Gospel writers accounts for the special nature of their literary work. They were not enshrining, protecting or promoting the memory or a dead master; they were explaining the universal significance of the life and death of someone whom they proclaim to be still alive and knowable. They were evangelizing. The fact that their *explanatory* evangelism [italics mine] was done by way of a narrative of Jesus' life accounts for the fact that, on the literary level, the Gospels may be classified as instances of Greco-Roman Biography.[73]

Summary

When one examines what early Christians believed and proclaimed according to the testimony *of the gospels themselves* (rather than external evidence from elsewhere in the NT or critical reconstruction), the following determinative results emerge:

(1) The gospels, like everything Christian, assent to the message that God raised Jesus from the dead.
(2) However, they do not express in written form any particular kerygma announcing this event.
(3) Nor are they hybrids of diverse or competing kerygmata.
(4) The gospels *report* the distinctive proclamations of the Good News by John the Baptist, Jesus, and the church.
(5) They do not explicitly claim to be kerygma or gospel.
(6) Responses to the Good News in these various forms are rarely (except for John's Gospel) expressed in terms of "faith".

These findings further affect one's view of the written gospels' nature and role:

(1) Their genuine narrative features must not be diminished by associating them directly with kerygma (or an inappropriate definition of kerygma).
(2) The gospels focus more on the *story about* Jesus than on the *person* of Jesus.
(3) The narratives stress what he said and did rather than who he was/is. Acclamation of status in the explicitly Christian confessional sense does not figure as prominently as recitals of words and acts.

(4) These logia and *erga/semeia* stem from God's (theology) power and authority rather than his own (christology).

(5) Such recitals were meant to *inform* (and perhaps convince) people about what God had done in Jesus, not to effect communion with him.

(6) Thus, the *earthly* Jesus rather than the heavenly Lord is the primary focus of attention.

(7) Any mediating of the present Jesus would have to occur by telling about his *past*.

(8) Whatever may be said about one's subjective relation to the risen Jesus, the gospels provide the *objective* ground for it.

(9) Thus, the manner of communication between Jesus and the reader/listener would not have occurred directly or immediately but *indirectly and "slant."* This has significant implications for how the gospels are to be regarded and read.

(10) One's reading of them can be informed by literature nearest to them in form, content, and function. Nothing from the level of internal evidence prevents comparing the gospels to Greco-Roman biographical and historical writing. Their uniqueness (their Subject lives) was conveyed through established and familiar literary conventions.

In the chapters that follow, I have attempted to deepen and broaden the base for these contentions.

2

MARK

Introduction

Over twenty years ago and against the developing consensus, especially among continental scholars, that the gospel was a creative theological work designed to support or correct the beliefs of Christians (i.e., for those who were advanced in the faith), C. F. D. Moule argued that Mark's aim was apologetic and evangelistic,[1] focused upon the outsider who needed to know the essentials of the story.[2] Even if Mark had intended his gospel for Christians, he wrote for believers engaged in evangelism to remind him of the facts[3] on which the superstructure of their faith stood or fell.[4] In being true to those rudiments of the account, the Evangelist knew and maintained the difference between the past of Jesus and his own situation[5] while at the same time desiring to "tell faithfully the story of how the former led to the latter".[6]

In support of his thesis, Professor Moule compared and contrasted certain themes of the second gospel with the prevailing concerns of the early church as reflected primarily by the Pauline literature, especially Romans. Wanting or rare and oblique in the gospel were such prominent features as an exalted christology, incorporation into the body of Christ, redemptive significance of his death, appropriation of its benefits, and a doctrine of the Holy Spirit.[7] In the absence of these ideologies, what remained were facts – not *nuda facta*, to be sure, but the results of an effort to preserve the story as it was, with as little adornment as possible.[8]

Although Moule's argument was not challenged directly, its main point and method did not prevail in those centres which came under the influence of redaction criticism as practiced on the Continent.[9] Even one sympathetic to his thesis might argue that such an approach wrongly presumed that Mark and Paul (in Romans) shared a common fund of beliefs or might object that the gospel's destination and the letter's were not necessarily the same.[10] But redaction critics, besides positing a greater degree of diversity within the New Testament, proceeded upon an unspoken and unargued tradition-historical tenet: that each document reflects the totality of what was believed by the Evangelist and his readers/audience.[11] Consequently, if Mark makes little or no reference to soteriology, it is because he has no developed one. The reason that nothing is said about incorporation into Christ as the mode of Christian existence is because following Jesus as a disciple constitutes the Christian life. Were any distinction to be made between Mark and any other form of Christianity, it should be to contrast Mark with himself; that is, to isolate the theology of traditions which he inherited from that of his own point of view. Such are the assumption and practice that dominate most redaction-critical analyses of this gospel.

In thus distinguishing between tradition and redaction, one is dealing in each instance with Christian points of view. While not denying that such analysis is possible and legitimate, Moule continued to insist that the Evangelists (at least on certain occasions) maintained the distinction between their own post-Easter beliefs and those of Jesus. In "Luke contrasted with Acts," he took an approach which avoided the objections raised about his analysis of Mark. Moule tested the Evangelist against himself and showed that he avoids putting the fully Christian sense of ὁ κύριος on the lips of the *dramatis personae* before Easter. Luke knew the difference and refused, by and large, to use it anachronistically.[12]

Might the same be said of Mark? Does his narrative primarily mirror the present of the Marcan community, as so many Marcan scholars claim?[13] The burden of this chapter will be to answer the opening question affirmatively. When the method Professor Moule adopted in Luke is applied to Mark, using a range of issues which transcend particular traditions and genres, then it is possible to contrast what Mark believed about the Christ this side of Easter with what the Jesus of his narrative proclaimed and taught before then. Certainly everything in the gospel reflects the "faith" (here broadly meaning "convictions *in toto*") of the Evangelist and at least some of his readers. But not all of it was communicated in the same categories, in the same manner, all of the time. Terminology and modes of expression were used discretely so as not to confuse the time of Jesus with that of the church.

However, in order to discern this distinction, it is necessary to keep to the goal announced in chapter 1 of concentrating on the redactional product, the finished narrative, rather than on the process of redaction. I shall steadfastly heed Wrede's injunction, now almost a century old, to avoid leaving prematurely "the terrain of the evangelists' accounts." Although he leveled this protest against the nineteenth-century biographers of Jesus, it is incumbent upon all of those who have with Wrede strayed from the ideal by using Mark prematurely to write the *church's* history. Yet he was correct to insist that "thoroughly illuminating the accounts on the basis of their own spirit" must become the foundation of all criticism.[14] The narrative, as narrative, should first be examined in its own right as an integrated whole.[15]

Analysis

The gospel

At the very outset, the Evangelist discloses the nature of his gospel and its christological component. With 1:1, in a statement external to the narrative itself, he entitles either the entire work or some segment of the first chapter as 'Αρχὴ τοῦ εὐαγγελίου 'Ιησοῦ Χριστοῦ.[16] The full phrase is unique to Mark and the NT, as is τὸ εὐαγγέλιον δ'Ιησοῦ Χριστοῦ.[17] Moreover, nowhere else does the Evangelist refer to Jesus with such fullness.[18] Of greater importance, however, is the fact that Mark's εὐαγγέλιον differs on two counts from that which he reports Jesus to have preached in vv. 14–15. While Mark's is christocentric, Jesus' is theocentric: τὸ εὐαγγέλιον τοῦ Θεοῦ (v. 14c).[19] Moreover, the content of the message is his Kingdom's having drawn near in a *previous* event: either John's ministry or Jesus' temptation, as the perfect tenses of πεπλήρωκεν and ἔγγικεν demand (v. 15a).[20] Mark's gospel about Jesus Christ presupposes the *subsequent* events of his death and resurrection as well as the Kingdom's full arrival in the future.

These important distinctions have been ignored or unnoticed by those who, like Willi Marxsen, interpret the gospel "kerygmatically."[21] However profound and true it is to say that Jesus is the gospel,[22] there is no basis for deriving such a formulation from this text. While the genitives of 'Ιησοῦ Χριστοῦ in 1:1 might allow apposition with εὐαγγελίου and make sense as "the beginning of the good news," i.e. "Jesus himself," such a rendering is impossible at vv. 14–15: "Jesus came into Galilee preaching the gospel [read, "Jesus"] from God ...; repent and believe in the gospel [read, "Jesus"]." It is patently clear from the narrative in general and the secrecy phenomena in particular that the Evangelist does not portray

Jesus as putting himself forth publicly or privately as Messiah,[23] or as the object of either εὐαγγέλιον or πιστεύειν.[24]

Elsewhere, he keeps separate what one does for Jesus' sake and the gospel's (8:35, 10:29).[25] Although the καὶ (...) τοῦ εὐαγγελίου might be epexegetic ("for my sake, that is, the gospel's"), it is still noteworthy that no direct connection is made. And, if the distinction with which the gospel opens is clear, then the likelihood that Mark continued it here is raised. In the other two occurrences of εὐαγγέλιον, the expression is absolute: the preaching of the gospel to the nations (13:10) and its accompaniment by the tradition of a woman's anointing Jesus' feet (14:9). Strictly speaking, then, Mark distinguishes between the gospel which Jesus proclaimed about the inauguration of God's Rule and the Evangelist's own kerygma that God had begun it in Jesus.[26]

Believing, following, receiving

Just as Jesus is not the content of the εὐαγγέλιον in the narrative, so is he not the subject or object of faith or believing. Only at 9:42 does there appear a reference to believing or trusting in Jesus approximating a Christian sense. Here he warns the disciples about scandalizing little ones (children or fragile Christians) who believe (τῶν πιστευόντων). Even if the longer reading, which adds εἰς ἐμέ, is original,[27] it would be atypical of the ways in which πίστις and πιστεύειν appear elsewhere in the gospel. All of the five occurrences of the noun have to do with a mighty work of healing. None has Jesus as the object of faith. One has God as the focus (11:22). Two imply faith in Jesus to perform a cure (2:5) or still the storm (4:40). In two others, it is faith that occasions the cure (5:34, 10:52). Similar features characterize the ten instances of the verb. The word to Jairus (5:36) and the father of the epileptic is to believe (9:23 and the father's comparable response in v. 24). Objects to believing appear six times: the gospel (1:15); that what one says, prays for, and requests will be forthcoming (11:23–24); that what John the Baptist said was true (v. 31); that the Christ is here or there because of signs and wonders (13:21, 22); that Jesus is the Christ, the King of the Jews (should he descend from the Cross, mock the Jewish leaders, 15:32). Once again, belief or believing has much to do with Jesus' or God's ability to do a mighty work of some sort. But Jesus is never the object of πίστις or πιστεύειν.[28]

Perhaps such a restricted usage has led Eduard Schweizer and others to maintain that Mark's concept of Christian existence lies in following Jesus (ἀκολουθεῖν and ἔρχεσθαι ὀπίσω μου).[29] But it may be that this term principally describes the relation of the disciples to Jesus before the resurrection, since another expression more clearly reflects the situation afterwards. Support for such a view comes mainly from two contexts. It is widely held, for substantial reasons, that chapter 13 provides the clearest window into the post-Easter *Sitz im Leben* of the gospel (see pp. 42–43, below). In an effort to prepare them for life in his absence, Jesus instructs an inner circle of disciples to recognize impostors who will come *in his name* (v. 6) and to anticipate hatred from all quarters because of *his name* (v. 13). In chapter 9, Jesus has earlier taught the Twelve about their life together in his absence, using similar language. He commends the one who may give them a cup of water *in his name* (v. 41). Consequently, when Jesus claims that whoever receives a child *in his name* receives him and in doing so, God himself (vv. 36–37), he is employing language appropriate to the post-resurrection period. Here, receiving Jesus (not following him) commences Christian existence. Before then, true to his usual manner, he speaks publicly about receiving the *Kingdom of God* as a child (10:14–15). Thus Mark has not only contrasted private and public teaching; he has also distinguished theocentric themes appropriate to Jesus' earthly ministry from the christological terminology of the Christian era (language which ends on a theocentric note).

Salvation

Scholars of most persuasions would agree that Jesus' statements at 10:45 and 14:24 reflect the Marcan soteriology, for here alone what Jesus' death achieves *pro nobis* appears clearly and unambiguously. The Son of Man came to serve and give his life as a ransom (effecting release of some sort) for the many.[30] His blood of the covenant poured out for the many secures covenantal (re)bonding.[31] Such statements are rare, being given privately to the Twelve alone. Never does Jesus speak publicly of his death and its import. On the other hand, the vocabulary of salvation and forgiveness which Jesus employs in the narrative is public and frequent but lacks a clear connection with the cross.

Of the thirteen instances of σώζειν (only the verb occurs), six mean little more than the healing or helping of persons who are physically ill (3:4; 5:23, 28, 34; 6:56; 10:52). Three refer to the eschatological time of salvation anticipated by Jews as well as Christians (10:26; 13:13, 20), and two have the sense of rescue or deliverance (of Jesus from the cross, 15:30–31). The nearest to a Christian sense appears at 8:35, where Jesus declares that the one who loses his life for his sake and the gospel's will save it. As our study above showed, even here there is not the full sense of τὸ εὐαγγέλιον 'Ιησοῦ Χριστοῦ (1:1). This distinction between Jesus and gospel (which is maintained at 10:29) cannot be ignored. Furthermore, the emphasis is more on human appropriation than christological achievement. Only obliquely does there appear to be a connection with taking up one's cross and following Jesus in 8:34. It is true that he had recently spoken privately to his disciples about the need for the Son of Man to suffer, die, and rise from the dead (v. 31). But even they are not informed about the significance or efficacy of that death. It is not clear what it achieves "for us and our salvation." (So it is with all subsequent "passion predictions" until 10:45: 9:12 [regularly ignored by scholars], 31; 10:33, 34.)

Jesus' encounter with the rich man in chapter 10 illustrates how one refused to meet the conditions for *inheriting eternal life* (v. 17) set forth in 8:34–38: selling all and following him (v. 21). When Jesus underscored the difficulty of a rich person's *entering the kingdom of God* (vv. 23–25), the astonished disciples wondered if anyone could be saved (v. 26). At Peter's reminder that the disciples had left all to follow their master, Jesus replied that such an act done for his sake and the gospel's would bring material and personal benefits in this age and eternal life in the age to come (vv. 29–30). Thus, the conjunction of these three expressions and their connection with following Jesus brings *eschatological* salvation. Although the christological element appears here (albeit without a particular title), the stress is once again upon human response. Nothing is said about why giving up riches and following Jesus completes what the rich man lacked.

The situation is much the same with the vocabulary of forgiveness. While the masses who repent at the Baptizer's preaching may find forgiveness (1:4), it is impossible for those who either blaspheme the Holy Spirit (3:28–29) or who find themselves among those to whom the mystery of the *Kingdom of God* has not been given (4:10–12). One's being forgiven by *God* is linked to forgiving others (11:25–26). Only once do both forgiveness and christology converge: at 2:5, Jesus provokes murmured accusations of blasphemy when he forgives the paralytic's sins (v. 7). Shortly thereafter (v. 10), Jesus informs the religious leaders of the Son of Man's authority to forgive sins upon the earth. However, this earthly role of the Son of Man relative to Mark and his readers is, of course, no longer possible. Only what is achieved by his death brings subsequent benefits.

So, we may infer that in the narrative of Jesus' ministry, soteriology (like gospel and belief) bears few, if any distinctly Christian (i.e. Marcan) features. And one may have to be cautious about detecting the Marcan soteriology even at 10:45 and 14:24. The christology of ransom and covenant (as well as forgiveness in 2:10) is exclusively that of the Son of Man,[32] a christological category which neither in its content nor formulation clearly suggests Mark's Christian point of view. In other words, it is not the subject or object of the Good News as "Christ" (and "Son of God"?) are (1:1). (As I shall argue in full shortly, the latter are the titles appropriate after the resurrection. Until then, they are to be suppressed or reinterpreted by "the Son of Man".) Nor does "the Son of Man" appear in any ascriptive or confessional statement as the others do. In view of these data, can one refer to a post-Easter soteriology at 10:45 without a post-Easter christology?

Christology

Before proceeding, I must repeat my aim of dealing with the final, redactional *product*, the narrative. In so doing, I shall propose a linear and complementary relation between christological categories which most of those who examine the redactional *process* claim to belong in a sort of lateral dialectic (especially when viewed under the so-called "kerygmatic" rubric).[33] Put negatively, I shall argue that the Jesus of the narrative avoids, qualifies, suppresses, or postpones until Easter christological categories which the Evangelist and his readers currently embrace. The latter happen to emerge in confessional or credal statements regarding Jesus' *identity* while his favorite term appears in expressions which narrate or portray his *role* (vocation).

Of the three major christologies, only χριστός appears in the title to the Christian gospel, which is about Jesus Christ, or Jesus the Christ (1:1). And the narrative also suggests that this term is more appropriate following Easter than before. In chapter 9, Jesus commends those who will relieve the disciples' thirst in his name (signifying his absence) because they belong to Christ.[34] Then, during the last days, false Christs will arise (13:21); but Christians are not to be led astray, even though the impostors attempt to substantiate their claims with impressive signs and wonders. "Son of God," too, belongs to the Christian era. While the case for thinking so would be strengthened were υἱὸς θεοῦ securely part of the text at 1:1, once again the narrative, as it anticipates the future, supports this contention. Although Jesus had customarily silenced all attempts to address him as such throughout his ministry, Peter, James, and John would be allowed to publicize it after the resurrection of the Son of Man (9:7–9).

Jesus, on the other hand, consistently avoids making positive use of "Christ" and "Son of God" both in public and in private. The only possible exceptions might be his attempt to elevate the status of the Messiah from being David's son to his Lord (12:35–37). However, as this rare initiative appears in an instance where no claim to the term is made, either directly or by implication, it hardly counts. And, although in all likelihood Mark meant to portray Jesus as referring obliquely to himself as the son of the vineyard owner, the reference is both indirect and unique (vv. 6–8). Certainly many have noted that Jesus alone defines himself and his role exclusively by means of "the Son of Man," whether this be privately or publicly: forgive sins upon the earth (2:10); exercise lordship over the sabbath (2:28); suffer, be rejected, die and rise (8:31; 9:12, 32; 10:33); serve, give his life a ransom for many (10:45) and come in glory (8:38; 13:26; 14:62). Yet, none of these functions ever is closely and clearly associated with "Christ" and "Son of God," the titles by which Jesus is known and addressed in Mark's church. Of course, even "the Son of Man" "belonged" to Christians with all of the other titles. But the point here is that they used them differently when affirming their convictions about him in the present than when narrating the story of his past.

Furthermore, the Jesus of the narrative qualifies or interprets those christologies to which Mark adheres. It is quite common for him to shift to "the Son of Man" when others use "Christ." When Peter confesses him as such in 8:29, Jesus forbids his disciples to make that information known (v. 30). Instead, he begins to speak of the need for the Son of Man to suffer, die, and rise (v. 31). When pretenders come claiming to be the Christ (13:21–22), his followers are to look for the Son of Man's coming in clouds with great power and glory (v. 26). This same move to interpret or qualify χριστός occurs finally at his hearing before the Sanhedrin. When Caiaphas asks Jesus directly if he is the Christ, the Son of the Blessed One (14:61), his affirmative, though perhaps indirect,[35] answer is followed by the promise that they will see the Son of Man sitting at the right hand of the Power and coming on the clouds of heaven (v. 62). And the divine declaration of Jesus' sonship at the transfiguration may be reported by the disciples only after the Son of Man rises from the dead (9:7, 9).

Several of the foregoing instances also illustrate yet another manner in which the christology of Jesus and that of Mark are distinguished. These phenomena belong to the so-called messianic secret (although in reality it is more like messianic reserve and Son of God secret because of the integrity with which each of the titles is used). Without exception, Jesus regularly suppresses all public acclamation by the demons about his special relation to God (1:25. N.B. the durative *Aktionsart* of the verbs in the editorial summaries at 1:34 and 3:11–12).[36] Even the case of Bartimaeus is not really an exception. It is true that, although the disciples had been prohibited from revealing Jesus' identity, the blind beggar is not prevented from addressing him twice with a quasi-messianic expression, "Son of David" (10:47–48). However, Jesus' actions in the Temple (and not the Roman garrison) are meant to stifle and interpret both the blind man's and the crowd's royal–political hopes for him (11:9–11, 15–17). Finally, the christology of Jesus in the narrative may be distinguished from that of Mark in the post-resurrection period by noting that the injunctions to silence about Jesus' identity are not meant to be absolute. As the narrative nears those events which separate the time of Jesus from that of the church, the veil is slowly pulled back. In the private hearing before the Sanhedrin, on the eve of his death and under duress, he admits (as we saw) to being the Christ, the Son of the Blessed One, albeit with the Son of Man qualification (14:61–62). Shortly thereafter, at the moment of Jesus' death, a centurion exclaims, "Truly this man was a [or "the"] Son of God" (15:39).[37] This postponement or delay had already been forecast following the transfiguration: the secret of Jesus' identity is not to be permanent. The resurrection of the Son of Man signals its end (9:7, 9). And so it did, for, as many have observed, "Son of God" and "Christ" (with "Lord") became for Mark and the early church the supreme categories of Christian confession, while ὁ υἱὸς τοῦ ἀνθρώπου fell away completely.[38]

Before concluding this point, it is important to note that the christological categories distinguished above appear in discrete kinds of statements. Without exception, "Christ" and "Son of God" (the titles of Mark's church) occur in acclamations of Jesus' status or identity: either of the supramundane Son of God, whom only the spirit world (both divine and demonic) and the lone centurion recognize,[39] or the Jewish Messiah-son of David whom the disciples and others perceive.[40] But never do we hear what the Son of God or Davidic Messiah is to do; they are predicates. The exact reverse occurs with "the Son of Man" (the title of the narration). While others have observed often enough that it never appears in a confession, either in Mark or anywhere else in the NT (with the possible exception of John 9:25), no one to my knowledge has made the point that this expression is the exclusive vehicle of narration and recital of his role or obligation (vocation).[41] Thus the titles adopted by Mark's church tell us who Jesus is: unique Son of God, Jewish Messiah (and also, Lord).[42] But the narrative christology tells us what he is to do, i.e. what constitutes sonship and messiahship.[43] It is not enough to say that "the Son of Man" is the title of the passion. A more comprehensive category is needed to do it justice: "the Son of Man" connotes action, function, and role.

The Holy Spirit

Three of the five references to the Holy Spirit belong to the pre-resurrection period: Jesus' baptism and temptation (1:10, 12) and his pronouncement regarding blasphemy (3:29). But two of them transcend the narrative, providing a clue to the Evangelist's pneumatology, of which little or nothing is made in the gospel. John the Baptist announces that the Coming One will baptize Israel with the Holy Spirit (1:8). This surely presupposes either Pentecost or some more remote eschatological event whose development never occurs within the body of the gospel. Likewise, there is nothing during the course of the narrative, either in the case of Jesus or his disciples, which corresponds to the sort of inspiration by the Holy Spirit which will guide their responses in the moment of trial (13:11).

Mission

One would have thought that an Evangelist who alone takes pains to inform his Gentile readers about Jewish rites of purification (7:3−4), who alone cites God's intent to receive their worship in the Temple (11:17), and who includes them in the gospel's post-Easter proclamation (13:10) would have reported more contacts with non-Jews. They are exceedingly rare: the Gadarene demoniac comes to Jesus (5:2). The local swineherds urge him to leave their territory (v. 17). Jesus does not deliberately evangelize or openly heal on

Gentile ground. He tries traveling through the regions of Tyre incognito (7:24). The Greek, Syrophoenician woman who found him is treated rather roughly in her efforts to gain her daughter's cure (vv. 27–29). Jesus intends his healing of the deaf mute in the regions of the Decapolis to remain secret (vv. 31, 36). There does not appear to be any deliberate effort to lay the groundwork in any direct way for the Gentile mission during Jesus' ministry. Of course, one can claim that Mark does so in all sorts of subtle ways.[44] This may well be true. In fact, it is so subtle that Matthew and Luke felt obliged to enhance Mark along these lines (although the extent to which they have done this has often been exaggerated, as chs. 3 and 4 will show).

Thus, the internal data of the gospel reveal that Mark maintained the difference between his own, post-resurrection point of view and that of Jesus in several critical aspects. In what follows I shall discuss the implications of these findings for current study of the gospels before suggesting in the final section a more comprehensive model by which the Evangelist might have related the career of the earthly Jesus to his faith in the risen Lord.

Implications about Mark's Ἀρχὴ τοῦ εὐαγγελίου

These conclusions run counter to several widely held and interdependent tenets in current study of the gospels. Günther Bornkamm and Willi Marxsen have led the way in maintaining that neither those who originally proclaimed the Good News and transmitted Jesus traditions orally nor Mark himself were concerned about the Jesus who was (and what he said and did) but about who he is (and what he says and does). And they make the incontestable assertion (which has unfortunately become a cliché) that the earliest Christians did not think or write with the standards of post-Enlightenment historiography.[45] But few these days would insist that the Evangelist wrote about the earthly Jesus with modern (or even hellenistic) standards in mind. Yet there is often the failure to realize that this issue is separate from whether or not he produced a narrative about Jesus' past. The two enterprises are not the same.[46] Thus Mark's story should not be judged by what would or would not have been the interest of Mark's predecessors in Jesus' character or career. One must take seriously the possibility that Mark believed the kerygma could have been served by *Bericht* or *Erzählung*,[47] if not by *Historie* or *Geschichte*.

Such a possibility demands more serious consideration when one realizes that the prevailing opinion often rests upon unargued and highly debatable traditio-historical assumptions. One is that separate and aggregate oral traditions served as vehicles for words of the risen Christ, not the earthly Jesus. Another maintains that they were complete,[48] self-contained, and comprehensive in expressing the christology of those who transmitted them.[49] Some of these points of view are allegedly antithetical: triumphalistic miracle stories could not happily co-exist with a passion narrative infused with the paradoxical kerygma of a crucified Messiah.[50]

In keeping with these assertions, Hans Conzelmann has maintained that, because Mark held a view of revelation which is always paradoxical, he employed the messianic secret in an ahistorical,[51] nonnarrative fashion to relativize traditions which declared Jesus' identity in an unambiguous way.[52] The secrecy phenomenon, as "the hermeneutical presupposition of the genre, 'gospel',"[53] allegedly ensured that the written εὐαγγέλιον retained the kerygmatic (i.e. paradoxical, dialectic) features of the spoken proclamation.[54] Consequently, the text which says, "Do not relate what you have seen [about the transfiguration of God's Son, 9:1–8] *until* the Son of Man rises from the dead" (v. 9) is supposed to mean, "we must not proclaim the gospel of Jesus Christ *without* proclaiming his death on the cross as the supreme manifestation of his sonship"[55] (my italics). In this view, the secret never really ends:

> its meaning, i.e. its truth, remains concealed to some extent even after Easter. For even after Easter, the Exalted One is visible only in such a way that he is also recognized at the same time as the Earthly One and that means the Crucified One.[56]

However, according to the analysis above, the secrecy motif was one of *several* ways of making christological distinction between the earthly Jesus and the risen Lord. (And the contrast among the titles was itself but one of several kinds.) Therefore, I concluded that it was a subordinate and narrative theme rather than a dominant and hermeneutical one. The chief reason for thinking so came from the most crucial text, 9:9, which shows conclusively, when its temporal conditioning is recognized, that the secret has no function beyond the resurrection, its terminus.[57] Furthermore, Conzelmann seems to have equated one's limited ability to perceive the mystery which perpetually attends all divine revelation, even at its most brilliant focus in Christ, with various moments in the history of the revelation. He does not allow that what was not permissible (yet possible) for the disciples to reveal about Jesus' divine sonship might be made public after the resurrection.[58] There is a real difference between the time of the announcement and one's capacity to understand it, both before and after, which should not be confused.[59]

Others, building on Conzelmann's work, have subsequently suggested that the super-christology of which he spoke was symptomatic of a *theologia gloriae*, either of a Jewish-nationalistic type[60] or of a hellenistic divine man variety, which Mark undercut by means of a *theologia crucis*.[61] Once again, whichever variation or refinement one follows, the net result is the same. The gospel is in no real sense a narrative about the issues which *Jesus* taught to his disciples regarding himself or his role. Rather, the story becomes an immediate, timeless address from the risen Lord about the *reader's* understanding of the Christ.[62] A shift has taken place from christology to anthropology, from revelation to epistemology. Certainly, both aspects concerned the Evangelist. The issue remains one of emphasis.

Now, there is no need to deny that the Marcan Jesus (and sometimes Mark himself) ever addresses the readers. He plainly does at various levels of directness. Jesus' word to the distressed father of the epileptic boy in 9:23 (πάντα δύνατα τῷ πιστεύοντι) transcends the ages. But there is no way that anyone beyond Jewish territory could have obeyed Jesus' command to the leper not to tell anyone of his cure but to get it certified by a priest (1:44).

The most telling places to witness various levels of immediacy occur in chapter 13. It opens with Jesus providing information about the end of the age to an inner circle of four disciples (v. 3), later includes a direct appeal to the reader (ὁ ἀναγινώσκων νοείτω, v. 14b), and ends with a most universal utterance: ὃ δὲ ὑμῖν λέγω, πᾶσιν λέγω, γρηγορεῖτε (v. 37). The common assertion that it is the risen Lord who speaks to his church directly through the traditions and the gospel, finds only qualified support in Mark 13. According to v. 11, the heavenly address is to be given by the *Holy Spirit* when believers find themselves arraigned before magistrates and rulers in times of persecution. Most important, however, is the statement that preparedness for the advent of false Christs depends upon Jesus' *advance* word: ὑμεῖς δὲ βλέπετε· προείρηκα ὑμῖν πάντα (v. 23). And it is this word of the earthly Jesus which abides forever (v. 31);

So the issue at stake is not whether or not the Marcan Jesus ever addresses the readers directly. That he does is patently clear from these instances in chapter 13. But they tend to support the thesis suggested above that, except for such occasions, the Evangelist maintains the distinction between what the earthly Jesus said about the gospel, faith, salvation, and himself and what the author believed about them. While such a purpose may not fit the category "kerygmatic" in the narrower sense, it certainly may in a broader one, particularly if Mark intended to provide an account of how the gospel began for inquirers into the faith or for those who would instruct them, as Professor Moule suggested. Having analyzed the gospel itself and criticized several of the current views, it remains for me to suggest an alternative in keeping with the findings of the preceding section and the concerns set forth in this one.

Alternative perspectives

If the messianic secret is not an hermeneutical device which forever maintains the christology of Mark's gospel in "kerygmatic" (i.e. dialectical) tension,[63] what might be an alternative? In the remainder of this chapter, I shall elaborate my thesis that it is a narrative motif which belongs to a genuinely narrative christology of Jesus' past (without begging the question either way concerning its historicity). Christologies stressing Jesus' status and prerogatives as well as his vocation to be God's loyal Son even to death have been articulated in a linear and fully complementary fashion. The same framework provides a means for relating the distinctions observed in the vocabulary of "gospel," "following-receiving," and "salvation."

A narrative model

The model is an ancient and conspicuously biblical–theological one: the covenant, consisting of two major components which may be refined further (Exod. 20, Deut. 5). The first recites (i.e. narrates) God's Sovereign and gracious election of Israel (Deut. 7:7–8; Ezek, 16:1–14) which collectively enjoys the status of being God's Son (Exod. 4:22; Hos. 11:1). A second element stipulates the People's obligations and defines their vocation in terms of loving obedience (Exod. 20:3–17). Both parts determine what it means to be Israel, God's Son.[64] Furthermore, this twofold model lies at the heart of the royal covenant made with David and his successors, especially as formulated in the deuteronomistic theology (1 Kings 9:2–9; cf. 2 Sam. 7:12–16). Having been "begotten" by God as his son, the King, like the People, is to behave as such. However, when Israel and its leaders fail in this capacity,[65] the prophets anticipate a future ruler who, obliged by the same terms, will obey perfectly (Isa. 11:1–5). In a more intensely eschatological context, God's People and/or their Representative, "one like a son of man," are to be vindicated by the Most High for loyalty to him, even though frail[66] and under pressure (Dan. 7).[67]

In Mark's Gospel, these two covenantal components appear to be expressed separately by the christologies under analysis. Put more sharply (and here claimed only for the Second Gospel, not necessarily for the historical Jesus), "Son of God", "Christ," and "Lord" are predicates found in confessions of Jesus' status or identity, with all of the prerogatives which it enjoys, while "the Son of Man" belongs to the recital of his vocation of obedience as Son and Messiah even unto death. Together, they provide a comprehensive response to two questions about Jesus (questions determinative of God's son, Israel and the king): who is he? What is he to do?[68]

This point is most apparent at two critical moments in the narrative: during the first "passion prediction" and at Gethsemane. Upon enjoining the disciples to keep his identity as Messiah secret (8:30), Jesus begins to speak boldly about the need for the Son of Man to undergo suffering, death, and resurrection (v. 31). While initially the $\delta\epsilon\tilde{\iota}$ seems deterministic, H. E. Tödt and others have argued that the "must" really amounts to the same as the $\gamma\acute{\epsilon}\gamma\rho\alpha\pi\tau\alpha\iota$ of 9:12b where the necessity of the Son of Man's suffering is "God's will as revealed in *Scripture*."[69] This point finds support in 8:33. After Peter protests this agenda in the strongest terms, Jesus attacks his "minding the things of men, not of God." C. E. B. Cranfield argues that $\tau\acute{\alpha}$ $\tau\iota\nu o\varsigma$ $\varphi\rho o\nu\epsilon\tilde{\iota}\nu$ means "to take someone's side," "espouse someone's cause." Consequently, the expression is better translated "for you are taking the side of men rather than the side of God." His will ($\delta\epsilon\tilde{\iota}$) is the way of the cross. In addressing Peter as "Satan," "Jesus regards Peter's attitude as a temptation to draw him away from the path of obedience to his Father's will."[70]

The final temptation is faced head on at Gethsemane, where there is a significant confluence of suffering, obedience, and sonship. Yet, contrary to what one might expect, the Son of God title does not appear. That Jesus is the Son is clear from his address to God, 'Aββὰ ὁ πατήρ (14:36). But the only christological expression which one finds in this passage is "the Son of Man" (v. 41). Here, Jesus' sonship comes upon its severest test. The temptation with which he is confronted is to avoid drinking the cup, i.e. undergoing the impending suffering, the destiny which he had so resolutely embraced earlier in the face of Peter's satanic rebuke. Now he stands alone, with neither angels (as in the original temptation by Satan, 1:13) nor friends to support him. Will he follow his own will, or will he choose God's way and pay the great cost which it involves (vv. 35–36)? The victory is not won with the first resolution to obey. Twice (and by implication, three times) he undergoes the agony of competing wills (vv. 39, 41).[71] With the disciples asleep, "at the end Jesus stood alone as the one fully obedient to God, i.e. as the Son of Man."[72]

Thus, at crucial points in the narrative, Jesus' role of obedient sonship finds christological expression via "the Son of Man": at first announcement of his destiny (8:31, and by implication, 9:31; 10:33–34; 14:21) and at the severest test of his desire to fulfill it. Such an emphasis on obedience provides substance and rationale for the suffering and death. Is it the Son of Man's death itself that is crucial or his obedience even to death, the index of its ultimacy? If the latter, then Mark's intent might not have been to undercut triumphalism with suffering so much as it was to articulate a narrative christology, using the age-old rubric of covenant election and fealty. Once this had defined the nature of Israel's vocation to be God's son. Later, the same two-fold criterion determined what it meant for the king, God's anointed, to be Son of God. Subsequently, the Evangelist employed it to explicate the twin aspects of Jesus' sonship.

Narrative and christology

So, while Mark himself does not say so explicitly, perhaps we might infer that he proposed to narrate how the one who was indeed the Son of God in status from the beginning nevertheless had to learn the complementary role of obedience through suffering (cf. Heb. 5:8–9). And this need for the perfection or completion of obedience unto death may provide the theological motive for the secrecy phenomena: to divulge knowledge of Jesus' status as the Son of God and Messiah before his role as such was fulfilled risked telling a half-truth. Once the obedience of the Son of Man was completed (not necessarily a foregone conclusion), then one could proclaim his identity as the Son of God openly. Such an interpretation would take seriously the temporal termination of the secret permitted in 9:9.

Because of these distinctions, we may conclude that the narrative must be read as an account of Jesus' past rather than as a foil for the present circumstances of the Evangelist and his audience, as so much of contemporary criticism claims. One need not deny that the gospel may be read synchronically (to use current, structuralist categories). Rather, the internal data show that Mark's narrative should be read diachronically, first and foremost. The contrast lies not so much between what the Evangelist held *vis à vis* contemporaries with whom he disagreed over the nature of christology and discipleship. Instead, Mark distinguishes that which he (and perhaps his congregation) confessed regarding the identity of the risen Lord, Christ, and Son of God from what he narrated about the earthly role of the Son of Man whom God raised.[73] The gospel narrative is as much about Jesus' becoming as it is about his being. Who he *was* and what he *became* (along with the how and why of it) belong inseparably together. Otherwise, one may not be able to understand correctly who he *is*.

Narrative and gospel

Because Mark narrates christology-in-the-making, one ought to expect movement, change, and process. But the question remains, what is the relationship between the narrative about Jesus Christ and the gospel about Jesus Christ? Were we to define the early church's proclamation in, say, Pauline terms (with the emphasis primarily, if not exclusively, upon death and resurrection), then Mark's entire work might be viewed as the beginning of or prolegomenon to the heart of the good news: *Bericht zur Botschaft*.[74] The Evangelist determined to narrate the foundation of the church's kerygma: how the gospel began rather than the good news *per se*. He recounted how Jesus of Nazareth, the elect Son of God, took upon himself the vocation symbolized by the Son of Man who, having obeyed God perfectly, even to death, became (upon his resurrection) the object of the Church's preaching.

Or, one may judge Mark's work as something more like *Botschaft als Bericht*.[75] In other words, unlike Paul's, the Evangelist's εὐαγγέλιον about Jesus Christ [the Son of God] included a recital of his career beginning with the events of chapter 1. In the process, care was taken to observe the contrast between the gospel preached *by* Jesus about the Kingdom's having drawn near (1:14–15) and the gospel *about* Jesus proclaimed by Mark to his church (1:1). Bultmann's famous dictum, that "The proclaimer became the proclaimed,"[76] can, as expounded in chapter 1 above, be read in such a way that Jesus' role as proclaimer is excluded from the Christian proclamation. (And the slogan tends to obliterate the *theo*centric continuity between the church's classically expressed kerygma[77] and the message which Jesus proclaimed.[78] Furthermore, as if to complement the mere confession of Jesus' identity which 1:1 suggests ("Jesus is the Christ, the Son of God"), the Evangelist narrates his vocation of loyalty which God vindicated in the resurrection. The good news about Jesus, according to this interpretation, begins with his announcement of God's Rule drawing near accompanied by an account of his perfect obedience to the One whose spokesperson and agent he was. Jesus' proclamation about God is paralleled by his obedience to God. In view of the foregoing analyses, it seems that Mark's narrative (whatever else might have to be said about the others) should be regarded as more than the prolegomenon to the gospel. The recital with which chapter 1 opens belongs to the good news itself, although the association is implicit rather than explicit, as chapter 1 showed.

Narrative and history

Throughout this study, I have repeatedly attempted to avoid historical judgments, either about Jesus or the church, until certain issues had been explored at the level of the narrative, the redactional product. However, historical implications, from whatever angle, cannot be postponed indefinitely.

There is still a widespread feeling among students of the gospels that attempts to recover the historical Jesus are liable to failure because the task is critically so difficult as to be impossible. The historical difficulty rests upon the conviction that our sources are virtually confined to prejudiced, internal data. Yet the foregoing conclusions, if sound, ought to temper such skepticism. Mark did not overlay or infuse his narrative with "faith" in the consistent and thoroughgoing manner often claimed. Consequently, the historian may find himself or herself some steps closer to the earthly Jesus than before. How many steps is uncertain, and one will still need to present the warrants anew and afresh. The theologian should be encouraged to pursue the question about the legitimate relation between history and theology (or at least the connection between a story about the past of Jesus and the reader's current knowledge and convictions about him). Mark's narrative is much more than a docetic cloak for the risen Jesus or a mere foil for the existential self-understanding of early Christians.

But this leads one to ask (if not answer) how far the distinctions which Mark kept had been maintained in the traditions inherited by him and in the framework within which they had been transmitted. In other words, how much of the phenomenon analyzed above may be credited to the Evangelist's account? Was he an innovator or himself a transmitter (albeit perhaps an exaggerator) of the consciousness between two times? Might it be that Mark, who was as much a bearer of tradition as its shaper, extended to his gospel what was there in the tradition before him and perhaps even from the start? The answer, of course, will depend in part upon one's estimate of Mark's sophistication as a pastor—theologian. And there are enough rumblings about his achievements to suggest that scholarly plaudits might have been too generous and uncritical. Far too many traditions have "slipped through the cracks,"[79] leading one to entertain the possibility that the tradents before him and even Jesus himself might have been responsible for the distinction. Of course, raising this to a possibility does not make it so. Rather, one is thereby encouraged to pursue a task whose historical potential and theological significance have yet to be explored fully.[80]

3

MATTHEW

Introduction

That Matthew wrote a "church book" *par excellence* might lead one to suspect that the distinctions maintained so valiantly by Mark would surely fall by the wayside here. Who can deny that Matthew enhances the disciples' and Jesus' images, both by upgrading their status and also by removing the unflattering warts which Mark for whatever reason retained? Surely, in the only gospel to contain "church," one could expect to see these and other ecclesiastical concerns of a later age being justified by their anachronistic presence during the time of Jesus.

It is not the purpose of this chapter to deny an editorial *Tendenz* in Matthew any more than to deny it to Mark. My only plea is that, whatever clear data and strong argument may lead us to believe about the First Evangelist's redactional activity, due notice be taken of those instances where his sense of before and after restrained urges to make Jesus the spokesperson for post-resurrection Christian doctrine and practice. This, of course, challenges what I have described in chapter 1 as perhaps the most influential redaction-critical interpretation. Its expression so far as Matthew is concerned may be summarized in the words of its erstwhile American spokesperson, Jack Dean Kingsbury:

> In writing his story, the first Evangelist was proclaiming his version of the kerygma of the life, death, and resurrection of Jesus Christ. In the kerygma, the risen Jesus is one with the earthly Jesus. As a result, the story about Jesus of Nazareth the first Evangelist fashioned is one that had immediate relevance for his post-Easter church.
>
> And because Matthew is kerygmatic in nature, the intended reader relates to it as a word of address to him or her. To describe this particular way of relating to a Gospel like Matthew, scholars have coined terms such as

"transparency," "typicality," and "simultaneity." Specifically, the contention is that the first evangelist so wrote about the life of Jesus that events, words, and characters of the past were made "transparent" for the present of his Easter church, i.e., they had immediate relevance of some kind for this church or its situation.[1]

Method

Bearing in mind the overall evaluation of this stance (and the analysis of kerygma and gospel in the introduction), it is now necessary to see if the particulars of Matthew's Gospel allow such a view to stand. As before, I shall strenuously maintain the integrity of this gospel's thought. Two opposite tendencies must be resisted: reading Matthew through the lenses of the other gospels and viewing it with the spectacles of a reconstruction of Christianity in the latter half of the first century. While redaction criticism has virtually succeeded in eliminating the former, it has not altogether prevented the latter. To illustrate my point, I cite the example of Georg Strecker who, although providing many fine insights into the gospel in a well-known essay, nevertheless begins with a revealing introduction, excerpts of which I quote and highlight:

> Matthew's understanding of history *presupposes* the change in the theological situation which took place around the turn from the first to the second Christian generation. This situation is characterized firstly by the necessity of considering the problem of "time" or "world" as the historical locus of Christian existence. This implies, secondly, the task of asserting the original relation of Christian existence to the eschaton. That sums up the question to be asked in analysing Matthew here: In what way has the redactor of the first Gospel taken account in his modification and compilation of traditional material, of the theological situation of his generation; and that means by what specific understanding of history does he respond to the problem that exists?[2]

Now, this may all be good and true. But should it not come as a *result* of a close reading of the text rather than as its *presupposition*? The task has to be conducted on a more inductive level in order to avoid or at least reduce the degree of circularity in which Strecker's position is locked. Consequently to find the clearest expression of Matthew's Christian belief, we must appeal first to the post-resurrection narrative. Here may be found the most obvious and undisputed formulation of the Evangelist's Christian thought (a luxury not available in Mark). When similar features occur elsewhere dominating large sections of text or controlling pivotal pericopae, then they provide strong clues about the nature and extent of the writer's editorial activity. Where these are absent or contrary, then one may suspect either an alternative Christian point of view (as redaction critics would be inclined to think) or an effort to relate the word and deed in a manner dictated by the desire to preserve the tradition accurately or to represent the situation authentically. Such a window into Matthew's world occurs at 28:18–20, the so-called "Great Commission".[3] Once this is exploited, I shall return to a consideration of the same and similar categories analyzed in Mark. But the exploration can be pressed further. How will Matthew treat his sources: Mark, Q, and M?

Post-resurrection narrative: the commission (28:18–20)

"All authority in heaven and on earth has been given to me"

Up to this point, Matthew has not made more of Jesus' authority than the other synoptists. With them, he relates reactions to Jesus' ἐξουσία as teacher (7:29//1:22//4:32), healer (8:9//Luke 7:8; cf. Mark 1:27), and critic of Temple practices (21:23–27//11:27–33//20:1–8). Once Jesus shares his authority to exorcize unclean spirits with the twelve disciples (10:1//6:7//9:1). But the most important instance for this investigation occurs at 9:6 in the healing of the paralytic. As in the other synoptics (2:10//5:24), Matthew reports Jesus himself interpreting the significance of the act for the hostile religious leaders: "so that you may know that the Son of Man has authority upon the earth to forgive sins." Convinced though he is that after the resurrection Jesus possesses *unlimited and universal* ἐξουσία, he nevertheless avoided anticipating it anachronistically.

"Therefore go and make disciples ..."

Heretofore, nothing is said about making disciples of any sort, Jewish or otherwise. There is no explicit sense in which they are told to replicate in others what Jesus had done with them. The disciples' mission as in the other synoptics previously had been cast solely in terms of exorcism and healing, proclaiming Jesus' message of the kingdom (10:1, 7−8//3:13−15//9:1−2), and bearing Spirit-inspired witness before hostile officials (vv. 18−20//13:9−11//12:11−12).

However, this injunction is unique to all of the gospels. In Luke 24:47, the risen Jesus commissions the disciples to preach (κηρύσσειν) repentance and forgiveness of sins in his name to all the nations. And "preaching" is the vocabulary of Mark 16:15, which uncritical readers of Scripture sometimes quote at this point: "Go into all the world and proclaim the gospel to the whole creation" (cf. also v. 20 and the so-called Freer Logion which concludes the account after v. 8).

"Of all the nations/Gentiles ..."

On the surface of it, the "therefore" (οὖν) identifying Jesus' empowerment as the cause of this Gentile mission bears certain affinities with Dan. 7:13−14, the most direct literary source for the Son of Man sayings in the gospels. Here, the Venerable Judge awards to "one like a mere mortal"[4] universal dominion, glory, and power that brings homage from all peoples (cf. vv. 18, 22, and especially 27, which suggests that this lowly figure represents in Daniel's dream the powerless people of God, whose loyalty under duress he vindicates).[5] In addition to the kingdom, the power, and the glory, they are to enjoy the service of all the nations as well. There is no question in Daniel as to who comes/goes to whom. But the movement in Matthew is in the opposite direction.

And the Evangelist's portrayal of non-Jews is more textured than most scholars allow. On the one hand, he prefixes the gospel with their appearance in Jesus' genealogy (1:5, 1:6[?]) and cites texts that prefigure their inclusion in God's saving purposes (4:15; 12:18, 21). In the parable of the evil vine-dressers, shared across the triple tradition, he alone specifies that another nation (ἔθνος) will inherit the Kingdom forfeited by the Jews (21:43//12:9//20:16). And the Canaanite woman from Tyre and Sidon does get fuller and more favorable treatment than in Mark (15:21−28//7:24−30).

However, although Matthew includes the Q account of Jesus' encounter with the Roman centurion (8:5−13), it is Luke who reports his high regard among the Jews (7:3−5). Furthermore, he does not multiply Jesus' encounters with non-Jews. And the Evangelist allows critical or awkward references to them *throughout the narrative* to stand. He refuses to remove or temper their potential offensiveness, as Luke does at one point (5:47//6:27). In all three accounts of the exorcism of Legion, the Gentile population asks Jesus to leave the region (8:34//5:17//8:37). Matthew alone omits all reference to the demoniac's reporting his cure in the territory. What a convenient pre-figurement of the Gentile mission it would have been. Matthew retains the synoptic datum that Jesus was killed by the Gentiles (20:19//10:33−34//18:32−33) and that he rejected their hierarchical standards of greatness (20:25−27//10:42−44//22:25−26). More striking is the fact that the First Evangelist maintains this critical stance even in his special material (6:7, 32; 10:5, 18; 18:17; 24:9, 14[?]; 25:32). In contrast to their current, universal commission, the disciples had been instructed earlier to preach exclusively to "the lost sheep of the house of Israel" (10:7). Gentiles and Samaritans were to be avoided (v. 6). With the resurrection, however, the embargo becomes lifted. Yet, at the end of the age, the nations will not all have been called "blessed" by the reigning Son of Man (25:34, 41). The Kingdom belongs only to those who ministered to Jesus when they attended the needs of "the least of his brothers" (vv. 40, 45).

Thus, despite his predilection towards Gentile interests, Matthew preserved the memory that Jesus had not taken initiatives to contact them, nor did he avoid using them as examples of attitudes and behavior to eschew. Such reserve becomes all the more noteworthy, since Matthew began his gospel at pains to identify Jesus as the Son of Abraham (1:1) who at last fulfills in this commissioning scene the promised blessing upon all the nations (Gen. 12:7).

"Baptizing them ..."

In spite of the prominence given to baptism here, during the course of Jesus' career nothing is mentioned about baptizing anyone, much less Gentiles, and certainly not in the name of the "Trinity." All of the focus, as in the other gospels, is upon John's activity (3:6, 11//1:5//3:16). But Matthew alone notes the awkwardness surrounding Jesus' own baptism at his hands (vv. 13, 14, 16). And it was John who taught about Jesus' future role as the one who would baptize with the Spirit (3:11//1:8//3:16) and with fire (Q), an event that none of the synoptists recounts. (Some see a "Johannine Pentecost" at 20:21−23.[6]) Matthew, like the other Evangelists, refuses to justify the rite of baptism by making it part and parcel of Jesus' own practice or teaching. It was exclusively a post-resurrection ordinance. Given the prominence of baptism throughout the church at large, such reticence deserves recognition.[7]

"Into the name of the Father ..."

As the task of baptizing finds no earlier mention, so we should not expect its mode or point of reference to appear prior to this statement. And while the names *per se* of each member of the Trinity do occur, the expressions "name of the Son" and "name of the Holy Spirit" are entirely absent. However, the first petition of the Lord's Prayer to God addressed as Father yearns for the hallowing of his name (6:9). And this is paralleled in Luke 11:2. A related category, "the name of the Lord" (21:9, 23:39), is found throughout the gospel tradition (Mark 11:9//Luke 19:38//John 12:13). Such *patri*centricity dominates the pre-resurrection narrative.

"And of the Son ..."

Likewise, even actions or speech done in connection with "Jesus" fail to occur. Matthew, like the other synoptic Evangelists, never reports him teaching anyone to pray in his name (nor do Christian scribes attempt to insert it into the textual tradition). However, in the post-resurrection era, it will be possible to prophesy, exorcize and do mighty works in that name (which will amount to nothing if not a function of doing the *Father's* will, 7:22). Disciples can expect universal hatred because of Jesus' name (10:22, 24:9//13:13//21:17). Yet some of the nations will hope in it (12:21).

Receiving him will come by receiving a child in Jesus' name (18:5//9:37//9:48). And his presence is assured when two or three are gathered together in his name (18:20). To have left all for the sake of Jesus' name will guarantee inheriting the Kingdom of Heaven (19:29; cf. Mark 10:30 and Luke 18:30). Impostors will use the nomenclature at the end of the age (24:5//13:6//21:8). Remarkably, before the resurrection *nothing* is said or done in Jesus' name. It functions exclusively in his absence. (Luke 9:49−50, not Matthew, parallels the Marcan account (9:38−9) of the "free-lance" exorcist who expelled demons in Jesus' name.)

"And of the Holy Spirit ..."

There has heretofore been no reference to "the name of the Spirit" or to baptizing in his name. Nothing in the gospel leads one to anticipate such a universal practice among Gentiles because of an analogous practice among the Jews. Nor does Matthew impose other post-resurrection convictions about the Spirit in an anachronistic way onto the narrative. Among the eleven references, nine find parallels in both[8] or one of the other synoptics.[9] Jesus' casting out demons by the "Spirit of God" (12:28) seems more at home in Luke who has "finger of God" (11:20).[10] But the main point is that this allocation of the three names falls far short of 28:19. The only clearly Matthean emphasis occurs at 12:18 where he quotes Isa. 42:1–4 regarding Jesus' silencing of those who had been cured (vv. 15–17). However, strictly speaking, it is the form of scripture quotation that bears the mark of Matthean redaction, not the content *per se*. Echoes of the beloved, spirit-bearing servant of the Lord had already been heard at the baptism (3:11, 16//1:8//3:16).

"Teaching them to observe all that I commanded you"

This is the only indication that Jesus chose disciples to be teachers of others. Previously, their charge had been to *preach* exclusively to the lost sheep of the house of Israel and to heal (10:6–8, parallel to Mark 3:4–15//Luke 9:2 apart from the exception). Although Matthew's syntax at this point matches that of 28:19 (πορευόμενοι δὲ κηρύσσετε and πορευθέντες οὖν μαθητεύσατε), both the task and subject matter differ. Prior to the resurrection, their message was the same as Jesus': the drawing near of God's Government (10:7//Luke 9:2; see 3:1–2, 4:17). The focus is *theo*centric.

This is true about the language of "observing commandments," which are the commandments of *God* (sometimes through Moses in the Law).[11] However, the risen Lord now commissions his disciples to make *his* ordinances the standards which the nations obey. Jesus is now the revealer *par excellence*. A shift towards christology has occurred.

Of course, some of this shift had already been anticipated within the narrative earlier, especially in the so-called "antitheses" of the Sermon from the Mountain (5:21–48) where Jesus in some instances seems to set his own authority above that of the earlier revelation of God (especially vv. 31–32, 33–37, 38–39). But even here the audience in view is Jewish, whose hope of entering the kingdom of heaven lies in doing the *Father's* will (7:21). The contrast introduced at 28:20 lies between Jesus as the new authority for Israel and the risen Jesus as the Teacher of the Gentiles through his newly commissioned followers.

"And see, I am with you always ..."

With this statement, the risen Jesus makes explicitly christological a theological emphasis introduced in chapter 1. The name by which he was to be called, Emmanuel, "God with us" (v. 23) never occurs subsequently. The only connection with the narrative that follows is a general phenomenon which Matthew shares with the other synoptists (and even with John, though in a different way). During his life, Jesus mediates the word, power, and authority of *God*. After the resurrection, it is *Jesus'* presence which is promised to two or three gathered in his name (18:20) and to the eleven who are to fulfill the commission which he gives.

"Even to the end of the age"

With this concluding comment, Matthew seems to allow for an indefinite interval before the end. That the Evangelist attempts to convince his readers of a delay in the time of Jesus' return is acknowledged by nearly everyone. Indeed, Matthew's redaction of the triple tradition, Q and the appropriation of M material in chapters 24—25 say as much. The end will not come until the gospel is preached throughout the whole world (24:14). Prepared and unprepared virgins sleep during the bridegroom's delay (25:5). Servants and Master settle accounts after his long-term absence (v. 19//Luke 19:15).

Yet such representative texts do not tell the whole story; and they appear late in the narrative in private teaching to the disciples. Earlier, contrary instruction about the end was neither altered nor omitted. The delay will probably not extend more than a generation. Matthew's call to discipleship concludes on a more precise and awkward note than Mark's (9:1) or Luke's (9:27). Jesus promises that some among the listeners will survive "to see the Son of Man coming in his Kingdom" (16:28). The other synoptists' references to the Kingdom's coming are much more oblique and therefore open to alternative interpretations. More striking still is Matthew's inclusion of the expectation of 10:23, of which Albert Schweitzer made so much.[12] Persecuted from town to town, the disciples are assured that they "will not have gone through all the towns of Israel before the Son of Man comes."

Matthew's handling of eschatology looks like a less-than-thorough-going redaction of tradition, ecclesial or dominical. Either he simply failed to make it consistent or he could not because the tradition was so well known. Yet, nothing obliged him to include 10:23; and he might have exercised the same freedom which his synoptic colleagues enjoyed with 16:28. Therefore, at every major point where the Evangelist's Christian stance is most explicit, he maintains a distinction between post-resurrection points of view and those expressed by Jesus beforehand. Such consistency is so comprehensive that it seems as unselfconscious as it is deliberate. Now it remains to be seen if this phenomenon can be detected elsewhere in the gospel.

The pre-resurrection narrative

One can best proceed along the lines established for Mark, 90 percent of which Matthew used, and then include Q and M material. If the First Evangelist can preserve the sense of before and after in the Marcan source and within other sources, then his achievement will have been notable indeed. Of course, the search cannot be limited to vocabulary common to all three. One must be ready to notice other terminology and phenomena that point in the same direction. Several rubrics will classify the data: christology, the benefits that come from responding to Jesus' call, the nature of that response, and the character of the respondents themselves.

Christology

The Son of Abraham
Given the prominence that this designation enjoys in the opening lines of the gospel, one expects it to be explicated throughout the narrative or in editorial comments. But nothing therein suggests that Jesus is the one through whom the promised blessing of the nations (Gen. 12:3; 22:18) will come. The closest that Matthew gets to this notion (one which the reader must infer) appears in the post-Easter commission to make disciples of all the nations. Otherwise, the Evangelists' attention to non-Jews is not distinctive. (They will get separate attention below.) Even his account of the eastern astrologers makes them come to "bless" the child Jesus (2:1–12).

The Son of David
Because Father and Son language has such a prominent place in the conception of the Davidic kingship (2 Sam. 7:14; cf. Psalm 2:7; 89:26–27), and because Matthew also introduces Jesus as the Son of David (1:1), a closer inspection of this christology, if that is what

it is, seems warranted. David appears four times as a convenient divider among the first and second sets of fourteen generations belonging to Jesus' family tree (1:6, 7). Yet, when the angel addresses Joseph as υἱὸς Δαυείδ (1:20), Jesus' status seems undercut, the expression in the genealogy lacking the article which might have meant *par excellence*. Subsequently, the first Evangelist will portray Jesus as Son of David mainly in his healing the sick and demon-possessed. Matthew inserts this title into material shared by one or the other of the synoptists (12:23, 15:22; cf. the doublet of 20:30, 31 at 9:27). A somewhat heightened royal–political aura surrounds the expression at 21:9 and 15 where the hosannas of the crowd are directed to Jesus as David's heir rather than to his coming Kingdom as in Mark 11:10.

However, like his synoptic "colleagues," Matthew reports Jesus' efforts to upgrade the experts' understanding by citing David himself who calls the Messiah κύριος (22:41–46//12:35–37a//20:41–44). Significantly, Jesus avoids any effort at self-identification here. And the treatment of κύριος below enables one to read the sense of David's remarks thus: "The Lord [God] said to 'my Lord' [i.e., 'my superior,' the Messiah ...]." Whatever Matthew or his readers may believe about him in this regard, no effort to make Jesus the spokesman for their convictions can be detected at this point.

The Son of God
Of the seventeen instances where Jesus' sonship is explicit or implied, ten have a parallel with one or both of the other gospels where no advance or retreat in the meaning can be detected.[13] As in the case of Mark, Matthew nowhere (even in his special material) reports that Jesus used this expression in public or that he received public acclamation as such. He does allow the Q saying in 11:27 (//10:22) to stand. According to the First Gospel, Jesus addresses God as his father in public (privately in Luke) and then speaks of the special closeness that both enjoy. And yet, the relationship is described by a human analogy, virtually proverbial: "who knows a father and his plans better than a son and *vice versa*?" Such intimacy makes a son the best spokesman (i.e., revealer) and agent of a father's "business."[14] Were this to be regarded in its full-blown christological sense (the special relation of Jesus to God can hardly be diminished), then the point still stands because of its *exceptional* nature.

Otherwise, the closest broaching of sonship occurs in the Parable of the Evil Tenants shared by all the synoptics (21:37//12:6//20:13). Jesus makes nothing whatever of the son and heir whom the owner expects to be honored (αἰτεῖν not προσκυνεῖν) when he comes to collect the principal share of the harvest. None of this vocabulary bears any "kerygmatic" features. The son's death achieves nothing. Nor is he raised to life. And Matthew alone avoids calling the son "beloved." Furthermore, in his version of Luke's parable of the Great Supper (14:15–24), Matthew merely mentions without further ado that a certain king gave a wedding feast for his son (22:2). And that is the last one hears of him. He remains a passive figure. Subsequently, the king's servants suffer and die, not the son (v. 6). The First Evangelist avoids "making kerygmatic hay" out of this golden opportunity.[15]

And even in private usage Matthew goes to special lengths to point out that such an estimate comes by divine revelation. Human insight did not inspire Peter's confession. That Jesus is the Christ, the Son of the living God, required God's disclosing it to him (16:17). Yet, the point is not maintained with the strictest consistency when Matthew, alone of the gospel writers, reports that the disciples did acknowledge him as such *before* Caesarea Philippi and without apparent supernatural aid (14:33). Furthermore, the crowds and Herod do no better here than in Mark when they posit some sort of resuscitation of a former prophet or the recently decapitated John the Baptist (14:1–2, 16:13–14//6:14–16, 8:27–28//9:7–9, 18–19).

It should come as no surprise then that Jesus cannot be found explaining the meaning of sonship to the public since he hardly ever broaches the subject, much less uses the term. The disciples get precious little in private. But Matthew surrounds his narrative with a kind of commentary, sometimes more explicit than at others. The reader gets the full-blown story starting in chapter 2. Although the First Evangelist has been much maligned for his citation of Hosea 11:1 as the prooftext for the return of the Holy Family to Nazareth from Egypt (2:15), scholars have begun to recognize a sense in which that "prophecy" had been fulfilled for the Evangelist and his readers. When Matthew aligns Jesus' experience with Israel's ("Out of Egypt have I called my son"), he is contrasting its sonship with his. Indeed, in these early chapters, including the temptation, Jesus emerges as the obedient son that Israel was meant to be but was not.[16]

A more explicit and individualistic development of the character of Jesus' sonship occurs in the temptation scene *per se*, although the connection with Israel remains intact. With Luke, Matthew relates the process by which Satan tries to make Jesus act as the independent son rather than the obedient son which his status obliges him to be.

In a context ostensibly christocentric, Jesus' replies are decidedly theocentric: he stresses the word of God (4:4//4:4), the reliability of God (4:7//4:12), and the worship of God (4:10//4:8).

Finally, Matthew adds his own touch to the crucifixion scene and provides content to the soldiers' confession (27:54), lacking in Mark 15:39. Religious leaders dare Jesus to save himself and descend from the cross, he who *trusted* God, calling himself God's son (27:42–43). Such theocentricity and subordination, dominating the gospel front and back, is something other than the "trinitarianism" of the Commission. But scholars routinely pass such distinctions by.[17] Matthew's redaction is neither monolithic nor monochromatic.[18]

Lord

The place to begin is with a celebrated point of departure: G. Bornkamm's analysis of this title in the essay examined in chapter 1 in another connection. In Bornkamm's estimation, Matthew (unlike Mark and Luke) has invested Jesus "not only ... with a human title of respect, but with a divine predicate of majesty. This is obviously [*sic*!] the meaning of *kyrie*."[19] According to J. D. Kingsbury, he has "put an end for all practical purposes to the dispute" on this issue.[20] In support of his contention, Bornkamm observed that non-disciples never address Jesus thus. Disciples and those positively disposed towards him only use κύριε and never call him διδάσκαλε. The sole exception to the Matthean rule occurs when Judas hails his Master ῥαββί (26:25). Such consistency does not occur in the other synoptic gospels.

Furthermore, it is Matthew who heightens the christology of his source at two notable places. Caught by a storm on the lake, the disciples cry out, "Lord, save; we are perishing" (8:25). Mark 4:38 has ῥαββί. A similar phenomenon occurs at the transfiguration (17:4) where Mark has Peter address Jesus as ῥαββί (9:5).[21]

These citations seem impressive indeed. However, closer and fuller inspection reveals more diversity and greater delicacy in usage. First, it should be observed that Matthew in keeping with the entire gospel tradition never reports that anyone confesses Jesus as Lord. In other words, nothing corresponds to the content of Christian proclamation and its response, κύριος ʼΙησοῦς and variations thereof. The First Evangelist will relate confessional expressions whose object is "Christ" (16:16) and "Son of God" (14:33, 16:16, 27:54) in keeping with synoptic patterns. But never does "Lord" appear in such constructions. This feature of the narrative corresponds to Matthew's role as narrator, *per se*. He employs ὁ κύριος exclusively and unambiguously in reference to God,[22] the corollary being that it is never so used by him of Jesus. These data should give one pause at the outset about ascribing divine, majestic connotations to "Lord" in Matthew.

Second, the weight of κύριε in the Stilling of the Storm pericope must be measured contextually. The account ends with the disciples asking in amazement, "Who is this that even the winds and sea obey him?" (8:27). D.A. Carson rightly notes that "The question is singularly out of place if by *Kyrios* they have *already* predicated 'divine majesty' of Jesus."[23] Another storm scene, found only in Matthew, contains the same sort of dynamics. During the gale, Peter asks Jesus ("Lord") for permission to join him across the waves (14:28). When the attempt goes awash, he hears his Master criticize the doubt and little faith that had brought about the failure (v. 31). And the drift of the story heads in the direction of another and higher christology: the acclamation of Jesus as truly God's Son (v. 33). This is hardly the stuff of rarefied post-Easter confession.

Subsequently, the appearance of "Lord" on the lips of "Peter the Confessor" (alone among the synoptics) occurs at the very moment of his efforts to dissuade Jesus from his grim destiny as the Son of Man (16:22). Its "value" becomes further diminished by Jesus' rebuke in the following verse. A similar relativizing of terms takes place at the transfiguration where only Matthew records that it was Peter who wanted to build three booths (17:4). Although he calls Jesus κύριε (again exclusively in Matthew), the Chief disciple ranks him *alongside* Moses and Elijah. But their removal by the cloud and his address by God (the Beloved Son, the one who pleases his Father, he alone is to be obeyed, v. 5) establish Jesus' supreme status.

Furthermore, Bornkamm's statistics may also be contested. Perhaps a single exception (only Judas among the disciples fails to call Jesus κύριε) will not disprove the rule, especially if it involves a traitor. But the claim that non-disciples (and those not sympathetic to Jesus) never use the expression ignores two revealing passages. Before the Judge, the workers of lawlessness appeal to him thus (7:21–3). At the Great Assize, the unrighteous of the nations address their Judge thus (v.44), having heard the awful sentence and the reasons for it. Consequently, the frequency of "Lord" in the speech of disciples and sympathizers need not necessarily or even probably be evidence of Christian connotations projected backwards. With disciples and teaching so prominent in Matthew's Gospel, it is especially suited to his role as their "Master." Moreover, although disciples (and sympathizers) never refer to him as διδάσκαλε *per se*, he does so himself. Thus, the disciples because they are brothers must not use ῥαββί and καθηγητής of themselves, for they have one alone who is ὁ διδάσκαλος; and ὁ χριστός alone is their καθηγητής (23:7 – 10).

Such evidence as there is of post-Easter usage comes from Jesus himself; but it is of a different order from that claimed by most critics. Both examples are set in the eschaton. On Judgment Day, correct confession (κύριε, κύριε) will not guarantee entry into the Kingdom of Heaven. Nor will prophesying, miracle working, and exorcism done in his name. That destiny is reserved for "the one who does *the will of my heavenly Father*" (7:21 – 2). Jesus' lordship, while higher than any human authority's, is not identical to the Father's. This instance from Matthew's special material (where his view is most clearly in evidence) corresponds to the rendering of a logion from Q. In his final use of the term in public, Jesus laments to the citizens of Jerusalem that they will hail him after the city is left desolate[24] with these words: "Blessed is the one coming *in the name of the Lord*" (23:39//13:35).[25] This is notable, indeed, for in the New Age *God* will be ὁ κύριος. Our hardest data regarding post-Easter nuances of this christological category show Jesus himself maintaining an unmistakable *patri-* and *theo-*centricity. These observations therefore justify taking the great bulk of honorific and gnomic uses in their *prima facie* sense: Jesus is called "Sir" or "Master." Parables refer to persons in authority in circumstances where their political, social, and economic activity serve as analogies for the Kingdom of Heaven.

So, it becomes necessary to part company with the stream of interpretation generated by Bornkamm. I concur with Kingsbury that ὁ κύριος has more of an auxiliary role.[26] But both have ignored certain vital elements in the text which vitiate their conclusions. Furthermore, a case could be made that their reading has been predisposed by the logic of criticism begun by M. Kähler and mediated by W. Wrede (see ch. 1). As I argued above, that line of thinking is highly contestable at several points. Other assumptions and readings of the data are at least as possible, and I would argue, more probable.

The Son of Man

It may be of some consequence that Matthew does not introduce brand new sayings about the Son of Man to the public proclamation of Jesus. The only possible exception might be his addition to the Q saying comparing Jesus and Jonah: the Son of Man's temporary stay in the heart of the earth will be like the prophet's spending three days and nights in the whale's belly (12:40//11:30). Otherwise, the Evangelist does not go beyond Luke[27] or Mark and Luke[28] in his narrative about Jesus' statements regarding the present activity of the Son of Man.

So far as private teaching is concerned, Matthew's logia belong to types already encountered: present activity (13:37), suffering (26:2), and eschatological return (10:23[?], 13:41, 24:30, 25:31). Within the triple tradition, sayings about the Son of Man are to be found at 16:27//8:38//9:26. Those fully parallel with the triple tradition[29] and with Mark[30] speak mainly about his death and resurrection[31] to the disciples alone.

When the data are examined thus, it is all the more remarkable how conservatively Matthew treats the tradition and his written sources. With them, he keeps the expression upon the lips of Jesus exclusively, and its setting (public and private) remains intact. The crowds are no more privileged with special information than elsewhere. They do not become better informed and therefore more accountable and blameworthy as such. And the term remains in Matthew the exclusive means of expressing what Jesus is about: this frail mortal will eventually experience the vindication by God of that frail mortal of Daniel 7.

Messiah/Christ

Having made so much of Jesus' descent from David (1:1), Matthew quite naturally introduces his gospel with the genealogy and birth narrative concerning "the Christ." Each of these comes from the narrator *qua* narrator (1:16–18 and 2:4; cf. 11:2). And this is the title at the scourging and trial (26:68; 27:7, 22) where Mark has an equivalent expression, "King of the Jews" (15:9, 12). In the triple tradition, Matthew twice supplies the title where it is only implied.[32] Otherwise, he and the other synoptics concur.[33]

The only time that Matthew really transgresses the restraint shown by Mark in disallowing its use in public (23:10) comes at a point devoid of kerygmatic or confessional quality. In denying the disciples high-powered titles of respect, Jesus makes the point that only the Christ is their master. And there is no explicit self-reference here. This rather low-key public usage is more than offset by another: Jesus' reluctance to appropriate the term before the Sanhedrin (26:64) contrasts with the overt or implied acknowledgment in Mark 14:62. According to the superior texts, Matthew has kept the "messianic" secret better than most give him credit for.[34]

Theology

In addition to all that has been said so far regarding christological titles, a word needs to be appended about theology. As in Mark, Jesus appears to the public as the great exponent and agent of the Kingdom of *Heaven/God*. And noteworthy in this connection is the fact that only Matthew reports that John the Baptist and Jesus preach the same message about it (3:2 and 4:17). How easily that lack of distinction could have been removed. (Likewise Matthew preserves the awkwardness of Jesus' baptism at John's hands.) Furthermore, all of Jesus' teaching about the Fatherhood of God is given in public without reference to himself as the Son who, because of his filial intimacy, can reveal him supremely. Only at 11:25–27 will this point be made (but in Luke 10:21–22 privately to the disciples). Thus, "God with us" (Emmanuel) means in the context: God's presence or accessibility through Jesus' teaching and action on his behalf.

Fulfillment

Although much has been made of Matthew's efforts (sixteen instances) to show Jesus fulfilling the word of the Lord (1:22; 2:15) or that of the prophets, especially Isaiah (4:14; 8:17; 12:17) and Jeremiah (2:17; 27:9), it is indeed rare to find Jesus asserting this of himself. Only once does he do so; and that is in private (5:17). Only at the moment of his arrest does Jesus speak of the scriptures (which?) being fulfilled (once to the sword-wielding disciple and once to the arresting crowds at 26:54, 56). Isaiah 53:4 is cited by Matthew in connection with Jesus' *healing* ministry (8:17) rather than his death. Once again, the Evangelist scrupulously avoids making Jesus claim what he, as a post-resurrection Christian, knows is true.

Benefits

Salvation

Jesus is so named because he will save his people from their sins (1:21). And the name by which he fulfilled Isaiah's prophecy (i.e., "Emmanuel") seems to define by its proximity (v. 23) the means of that salvation: to mediate the presence of God. Yet "Emmanuel" is never again the name by which Jesus is known. And this under-standing of salvation is not subsequently carried through. Elsewhere, Matthew retains the Marcan uses of σώζειν (healing, rescue, escha-tological salvation) and extends them into M material (14:30). The First Evangelist preserves the Q saying about the Son of Man's coming to save the lost, but its thrust is pastoral: to rescue one of the little ones who already believe in him (18:6; cf. vv. 2, 14).[35]

Forgiveness

In only one instance is forgiveness of sins linked to the death of Jesus. Matthew's words of institution at the Last Supper add that the blood of the New Covenant, shed on behalf of the many, is "for the forgiveness of sins" (26:28). Otherwise, there is nothing distinctive about his position. The Evangelist shares with the other synoptics the account of Jesus healing the paralytic and forgiving his sins by virtue of the Son of Man's authority to do so (9:2, 5−6//2:5, 7, 9−10//5:20−21, 23−24). How such forgiveness compares or differs from that granted in Jesus' death, the Evangelists do not discuss. The difference may lie "merely" in that the latter is for "the many" (26:28 and Mark 14:24). In other words, forgiveness granted locally and to individuals comes to everyone everywhere through the cross. As with Luke and Mark, the latter theme forms no part of Jesus' public proclamation or private instruction. Nor does it occur as part of the so-called Great Commissioning scene in 28:18−20, although Luke makes it part of his charge in 24:47.[36]

The remainder of Matthew's teaching on forgiveness is decidedly theocentric. With Luke, he reports the Lord's Prayer as a direct appeal to God without christological mediation, where divine forgiveness is linked to the human (6:12, 14, 15//11:4). Such is the expansion of that teaching in chapter 18, where its application to the communal life of the church is most evident (18:22//17:4; see especially the parable of the unforgiving servant found in Matthew alone: 18:27, 32, 35). Were John the Baptist to be included, then Matthew would join the other synoptics in relating that forgiveness is granted (at least by implication at 3:6) to those who confess their sins in response to his preaching. How all of these differ in quality from one another, none of the gospel writers says with clarity. One thing is clear, however: Matthew did not take a clearly articulated Christian position and impose it upon his sources and traditions in order to make Jesus an advocate of it.

Kingdom secrets

Since William Wrede's monumental book on the gospel of Mark,[37] various efforts have been made to overturn or refine his conclusions about the secrecy phenomena in the gospels.[38] Recent studies have challenged his attempts to subsume all of them under a single rubric.[39] But little if any attention has been given to the rather cavalier claims that he made about Matthew. In a nutshell, Wrede asserted that he virtually "spilled the beans." The First Evangelist could not keep the secret. Of primary significance to Wrede's thesis was his analysis of Mark 4:10−12 (Matt. 13:10−13//Luke 8:9−10). Not only did Matthew replace one grand secret of Jesus' person with esoterica about the Kingdom of Heaven; but he also reinterpreted the significance of Jesus' parabolic teaching: from the means of obfuscation and damnation (ἵνα in 4:10) to the media of illumination and repentance (ὅτι in 13:13). Yet, both before and after, the Matthean version is equally harsh. The have-nots will have even less (v. 12; cf. Mark 4:25); and those not sharing the disciples' privileged status will bear the brunt of Isaiah's terrible prophecy (6:9−10), quoted in full (vv. 14−15).

Furthermore, a more sensitive study of the secrecy phenomena has distinguished mystery regarding the Kingdom of God from christological reserve and secrecy.[40] Here Matthew is completely in line with Mark and Luke. During the *public* ministry, Jesus suppresses the demons who address him as "the Son of God"; and he enjoins his disciples neither to speak of him as the Messiah (16:20//8:30//9:21), nor to reveal what they had seen of him during the transfiguration until the resurrection of the Son of Man (17:9//Mark 9:9). Admittedly, Matthew (17:22) does seem to remove Mark's note that Jesus desired to travel incognito through Galilee (9:30). Yet he alone includes Jesus' severe injunctions to silence upon the two blind men who had been cured (9:30).

The Responses

Believing, faith

Only at 18:6 does there appear distinctively Christian language. As in Mark 9:42, Jesus warns against offending children or immature disciples: ἕνα τῶν μικρῶν τούτων τῶν πιστευόντων. Matthew adds εἰς ἐμέ. Yet, this single exception to the rule is notable. Otherwise, believing as in Mark is in Jesus' or God's ability to heal or do something extraordinary. Or it is simply the person's faith (without an object) that triggers the cure. Never in public does Jesus call for belief in himself. The sole instance at 18:6 occurs in a private setting with disciples regarding life together in the church. This reserve prevails in Matthew, whatever the source. (It is in fact characteristic of the entire synoptic tradition.) The gospel authors and the tradition before them knew that Jesus had not explicitly applied the vocabulary of faith to his person. We would hardly have expected such astounding consistency, given the repeated assertion that the early church projected its "faith" upon the Jesus tradition. Without denying that it did, one will nevertheless have to be much more precise as to what that claim means, in view of such evidence.

Following

Matthew has not exceeded Mark in principle so far as this category is concerned. While there is an increase in the number of instances where the crowds or disciples follow Jesus, i.e., accompany him, there are no especially Matthean occasions where persons are called to become his followers. Some kind of parallel occurs in the triple tradition, in Q, or in Mark.[41] More significantly, the First Evangelist maintains an important distinction in vocabulary that points, once again, to the sort of discrimination for which I have been arguing throughout. In the previous chapter, I maintained that for Mark, and contrary to prevailing opinion, the language of following Jesus principally describes the relation of disciples to him before the resurrection.[42] "Receiving" him, on the other hand, more aptly reflects the response to Jesus afterwards. The same holds true for Matthew (10:40; 18:5).

Worshiping

At first glance, the rather neat distinctions maintained up to this point appear to break down with the vocabulary of worship, which is found in every source, segment, and audience. It seems that here is one term or idea that has escaped the centripetal restraint demonstrated so far. Nevertheless, before conceding that Matthew's post-resurrection views have for some reason surfaced here primarily (and perhaps with "understanding," below), it will be well to handle the evidence with as much deftness as the raw data permit. Twice in the triple tradition, Matthew recounts that those who came to Jesus for healing worshiped him (8:2; 9:18//1:40; 5:22//5:12; 8:41). And in the only other public setting, Matthew exceeds Mark in recounting that the Gentile woman, coming on behalf of her possessed daughter, worshiped Jesus (15:25//7:25).

Yet there is another level of usage that may qualify these "high-powered" instances. Προσκυνεῖν expresses the proper attitude towards royalty. The Canaanite woman shows obeisance to Jesus whom she had called Son of David (v. 22). The astrologers and Herod seek to worship the newborn King of the Jews (2:2, 8, 11). The mother of the brothers Zebedee asks Jesus for royal favors on their behalf when he comes in his kingdom (20:20–21. Mark 10:35 has "glory" instead of "kingdom".) But Jesus is quick to declare that such prerogatives belong to God alone (v. 23).

Ostensibly, the disciples' worship would be of a higher order. However, the two instances usually appealed to indicate something more subtle. After Jesus rescues Peter, whose little faith and doubt caused him to sink (14:31), the others in the boat worship, declaring him to be God's Son (v. 33). Yet this confession may be of a different order than Peter's acclamation of Jesus' sonship at 16:16, which came by divine revelation rather than human insight. Yet after Easter, although joyful disciples worship the risen Lord (see Luke 24:52), some doubt (28:17). Such mixed responses to Jesus, both before and after the resurrection, make one wonder if "worship" in its absolute sense is in view here. Of course, Matthew may be making the fine point here that this kind of dialectic always accompanies one's response to him.[43]

Finally, the nuance of προσκυνεῖν[44] will perhaps be appreciated better by relating it to my observations above about κύριος: just as references to Jesus as "Lord" can mean something greater than "Sir" or "Master" but less than "God," so the προσκυνεῖν of Jesus may be something more than reverence/obeisance but less than worship *per se*. However, if Matthew's Christian convictions do show through here, they are exceptional as indeed may be the final study of how responses to Jesus have been articulated in this gospel.

Understanding/Knowing (συνίεναι/νοεῖν)

The capacity for understanding figures largely in Matthew, principally in the parable chapter, as the means of responding to the word about the Kingdom (13:13–15, 19, 23). To Jesus' query if they understand all that he has said, the disciples reply with a confident "yes" (v. 51). In editorial comment, the Evangelist will underscore their ability to perceive (16:12; 17:13). Mark, of course, never allows them to get the point; so one may be tempted to conclude that we have here an example of a Matthean cover-up. However, such a judgment becomes vitiated when two intervening narratives are inspected. Having failed to understand Jesus' teaching about the internal origins of purity, the disciples must bear his stinging rebuke: "Even yet are *you* also without understanding' [ἀκμὴν καὶ ὑμεῖς ἀσύνετοί ἐστε;]?" "Do you not know?" (15:16–17//Mark 7:18). Likewise over the conundrum about leaven and loaves, Jesus charges them with little faith (no parallel in Mark), lack of knowledge, and failure to remember (16:8–9//Mark 8:17–18, 21). At best, the situation is mixed, Matthew tempering editorially the harsher narrative which he nevertheless allows to stand. Simple removal of the awkwardness could have solved the problem but for the patent restraint.

The respondents

Disciples

There is no doubt that Matthew has, in some instances at least, enhanced the disciples' reputation by removing the harshness of Mark's treatment of them. Not only does the Evangelist omit Jesus' rebuke of their culpable incomprehension (13:18//4:13), but he also credits them with understanding (13:16; 16:12; 17:13). Yet, sometimes the criticism is allowed to stand (15:16//17:18). The same may be said of Matthew's reluctance to report the disciples' lack of faith during the storm (Mark 4:40//Luke 8:25). He merely relates their little faith (8:26). Yet, at a more crucial moment, namely Peter's failed attempt to walk on water, Jesus upbraids him for his little faith and *doubt* (14:31). Nevertheless, the Matthean account concludes on a high note with the disciples worshiping Jesus as the Son of God (14:33), whereas the Marcan version ends in their lack of understanding and hardened heart (6:52). However, Matthew preserves the synoptic account of the disciples' inability to heal the lunatic/demon-possessed boy. They bear the brunt of Jesus' diatribe against the faithless and perverted generation (17:16–17//9:18–19//9:40–41).

In the first debate over rank in the Kingdom of Heaven, Matthew does avoid the embarrassing and self-serving dimension to the disciples' question (Mark 9:34//Luke 9:46). Yet, in expounding on true greatness and before answering directly, Jesus (only in Matthew) warns them that becoming humble as children is as much a prerequisite for entering the Kingdom as it is for gaining prominence in it (18:1–4). And he will not avoid showing the disciples their mistaken connection of riches and salvation (19:23–30//10:23–31//18:24–30).

When the point about status must be made again, it is in the wake of the mother of the (unnamed) Zebedee brothers' request that they be Jesus' right- and left-hand men (20:20–21). Scholars often cite this as yet another of Matthew's efforts to lessen the sting. Perhaps so; but Jesus' rebuke of such boldness is directed to the brothers as well (v. 24//Mark 10:41). Matthew, unlike Mark, relates the disciples' amazement over the fig tree's withering. Both relate Jesus' insistence on the need for unwavering faith (21:20–22//11:21–23). The First Evangelist joins the others in reporting the failure of Jesus' own followers to perceive the significance of his anticipatory anointing by an unnamed woman (26:6–13//14:3–9//7:36–50). Matthew, too, recounts the thrice-aborted vigil in the Garden of Gethsemane (26:36–46//14:2–42//22:39–46).

So again, the portrait is more complex and subtle than general allegations often allow. A more accurate assessment of Matthew's treatment ought to claim that he, rather than being guilty of a wholesale removal of criticism against the disciples, in an age when their status would have been growing among Christians, attempted to balance what some have gone so far as to call Mark's unrelenting vendetta.[45]

Peter

No one would deny that he occupies a special place in Matthew's gospel. His prominence as chief of the church's apostles appears only here. And yet the First Evangelist himself makes the point that Peter's authority is shared authority. His power to "bind and loose" with heavenly effects (16:19) belongs to other disciples (18:18). Likewise, Peter comes in for special praise because he has confessed the true status of Jesus revealed to him by God (16:16–19). But this makes Peter's resistance to the messianic role as defined by Jesus all the more shocking. Only in the First Gospel are the very words of protest related (v. 22) as well as the terrible σκάνδαλον εἶ ἐμοῦ of the Lord's rebuke (v. 23).

A similar multi-sided rendering of Peter occurs during the transfiguration. According to Matthew, it is he who volunteers to build three booths himself. And, although addressing Jesus as κύριε (17:4; ῥαββί in Mark 9:5; ἐπιστάτα in Luke 9:33), Peter nevertheless wants to accommodate Jesus, Moses, and Elijah together. However, the disappearance of these ancient worthies neutralizes this egalitarian move. Jesus alone emerges as the one who must be obeyed (v. 5 and para.). This suggests that κύριος is honorific here rather than a full-blown "confession" by the chief apostle. At the close of the episode, the inner circle of disciples lies prostrate with fear (vv. 6–7), a reaction omitted by Mark and Luke.

The complex figure of Peter is drawn most poignantly during Jesus' hearing before Caiaphas. As the narrative draws to a close, Matthew maintains the balance which keeps his efforts from becoming hagiography. Peter's denials appear more vehement in this gospel, for under the relentless interrogation of servant girls and bystanders, he twice refuses to know Jesus (26:72, 74). The intensity of this exchange is measurably greater than in the Marcan parallel at 14:68–72.[46]

Finally at the moment of parting, the Eleven are described as worshiping the risen Lord. Nevertheless, as noted above, Matthew concludes their response to him with the astonishingly frank observation that "some had doubts" (26:17). Such a finely wrought work may not in the first instance be claimed as historical; i.e., "complex, therefore authentic." Rather, the data here presented ought to make one extremely cautious about routine, but unsupported, assertions about the First Evangelist's version of Jesus' intimate protagonists. Far from exhibiting a failure of nerve, Matthew has given us a picture which is many-sided and anything but whitewashed.

The crowds

Rather than catalog the entire range of their responses to Jesus, I shall simply relate Matthew's report of the highest opinion that the people achieve of him. In the First Gospel there is only one such estimation rather than two as in the other synoptics (6:14–16//9:7–9). At 16:13–14, Matthew claims no more, really, than the others (8:27–28//9:18–19), perhaps because of redundancy. Jesus, say some, is John the Baptist, or Elijah, or Jeremiah, or one of the prophets. Each of these, important in his own right and more so since they are *redivivi*, nevertheless falls short of the true perspective possessed by Peter and the disciples through special revelation (16:17, 17:5). And yet, the crowds do attribute to Jesus "messianic" dignity in calling him the "Son of David" at the triumphal entry (21:9). But Matthew, in company with the other synoptists, shows Jesus pointing out the inadequacy of this title (22:41–46//12:35–37//20:41–44).[47]

Conclusions about Matthew's Βίβλος γενέσεως

The evidence marshaled above leads to the conclusion that Matthew maintained the distinction between before and after in a thorough-going, comprehensive manner. Nuances of terms typical of the post-resurrection narrative but foreign before are not commonly projected backwards. Vocabulary characteristic earlier is not projected forwards. The First Evangelist's achievement might even be said to have sur-passed Mark's, for there was so much more text to control. Matthew retains the ethos of his Marcan source. Furthermore, he carries it over into his other "sources," Q and M (unless, of course, this conserving tendency was already at work in them). Neither the deeper convictions about Jesus' grander human and divine ancestry, nor the supernatural phenomena accompanying his birth were allowed to intrude decisively upon the task of keeping his story distinct from the gospel writer's. Finally, despite an inclination to improve the disciples' image, Matthew cannot be accused of revisionism. In fact, there are points at which his portraits of Jesus' followers are even more severely painted than Mark's.

Although post-resurrection convictions do occasionally surface, they are rare and confined to private teaching of the disciples. Perhaps the most obvious examples of such inappropriate idiom are to be found in the mission instructions to the Twelve (ch. 10) and in the teaching about the church, both in its universal and local manifestations (chs. 16 and 18). Even so cautious a critic as F. F. Bruce acknowledges that in the former there occurs an "unusually clear opportunity of dis-tinguishing two or more settings."[48] The first relates Jesus' deep compassion for the crowds who seemed like sheep without a shepherd (9:36). In a change of metaphor, he compares them to a field ripe for harvest but lacking in workers (v. 37). The Twelve are therefore chosen to continue Jesus' preaching of the Kingdom of Heaven and healing all maladies. But they are both restricted to "the lost sheep of the house of Israel" and prevented from contacts with Gentiles and Samaritans (vv. 5–6).[49] In vv. 16–23, without any transition, the tone and theme change drastically. The disciples receive instructions about how to cope in the hostile Gentile world which they were recently forbidden to enter. As F. W. Beare points out, the issue is not the genuineness of these latter sayings but the appropriateness of their setting.[50] Thematic considerations about mission have overcome the attempt to maintain the "historical"[51] (i.e. narrative) and idiomatic sensibilities which Matthew has sustained throughout.

The second place where the Evangelist is said to have lapsed is with the appearance (only here in the gospel tradition) of ἐκκλησία in 16:18 and 18:17 (twice) in a sense that seems obviously Christian. However, R. T. France argues for a meaning that fits a narrative setting in Jesus' ministry: "the Assembly of God" under the Old Covenant is now being fulfilled with new foundations in *"My* Assembly" (16:18).[52] And Bornkamm notes that these represent only "the most meagre beginnings of a clear ecclesiology."[53] Lacking are technical terms such as "true Israel," "saints," and "the elect." Absent, too, is evidence of special offices and officers. In fact, "Matthew's Gospel confirms throughout that the congregation which he represented had not yet separated from Judaism." "The struggle with Israel is still within its own walls." "Thus Matthew's conception of the Church remains imprisoned[!] in the Jewish tradition."[54] If this is true (apart from the value judgment in "imprisoned") even for the language and setting of chapter 18, then 5:22−24 suggests an idiom clearly appropriate to a narrative *Sitz im Leben* during Jesus' ministry. It speaks of another manner of settling disputes among brothers. The use of abusive language makes one accountable to a *sanhedrin*; broken relations interfere with the effectiveness of gifts brought to the *altar*. The possibility of anachronisms in places like chapters 10 and 18 cannot be ignored. However, the important question is this: are they significant enough to have vitiated the overall thesis?

If not, then one is in a position to evaluate the view expressed by Kingsbury on behalf of certain redaction critics early in this chapter. While not denying that Matthew like all of the Evangelists wrote on two levels, I cannot support those who advocate the directness and immediacy of address that words such as "transparent" and "window" convey. With Luz (n. 61) and Kingsbury (n. 1, pp. 457−9), I conclude that the messages intended for the Matthean community were anchored firmly in a narrative of Jesus' earthly ministry whose "pastness" was conveyed by an idiom appropriate to the time yet intelligible by the reader/listener.

4

LUKE

Introduction

With Luke, the contrasts which I have been underscoring could be made more easily by an appeal to Acts. Here, the post-Easter life of the church as he interpreted it meets us with clarity and force. However, I shall avoid this natural move, since the point of the entire exercise has been to rely upon internal evidence exclusively. And an abundance of it exists in chapter 24: except for John, the most extensive account of Jesus' post-resurrection activity in the gospels. As with Matthew, I shall use this material to provide the major sections and sub-categories for the data. Finally, the Prologue will contribute its special brand of evidence to the argument.

Post-resurrection narrative (24:13−53)

On the road to Emmaus

The two men whom Jesus joined on the journey are otherwise unknown, belonging to the outer circle of disciples (the πᾶσιν τοῖς λοιποῖς of v. 9; cf. v. 33b). Yet Cleopas and his partner are inside enough to refer to "some of our women" who brought them the startling reports of the risen Jesus (v. 22). Likewise, the contingent of men who subsequently inspected the site are called "some of those with us." Their reactions afford a further insight into the pre-Easter mindset among the band of disciples. Through his miracles and preaching, Jesus had reminded them of Yahweh's historic spokesmen.

"A man, a mighty prophet" (v. 19)
Not yet enlightened with the supreme estimate of the risen Lord, these two reflect what the earthly Jesus had said of himself. The proverb of prophets unappreciated on home ground applied to him, too (4:24),

74

a contention recorded by Matthew (13:57) and Mark (6:4). However, Luke alone relates a more direct association. In 13:33, to the Pharisees, Jesus claims that his agenda will be completed or perfected (τελειοῦν) according to the prophetic precedent: it is unthinkable for a prophet to perish outside of Jerusalem (13:32–33). The prophetic model appears again but along different lines and without even the hint of death. Luke seems to be avoiding the connection at 11:29–32. Matthew has Jesus appeal in public to the sign of Jonah as prototypical of his three days and nights in the whale's belly (12:38–42). But Luke makes Jonah's significance lie in his preaching of repentance to the Ninevites. While for him and Matthew Jesus is greater than Jonah (and Solomon), the precise understanding of that greatness is not spelled out by the Third Evangelist.

Could such a self-consciousness have fed popular perceptions as recorded in 7:16? In the wake of Jesus' restoring the widow's son to life, the crowd glorified God saying " 'a great prophet has been raised up among us, and God has visited his people'." This fits closely both the opinion of Herod and of the general populace (9:18, 19 paralleled in Matt. 14:1–2; 16:14, and Mark 6:14–16; 8:28; see also Luke 9:7–8). One will have to wait until Luke's second volume to find a testimonium to the specifically Christian understanding of Jesus as the eschatological prophet spoken of by Deut. 18:15 (3:22–23; cf. 7:37).[1]

But the violent actions of their leaders had dashed all expectations:

"We were hoping him to be the one to redeem Israel shortly" (v. 21) The poignancy of this statement exceeds even that of the imprisoned Baptizer whose apocalyptic agenda Jesus had failed to fulfill (11:2–3//7:8–20). Although it is true that the hopes expressed here are not necessarily erroneous or canceled,[2] they were clearly misplaced as to the time and mode of fulfillment. Luke has a broader vision, to be sure, which may include and transcend any particularism suggested by the statement;[3] but the point is that he allows the report of its inadequacy to stand in its prima-facie sense. Thus, there appears to be no "advance" over the Spirit-inspired prophecy of Zechariah, who blesses God for visiting his people and making redemption for them (1:68). Anna's talk about the infant Jesus bears the same quality. She blesses God in the presence of all those who were expecting the redemption of Jerusalem (2:38). No further uses of this word group occur in the gospel or Acts. Luke lacks the λύτρον saying about the Son of Man in Matt. 20:28 and Mark 10:45 (and found only here in the gospels). Although such vocabulary can be given greater or other meaning by the reader, the specific language maintains its integrity within the narrative.

In his critical rejoinder, Jesus calls them "foolish men and slow of heart to believe all that the prophets had spoken" (v. 25). Such references to prophetic witness will subsequently occur five more times (vv. 27, 44–46), illustrating the importance of biblical attestation for Luke. Nevertheless, its significance does not emerge in the same way prior to Easter. Here, the christological content of that witness takes on different features.

> Was it not necessary for the Christ to suffer these things and enter into his glory?" (v. 26)

With ὁ χριστός on the risen Lord's lips, there is dramatic evidence of christological precision which Luke, along with the other synoptists, has maintained to the end. In the L material, the title is an exalted one, indeed. The angels announce to the shepherds the birth of "a savior who is Christ the Lord" (2:11). Simeon had been promised that he would live until he had seen "the Lord's Christ" (2:26). Yet the settings are private, and the reference is to Jesus ultimate, eschatological significance rather than to anything that he will achieve prior to Easter. Furthermore, John the Baptist stimulates messianic expectations among certain groups (3:15). Luke joins the other synoptists in relating that, during the public ministry, Jesus avoids using the title of himself in any way. And he forbids its usage by the disciples (16:20//8:30//9:21). The point about the Messiah's relation to David is, as in the other gospels, an academic question with no application made (22:41–45//12:35–37//20:41–44). No new instance in Q or L is introduced. After the resurrection, however, the phenomenon changes drastically. It is the only title that Jesus employs in his two post-resurrection appearances. (See also v. 46.)

Furthermore, prior to the resurrection, Jesus never speaks of the Messiah's suffering (ἔδει παθεῖν τὸν χριστόν). In keeping with the Marcan tradition, this theme remains confined to the Son of Man, δεῖ τὸν υἱὸν τοῦ ἀνθρώπου πολλὰ παθεῖν (e.g. Mark 8:31//9:22; cf. 17:24–25, and 22:37).[4] So it goes with scriptural fulfillment, here spoken of as "necessity." Although the risen Jesus maintains that the Messiah's suffering had been predicted by the prophets, the earthly Jesus cites a particular text in public which suggests that the accomplishment of the messianic task lies in a different direction. True, the noun χριστός does not occur; the verb does: the Spirit anointed Jesus (i.e., made him Christ: ἔχρισέν με) to fulfill the agenda set by Isa. 61:1–2: to announce good news to the poor, release to the oppressed and captive and to cure the blind (4:16–21). Later, Jesus informs the disciples that journeying to Jerusalem will complete (τελεσθήσεται) "all the writings through the prophets regarding (τῷ) the Son of Man" (18:31–32). This is never said of the Messiah until after Easter.

Thus, to the Pharisees, Jesus anticipates death in keeping with prophetic precedent (as described in Scripture). To the disciples before the resurrection, he refers to it as the agenda set by scripture for the Son of Man. Only on this side of the resurrection, however, does Jesus instruct them about the *messianic* significance of these prophesied events. Can this be merely fortuitous? Or, do we have here a conspicuous effort to match idiom with audience and time? Could it be that controlling Luke's narrative is the conviction expressed by Peter that it was *at the resurrection* that "God made ... [Jesus] both Lord and Christ?" (Acts 2:36; cf. 13:33 and Rom. 1:3–4).

Such alleged carefulness about titles might risk the charge of splitting hairs or quibbling, especially since "Son of God" and "Christ" seem to be equivalents at 4:41. Yet this is an editorial comment, indicating a conjunction of the two in Luke's mind. In the narrative of the trial, the two terms are separated (22:67–70) in a way that they are not in Matthew and Mark (26:63//14:61). So far as Jesus' public ministry is concerned, the Third Evangelist does not multiply the occasions when he is addressed as ὁ υἱὸς τοῦ θεοῦ. And no novel use is introduced. Jesus' attitude towards it remains constant: suppression when demons recognize him thus.

In private settings, Luke takes only one opportunity to increase the instances in the L material (the Annunciation to Mary in 1:35). Nothing new is added to Q in the Temptation narrative (4:3, 9), where Jesus' special status undergoes relentless testing. He is supremely the Son because he knows that a person's needs transcend the physical (v. 4), worships and serves God alone (v. 8), and refuses to put him to the test (v. 11).[5] Yet Luke will surpass even this level of care by a startling substitution. In Matthew and Mark (27:54//15:39), the centurion's acclamation of Jesus as God's son forms the climax to the narrative. Finally, what only supernatural beings (divine and demonic) know and what the Jews have not perceived, a Gentile "confesses." Surely, Luke would be expected to follow suit; but he reports the soldier's glorifying *God* and acknowledging that Jesus was truly δίκαιος (23:47), a quality predicated of Simeon (2:25) and Joseph of Arimathea (23:50). Admittedly, the term could suggest υἱὸς θεοῦ, since the two are equivalents in the Wisdom of Solomon 2:13, 16, 18.[6] Or, it might simply mean "innocent."[7] Either way, Luke requires his reader to infer what the other Evangelists have spelled out. And before Easter, he avoided associating suffering and "the Son of God" with the same care that he refused to link suffering with the "Christ."

It is not enough for Jesus to criticize the disciples' failure to trust the prophets' witness. Rather, he adopts a positive and more comprehensive approach.

> "Beginning from Moses and from all the prophets he explained to them in all of the scriptures the things concerning himself" (v. 27)

The language of Jesus here is Lucan, to be sure. In the parable about "Dives" and Lazarus, Abraham uses the expression "Moses and the prophets" twice (16:29, 31). These, if obeyed, will enable one to avoid the torments of Hades, says the patriarch. However, the absence of a christological component is made even more stark in Abraham's insisting that a warning to errant brothers delivered by one risen from the dead (!) would have no effect (v. 31).

Furthermore, the term "the scriptures" (γραφή in the plural) does not appear earlier than chapter 24. The singular may be found exclusively at 4:21. Otherwise, Jesus uses only the singular and plural participles (τὰ γεγραμμένα, and τὸ γεγραμμένον: 18:31, 20:17, 22:37) in the citation of Scripture. And merely twice before does Luke report Jesus' reference to it in direct connection to himself (18:31, 22:37). Nothing like this sort of explanation (διερμηνεύειν) occurs beforehand. Jesus does not carefully and systematically interpret his mission. The reader is tempted to wonder why, given the disciples' penchant for dull-wittedness and misunderstanding, the Master Teacher waited so long to provide this much-needed information. (And, of course, the crowds are less informed still.) Luke even avoids informing the readers about the significance of Jesus' words and actions in the way that Matthew does: such and such was done/said in fulfillment of what the scriptures prophesied.

To the band of disciples

The same points may be made about the second resurrection monologue, though its particular features merit special attention. What occurred in the first encounter was not accidental. Once again, Luke maintains the distinctions between before and after with the same care. It is a matter of deliberate narrative technique based upon theological convictions.

On returning to Jerusalem, after perceiving that the stranger is none other than Jesus himself, the two disciples are greeted with corroborating news.

> "The Lord is risen indeed ..."

This way of referring to Jesus in the absolute occurs only here, in the wake of the resurrection (Luke makes an editorial reference in v. 3 to "the Lord Jesus"). Earlier, no one from the public had used the title. In private, it cannot be found on the disciples' lips. The two potential exceptions are contestable. Elizabeth greeting Mary as "the mother of my Lord" could mean "Master" (1:43); Zechariah's "before the Lord" (v. 76) more naturally refers to God.[8] So, rarely, if ever, does Jesus or anyone within the narrative before Easter use ὁ κύριος in the fully fledged Christian sense.[9]

To the Eleven and others assembled in secret, Jesus appeals first to his customary practice.

> "These are my words which I spoke to you while I was with you" (v. 44)

However, one searches in vain for what follows, both in the statement's form and content.

> "It was necessary for all things written in the Law of Moses, and the prophets and in the psalms concerning me to be fulfilled" (v. 44)

This appeal to a tripartite "canonical" witness is as unprecedented in Luke as the "Trinitarian" baptismal formula is in Matthew. Each component (or a near equivalent) is cited separately throughout the narrative,[10] but never collectively. How much of this discrimination occurred self-consciously, one cannot know. If it belongs to an unconscious phenomenon, then the distinction becomes more noteworthy.

Furthermore, so far as content is concerned, Jesus did not previously appeal to texts from the writings of Moses or the psalms to substantiate the messianic agenda which he outlines subsequently, according to the Evangelist. Moreover, neither alleged earlier instruction nor that which is to follow stems from a plain reading of the biblical texts. In other words, the Scriptures do not speak for themselves. A special act by the Risen Lord is required to read them aright:

"He opened their minds to understand the Scriptures" (v. 45)
Luke thus implies that the disciples could not have made sense of them
beforehand. This inference finds support earlier on. In the one clear
instance where the appeal to prophetic scriptures did occur regarding
the Son of Man's fate (18:31–33), Luke reports that the disciples "did
not understand any of these things, and this word was hidden from
them; and they did not know what was being said" (v. 34; see 9:44–45
for the same statement except for the prophetic reference). Now
enlightened, the disciples may receive Jesus' instruction without
obstacles:

> "Thus it has been written: the Christ is to suffer and rise on the
> third day" (v. 46)

In this statement, the necessity of the Messiah's suffering has been
defined as *scriptural* necessity: events have proceeded according to
the sacred texts (however obscure to us their precise location may be).
Divine will, prophetic precedent, and now biblical warrant converge
as determinators of the drama. As before (v. 26), the christology is
"messianic" in the strict sense. The passion figures in both. In the
earlier text, entry into glory followed suffering; here the commoner
reference to resurrection occurs. Twice now, the risen Jesus speaks
in a manner atypical of the prior narrative. If he here uses the
vocabulary of the early church, then it has not been imposed
previously.

> "And repentance leading to forgiveness of sins is to be proclaimed"
> (v.47)

The language of this clause sets forth the preaching agenda for the
church, without a doubt. How does it square with prior terminology?
Will its program have been anticipated by Jesus? An uncritical
comparison will answer affirmatively. One can appeal to the typically
Lucan stress upon repentance. Both μετανοία and μετανοεῖν occur
more frequently (fourteen times) in this gospel than in Matthew and
Mark combined (ten times). In Luke alone, Jesus describes his
vocation as calling sinners to repent (5:32). And he joins Matthew
in recounting Jesus' rebuke of entire cities for refusing to do so
(11:20–21//10:13).

Furthermore, the church's proclamation of forgiveness could be
linked to Jesus' granting forgiveness during his ministry. All of the
synoptists relate how this belonged to the authority of the Son of Man
upon the earth (9:6//2:10//5:24). All three recount the incident of

Jesus' anointing by a woman (26:6–13//14:3–9//7:37–49). But Luke identifies her as Mary Magdalene whose sins Jesus forgives in consequence of her saving faith (v. 50).[11] The Third Evangelist includes the Lord's Prayer from Q, with its petition to God (without any christological mediation) for release from sins, linked to forgiving other sinners for wrongs incurred (6:12//11:4). And the sinning brother must enjoy unlimited forgiveness (18:21–22//17:3–4). But these are hardly characteristically Lucan. Neither he nor the other synoptists report that Jesus forgave the disciples. Nor does he bestow forgiveness with every cure or to every sinner. And no connection whatever is made with Jesus' death.

The task given to Christians of proclaiming repentance that leads to forgiveness (v. 47) does not fall within the description of Jesus' role. Instead, it characterizes the ministry of John the Baptist which Mark and Luke together report (1:4//3:3; see 1:77). The vocabulary is quite remarkably similar:

κηρυχθῆναι ἐν τῷ ὀνόματι αὐτοῦ <u>μετανοίαν εἰς ἄφεσιν ἁμαρτιῶν</u> πᾶσιν τοῖς ἔθνεσιν
κηρύσσων   βάπτισμα   <u>μετανοίας εἰς ἄφεσιν ἁμαρτιῶν</u>

Of course, the differences are patent enough. John required baptism of Israel. The church was to mediate forgiveness arising from repentance through Jesus' name to the nations. Yet, though mode and scope differ, the offer remains the same. (One could argue that the similarity in this instance is the more awkard feature.)

But the real distinction lies between the church's task as given by the Risen Lord and that of Jesus' self-proclaimed mission at Nazareth. Indeed, the ministry of John and the church seem closer to each other than that of the church and Jesus (at 4:18):

<u>κηρυχθῆναι</u> ἐν τῷ ὀνόματι αὐτοῦ μετανοίαν εἰς <u>ἄφεσιν</u> ἁμαρτιῶν πᾶσιν τοῖς ἔθνεσιν
<u>κηρύξαι</u>   αἰχμαλώτοις   <u>ἄφεσιν</u>

What makes these two statements so important for inspection is that both refer to the Messiah's (ἔχρισεν) and the church's charge to preach (κηρύσσειν); both are descriptions of a fundamental agenda; and both are functions of a Spirit-endowed ministry (see 24:48). Consequently, their disjunction becomes all the more impressive. Proclaiming release to captives has little or nothing to do in an obvious sense with announcing repentance that leads to forgiveness. So, when it comes to describing what lay at the heart of Jesus' and the church's mission, Luke refuses to justify the Christian blueprint by making it a carbon copy of Jesus' sense of calling.[12] Although at some extra-textual level, continuity might well be identified, the point is that Luke refused to achieve it within the text.[13] Past and present, before and after retain their (sometimes awkward and painful) integrity.[14]

Further evidence of such restraint comes from two accounts of mission conducted by the Twelve (9:1–6, 10) and by the Seventy ([-two] 10:1–17), the latter unique to Luke. Jesus' instructions to both groups bear clear similarities in seven categories.[15] But each differs from those in chapter 24 along several notable lines. The subject preached is the Kingdom of God (9:2; 10:9, 11) rather than forgiveness of sins. In chapter 10 it is quite specifically the Kingdom's drawing near (ἤγγικεν (ἐφ' ὑμᾶς)).[16] The focus is theocentric. Whatever christology there is belongs to the "ambassadorial" type, whose ultimate reference is God, not Jesus or his name: "Whoever hears you, hears me; and whoever ignores you [ἀθετεῖν], ignores me; but [ὁ δέ] the one ignoring me ignores him who sent me" (10:16). Finally, without denying that Luke anticipated the Gentile mission in the Seventy (a number, with Seventy-two, which stands for the nations of the world in Jewish reckoning),[17] it must be borne in mind that they extend *Jesus'* message and activity, confining their itinerary to those places where he would *subsequently* visit (10:1).

Somewhat less dramatic, but no less important, stands the related topic of the Lucan "soteriology." The cognates belonging to the vocabulary of salvation retain several distinctions among them. In the celebrations of Jesus' birth, salvation is theocentric and nationalistic. Thus, Mary rejoices in *God* her Savior (1:47), while angelic hosts declare to shepherds that a Savior has been born for all the people (of *God*, παντὶ τῷ λαῷ, 2:10). Earlier, Zechariah had praised God for providing salvation from David's line which includes national liberation from Israel's enemies (1:69, 71).[18] Gentiles are to be embraced, to be sure. Simeon blesses God for allowing him to see in Jesus salvation for all (2:30–32). This is the promise of the Old Testament (Isa. 40:3–5) quoted in 3:6. But it is their *future*, post-Easter inclusion. Nothing on this order occurs in what follows.[19] Until eschatological fulfillment begins in earnest, John the Baptist will give knowledge of salvation through the forgiveness of sins (1:77). Although angels hail Jesus as Savior, no one in the narrative does. (Yet he brings *immediate* salvation to Zaccheus because he is a son of Abraham, 19:9.) Thus, while the prelude and postlude of the Third Gospel roughly correspond in outlook, the narrative in between differs both in point of view and idiom. Again, there need not be conflict among them; but Luke has not constructed an obvious harmonization.[20] If it is to occur at all, it must be done by others and at another level of interpretation.

Before concluding this section on what must now be regarded as a much more complexly wrought Lucan soteriology. I shall include two related subjects. Besides the granting of forgiveness and the mediation of salvation by his presence, Jesus teaches the way to eternal life by applying what has already been established by Moses and recognized in Judaism.[21] Unlike Matthew and Mark, Luke does not report that Jesus taught that love for God and neighbor lay at the heart and head of Torah (22:35–40//12:28–33). Rather, to the lawyer's question about inheriting eternal life, he responds with another: "What does the Law say?" This prompts the νόμικος himself to join Deut. 6:5 and Lev. 18:5. Jesus then urges him to "do this and live" (10:25–28), just as Moses, speaking for God, had said (Lev. 18:5). Jesus' only role here lies in lending his authoritative support to what had already been revealed. Nothing is made of the fact or the significance of his person or role.

The same may be claimed for righteousness. Already, Zechariah and Elizabeth have this standing before God (1:6), as does Joseph of Arimathea (23:50). The publican, by virtue of his acknowledgment of sin and appeal to the mercy of God, returns home justified (18:14). Again, the christological component in the process is entirely absent. That Jesus underscored and confirmed the tax collectors' attitude before God seems adequate for Luke. How then does Jesus fit in the proclamation of the Church? How is repentance leading to forgiveness to be preached?

"In his name"

Up to this point neither repentance, nor forgiveness, nor preaching of any kind has been done in the name of Jesus. The disciples have invoked it to subject the demons (10:17);[22] but neither their proclamation nor his ever has a contemporary christological referent of any sort. Of course, as in the case of Matthew and Mark, Jesus does teach the disciples about activities done in his name: receiving a child (9:48), the coming of impostors (21:8), and enduring opposition (vv. 12, 17). But these clearly point to the era of his absence introduced by the Easter event which, as chapter 24 shows, changes everything.

Striking here is the absence of any reference to the cross, even though the risen Jesus cites Scripture predicting the Son of Man's suffering and death. Neither before nor after Easter do these pointers to Calvary ever indicate what his death was to achieve. Nor is it ever described as *pro nobis*. The closest hint comes in Luke's account of the Last Supper which by its association with Passover implies deliverance and explicitly claims covenant bonding (for many [= all] in Matthew and Mark, 26:28//14:24; for the disciples in Luke 22:20, *si vera lectio*).

Could it be then, that repentance leading to forgiveness in his Name suggests that, for Luke, it is the entire career of Jesus (i.e. his history, past and present) which saves rather than a particular segment or moment of it?[23] Does Luke mean to say that what Jesus granted to Israel during his life now by virtue of his death and resurrection becomes a universal legacy?

"To all the nations"

Jesus did not demand repentance from and offer forgiveness to Gentiles. This is an astonishing fact, though it and related data are nearly always overlooked in studies of the gospel for the Gentiles. Consequently, a more detailed analysis must be conducted among various sources.

The double and triple tradition

One might have expected Luke to increase the number of contacts with non-Jews. Yet, this is not the case. He does not, for example, reproduce Jesus' exorcism of the Syrophoenician woman's daughter (15:21–28//7:24–30). Strangely, the Evangelist fails to mention as Mark 5:20 does that the former demoniac reported his cure by Jesus in the Decapolis, cities established on a hellenistic model. Instead, he simply announces it throughout the whole city (Luke 8:39). And the "backlash" to the event takes on larger proportions: "the entire multitude of the region of the Gerasenes" asks Jesus to leave (v. 37).

When Luke relates the final passion prediction, his description of what Jesus is to suffer at the hands of the Gentiles is fuller than in the other synoptics (20:19//Mark 10:33–34//18:32). Nor does Luke soften Jesus' description about the power by which Gentiles rule (20:25//10:42//22:25). Unlike Matthew, he does not take the opportunity to name "the others" who will inherit the vineyard seized by murderous tenants as another "nation" (21:41–43//12:9//20:16). At 21:24, Luke alone aggravates the role of the Gentiles during the attack on Jersualem: taking the people into exile and trampling the Holy City during its prescribed occupation. How noteworthy, too, is Luke's omission in the Olivet Discourse of witness-bearing or gospel proclamation before the nations and their rulers (10:18// 13:10//21:12−13).

At the crucifixion, while Matthew and Luke report the centurion's confession of Jesus as God's son (which may perhaps carry less christological weight if "Colwell's Rule" cannot be invoked), Luke has him declare that Jesus was δίκαιος (22:54//15:39//23:47). This designation may, of course, carry its own christological freight; but it may also be saying something less; or at least the Gentile centurion is not being credited with a confession made rather frequently in Acts.[24]

Q

Luke retains the pericope relating Jesus' cure of the centurion (7:1−10) but takes special pains to describe the favor that he already enjoyed among the Jews (vv. 3−5) and the humility that prevented him from appealing to Jesus directly (vv. 6−7). Otherwise, the point about faith was the same: unexampled in Israel (v. 10) and not, strictly speaking, "in" Jesus. Also one might have expected Luke to omit the unfavorable comment about the Gentiles anxiously seeking material security (6:32//12:30) since he seems to have done so at 6:33 (//Matt 5:47). But this can hardly be called a tendency or pattern.

Given such a less-than-thoroughgoing redactional program, one cannot read Luke's version of the parable of the Great Supper as most critics tend to. On seeing the hall not filled by the needy from the city, the host commands his servants to complement their number with people from the "highways and hedges" (14:21−23). Yet, even if the city here refers to the Jerusalem of the Christian mission, outside still lies all of Judean and Samaritan territory (Acts 1:8) before one sets foot on "Galilee of the Gentiles" and beyond. Volume II of Luke's work should help to prevent such eisegesis. But even within the pericope itself, the distinction is being made among Jews themselves.[25]

L

In the examination above "salvation" had been anticipated by Simeon as enlightenment for the Gentiles (2:32). Indeed, one may also cite Luke's genealogy, whose range extends behind Abraham (the first Jew) to Adam, who was God's son (3:23−38). But the point could be as much a christological one: Jesus successfully resisting Satan's temptation makes him God's *obedient* son. Be that as it may, nothing specific is made of the family tree *per se*.

One might be tempted to refer next to Jesus' inaugural sermon at Nazareth. To be sure, references to Gentiles are not part of the sermon proper, nor are they explicit. Only when the crowd illustrates the proverb about prophets being honored by others rather than their own does Jesus cite the experiences of Elijah and Elisha. The point, however, is extended. Because these men of God were not honored by their own people, they honored others: they channeled the power of God to a widow of Zerephath and Naaman the Syrian (4:25–27).

Although scholars routinely claim that Jesus' journey through Samaria is really a prefigurement of the church's subsequent Gentile mission there, Luke's treatment is rather mixed. The only thankful one of ten lepers cleansed is a Samaritan, also called a foreigner by Jesus (ἀλλογένης, 17:16–18). And a Samaritan becomes a Jew's savior, not *vice versa* (10:29–37). But earlier an entire village refuses to receive Jesus and his company (9:52–56). This is quite unlike the uniformly positive response of Acts 8. And, although apostolic confirmation suggests a certain reluctance or reserve about Samaritan conversions, this is certainly a long way from the disciples' earlier desire to call down heavenly fire upon the inhospitable villages (9:54).[26] Such a mentality will eventually be overcome as the gospel becomes launched from Jerusalem where they are to receive a divine gift.

"I will send the promise of my father upon you" (v. 49)
With this word, Luke implies that Jesus had earlier spoken of this event in these terms. Yet, such is not the case. In fact, the only vocabulary occurring beforehand is ἀποστέλλειν and ἐπαγγελίαν. Otherwise, it is John the Baptist who deflects messianic acclaim by predicting that the coming Stronger One will baptize the people in the Holy Spirit and fire (3:16), an expectation reported by Matthew and Mark, too (3:1//1:8).[27] Yet Luke does not make Jesus in the narrative reinforce either John's pre-Easter or his own post-Easter convictions.

Such restraint appears in a gospel which all recognize to be especially devoted to documenting the operation of the Spirit. Jesus in particular, conceived by the Spirit, is led and motivated by him, as the "L" material makes especially clear (1:35; 4:1, 14, 18; cf. 10:21 and Matt. 11:25). However, that same "source" shows that others are said to be led and filled by the Holy Spirit: Elizabeth, Zechariah,

John the Baptist, and Simeon (1:15, 41, 67; 2:25–27). Already, these choice servants share in the experience of God's revelatory Spirit. Yet, a day is coming when Jesus' followers will encounter him in another capacity.

"You will be empowered from on high"
If "promise of the Father" is an exceptional concept in Luke's gospel, then the promise of heavenly power is, too. Previously, Jesus had given them authority (ἐξουσία) over serpents and scorpions and even over the power (δύναμις) of the Enemy himself, enabling them to subject unclean spirits in his own name (10:17–20, L). Acts shows that such power was not retracted. But something else needed complementing. Just as a special act of the risen Jesus made the Scriptures' witness to him intelligible (v. 45), so now their own witness (v. 47) becomes empowered, as Acts 1:8 will bear out. Although the designation of Jesus' followers as μάρτυρες is exceptional in the gospel here, it will become standard in volume II.

With this promise, the logia of Jesus come to an end. Luke concludes his account thus: leading the disciples out towards Bethany, he lifted his hands in blessing.

"And he departed from them, and was being borne up into heaven"
(v. 51)
Even if the second clause did not appear in the autograph, both the event of ascension and the means of referring to it are exceptional. (Διιστῆναι occurs only once before [22:59], in a reference to the passing of time;[28] ἀναφέρειν is found here alone.) Luke's reference to Jesus' ἀναλήμψις at 9:51 is unclear. Interpretations of this *hapax* oscillate between the ascension itself (see ἀνελήμφθη in Acts 1:2) and all of those moments (τὰς ἡμέρας) belonging to his ἐξοδός (9:31).[29] There is no stock terminology in Luke[30] and certainly little if any prior notice of such an occurrence.

"And they worshiped him ..." (v. 52)
The Third Evangelist is perhaps the most careful of the synoptists in restricting the worship of Jesus to this point. Not even the sense of προσκυνεῖν as "obeisance/reverence" precedes the resurrection. Luke 4:7–8 relates Jesus' insistence that the worship desired by Satan belongs to *God alone*. And fitting though the worship of Jesus is from here on, the disciples' Temple service is conducted as *divine* liturgy.

"Praising God" (v. 53)[31]

Whether or not the "non-interpolations" of vv. 50b—53 are genuine, they display Lucan sensibilities seen elsewhere. Perhaps this datum from internal evidence lends weight to the massive external evidence in favor of the longer readings.[32]

The Prologue

Besides joining the other synoptists in distinguishing between the idioms of pre- and post-resurrection eras, Luke goes a step farther. Unlike them, he betrays yet a third — another post-Easter "dialect." It occurs in the much-examined Prologue (1:1—4) where the Evangelist clearly states his purpose in writing. In thus revealing his intent, Luke resembles the author of the Fourth Gospel at 20:30—1. But whereas John's statement corresponds in its essential idiom with that of the preceding narrative (see the next chapter for a full discussion), Luke's does not. It stands apart from what follows in vocabulary and theme. A moment's glance at the two passages set side-by-side discloses striking similarities between eleven categories in each.

Luke 1:1—4	John 20:30—1
(a) διήγησις	(a) τῷ βιβλίῳ
(b) τῶν πληροφορημένων	(b) πολλὰ ... ἐποίησεν ᾽Ιησοῦς
(c) πραγμάτων	(c) σημεῖα
(d) αὐτόπται	(d) ἐνώπιον
(e) ὑπηρέται[33]	(e) τῶν μαθητῶν
(f) γράψαι	(f) γέγραπται
(g) ἵνα	(g) ἵνα
(h) ἐπιγνῶς	(h) πιστεύ [σ] ητε
(i) περὶ ὧν λόγων	(i) ὅτι ᾽Ιησοῦς ἐστιν ὁ Χριστὸς ὁ Υἱὸς τοῦ Θεοῦ
(j) κατηχή/ηθῆς	(j) ἔχητε
(k) ἀσφάλειαν	(k) ζωήν

But the differences within the Third Gospel are even more evident. Nothing that Luke wants to do for Theophilus corresponds to what Jesus sought to accomplish with his disciples *before* Easter. At this level, there is no evidence to support the dominant redaction-critical claim. Nor do the Evangelist's efforts on Theophilus' behalf mirror anything that Jesus said to his disciples *after* the resurrection. Again, the classical assertion of redaction critics is vitiated when examined from this perspective. The language of the Prologue has lent nothing to the *patois* of those eras; nor have they contributed to the idiom of the Prologue.[34]

Conclusions about Luke's διήγησις

Now with the analysis of Luke complete, I must reiterate the point that at no instance has my aim been to vindicate him as an historian. Instead, the goal has been to study the Evangelist's narrative art. I say "narrative" because there exist estimates of his work as *art* which are much too general and exclusive. For example, N. Q. King pits art against history in a treatment of the gentile mission as if these were the only possible categories, and antithetical ones at that.

> Clearly St. Luke was universalistic in his outlook in that he envisaged the Gospel's being carried to the non-Jews. But in his gospel, with consummate skill, he does not obtrude this. Rather, there is a partial κρύψις of his universalism while he is writing the Gospel. He indicates that the preaching to the gentiles is to come after the Jews have done their worst to the Messiah and he has triumphed in the power of God. One would like to suggest that he is too good an historian to commit the anachronism of inserting a fully fledged gentile mission into the Lord's own ministry, but of course, that is thinking in the categories of a modern historian. Rather, one may say it is the sure touch of an artistic genius. The theme which he played over earlier and had repeated now and then, has to wait until the second part of the work (that is, Acts) for its crescendo.[35]

One can concur, for the most part. But why bring in "the modern historian" (as if there were not historians of various "schools") at all? Luke at least ought to be credited with sensitivity to the historical, something lacking in medieval art that represents scenes from the gospels in the costume and architecture of the painter's age. (Are some redaction critics accusing him of a literary version of this?) And why make the avoidance of anachronism a virtue of modern historiography? The ancient Greek tradition held to the ideal, whatever the lapses in practice.[36]

John Drury makes the point more adequately:

> He simply knows that Jesus' ministry was at a particular time; not in his own time or the time of the Old Testament, but the link between them. It was yesterday – not today, or the

day before yesterday. He is, for example at pains to keep the gentiles off stage in his gospel. Mark's Syrophoenician woman disappears and Matthew's centurion is kept off the scene by hectic stage management. For Luke knew that the mission of the gentiles was later and avoids the anachronism. This finer sense of time distinguishes Luke.[37]

My contentions go farther (without begging the question of historicity). Once the narrative is analyzed on several fronts (so as to avoid all suspicion of idiosyncrasy), the conclusion must follow that Luke, perhaps more than Matthew and Mark, maintained an almost severe standard in portraying Jesus' past. Neither the Jewishness of the infancy narratives nor the obviously Christian character of chapter 24, nor the narrator's arrangement and adaptation of what lies between has intruded decisively upon the Jesus story. Of course there is a Lucan redaction. But detection of its character and scope must take into account the clear evidence that he resisted the pervasive encroachment of post-Easter convictions within the story of "all that Jesus began to do and teach."[38] As a result there now exist data to describe more adequately the nature of that διήγησις which the Evangelist ordered for the most excellent Theophilus (1:1–4).[39]

5

JOHN

Introduction

It might occasion some surprise that evidence for the synoptic evangelists' care in maintaining "an appropriate idiom and a sense of time" should be sought in the Fourth Gospel. To be sure, nearly everyone allows that John makes quite clear to the reader that his own era and that of Jesus are different. The most obvious evidence is that, since the resurrection, another Advocate takes Jesus' place (7:39, 14:15–17, 26; 16:7–15). The disciples afterwards are endowed with a heightened memory and understanding both of the Scriptures and of Jesus' teaching and action (2:22; 12:16; 13:7, 20). However, such distinction-making amounts in the main to simple periodization. How other is the idiom, how comprehensively John has distributed and integrated it throughout the narrative, how kerygmatic it is. Each of these differences warrants some elaboration, if only to underscore the extent to which the well-known "Johannine Problem" both obscures this sort of investigation and will be transcended by it.

Idiomatic homogeneity

The otherness of the Johannine idiom stems from the "wholly other" christology that one finds. Though from Nazareth, Jesus is from above (6:51, 62). He is even "from below" in the sense that he provides the "ground" of one's spiritual being as bread (6:35, 48), water (7:38), and light (8:12; 9:5) nourish one's bodily existence. But he is pre-existent as well as transcendent. Jesus outstrips John the Baptist and Abraham in rank because he existed before them in time (1:15; 8:58). The Word was in the beginning with God (1:1–2; 17:5). And this is announced with a public self-consciousness that differs both in degree and kind from the synoptics. Salvation is of a different order, too; and the stakes seem higher: to choose between life and death with eternal consequences that begin in the here and now (3:18; 6:35, 58). Appropriating so great a salvation also requires as profound a response. One must believe on Jesus, chew his flesh, drink his blood (6:30–58), participate in the most intimate divine–human interchange (ch. 15) called "knowing" (17:3). No wonder then that the Jesus of John's Gospel utters "words that sound like castles."[1]

This fortified theological idiom is also comprehensively distributed. Wherever one looks – prologue, body, and epilogue – and whatever the audience, there is one mind and voice throughout. To disciples (1:51), individuals (9:35), and the crowds (5:27; 12:34) Jesus speaks of himself as the Son of Man. He makes himself known to the Samaritan woman as the Messiah (4:26). As the Son of God, Jesus obeys God's agenda rather than his own (4:34; 5:30; 6:38). And people acknowledge Jesus in these terms. Early on, the Baptizer bears witness that he is the Son of God (1:34), as do the early disciples (1:49), the Twelve (6:69), and Mary (11:27). In the same breath, she also believes him to be the Messiah, as did the Samaritans and Andrew before her (4:29; see v. 42 and 1:41). The cured blind man, in a manner wholly atypical of the synoptics, believes on Jesus as the Son of Man (9:35).[2] Throughout, the benefit of such responses to Jesus is overwhelmingly this: eternal life now and hereafter (3:35–6; 5:24–8; 6:40; 11:25–7; 17:3; 20:31).

As marked and comprehensive as the theological idiom is its kerygmatic nature. The two go hand in hand. John not only tells the story, he addresses the reader directly and indirectly, making an offer and eliciting a commitment. The appeal for response and promise of benefits, so typical of the kerygma elsewhere, are conspicuously absent in the synoptics. This has been enough to convince some scholars that they cannot be regarded as the kerygma in written form.[3] But such objections cannot be sustained in John. His statement of purpose is clear. He intends to promote life by getting the reader to believe that Jesus is the Messiah, God's Son (20:31). This was the point of the Prologue, too: not only Jews by birth but all who received him, those who believed on his name, received authority to become God's children (1:2). And sandwiched in between, the christology, the promised salvation, and the means of appropriating it are the same.[4] Furthermore, Jesus' absence should make no difference in the possibility or the quality of the results. The reported signs function in the same way that the original ones did. He is the Man for all seasons.[5]

A common explanation for this other, comprehensive, and

kerygmatic idiom is that John has projected his Easter faith backwards upon the narrative in a radical way. What lurks between the lines in the synoptics lies on the surface in the Fourth Gospel for all to see. But this analysis misses the more profound theo-logic that underlies the characteristic language and thought of the gospel. The point is not that Jesus is the Messiah and Son of God in spite of the crucifixion and because of the resurrection, events which effect salvation by faith. No, the death is not a scandal. Rather, Jesus' being lifted up on the cross is the moment of glorification. On that occasion, Satan is to be cast out and stripped of his role as ruler of this world (12:27–33). However, important as these events are in John, they complete (τελειοῦν) what had been initiated much earlier (4:34; 5:36; 17:4; 19:30). Put most sharply, salvation is revelation rather than redemption. Not death and forgiveness but incarnation and knowledge integrate the idiom of Johannine theology, christology, and soteriology. This calls for some elaboration and justification.

Whatever the titles applied to him, Jesus' person, words, and actions reveal God. He is God's exegete (1:18), a role that starts at the incarnation. He is "Word of the Father ... in flesh appearing." As the obedient Son, Jesus does nothing and says nothing on his own (5:19, 30). Thus, to see and hear him is to see and hear the Father (14:8–10). This way of understanding the Fourth Gospel also explains the early and frequent recognition of Jesus by all sorts and conditions of men and women. It is simply not the case in John that Jesus could only be known authentically after and by virtue of the cross. No, if revelation occurred in the incarnation, then it is not surprising that perception of Jesus as Revealer should be possible thereafter at some fundamental level. This ability to acknowledge him during his life as God's last and best word-in-action also enables one to understand how the disciples, the masses, and erstwhile opponents could before the resurrection come to believe or rely on Jesus as the supreme expression of God's character and will.[6] It fits the logic: if the knowledge of God is eternal life (17:3), if Jesus reveals such knowledge, and if one trusts him for it, one should experience this level of existence before and independent of Easter.[7] The movement of Johannine thought is not simply or even primarily backwards from the resurrection but forwards from the incarnation.

Quite naturally, one may ask, "If all of this was in John's view available prior to Jesus' death and resurrection, what advantage do those have who came after?" To begin with, the sheer number of those who find life becomes increased. What were once the prerogatives of the few become available to the many. Accomplishing such universalization is one of the publicly stated functions of Jesus' death. Once a solitary seed dies, it produces abundant fruit (12:24). When Jesus is lifted up, he will draw all people to himself (12:32; in v. 34 the crowd understands this as a reference to his death). Furthermore, they are to experience the greater understanding which the Spirit will mediate: all truth grounded in an accurate recollection of Jesus' earthly teaching (14:26; 16:12–15).[8] The only disadvantage seems to be that one will have to believe without seeing Jesus and the signs that he performed to encourage reliance in his exposition of God's character. But there is the *report* of signs which the Evangelist supplies. And these are sufficient to extend to subsequent generations *the same benefits on the same terms* (20:31). No wonder that the pre- and post-resurrection idiom is virtually identical.

Finally, these grand themes (so comprehensively worked through, so closely integrated, and so passionately advocated) are presented in a uniform style quite unlike anything that one finds in the other gospels. While the task of detaching tradition from editorial framework and identifying sources has been relatively straightforward in the synoptic tradition (because so much of it is shared material), the same has not been true for the Fourth Gospel. Despite prodigious attempts to identify a "signs source" in John,[9] the results have been inconclusive, and no broadly based consensus has emerged,[10] so seamless has the garment been woven. The same is true at the literary level, Jesus' dialogue with Nicodemus being the most often-cited example: after a dozen or so verses, it is not clear whether one is reading the words of Jesus or those of the Evangelist. R. A. Culpepper reflects the majority view in concluding that

> in the gospel generally, there is a remarkable uniformity in the idiom of the narrator and Jesus. There is certainly the theoretical possibility that the author has adapted the speech of his narrator to Jesus' idiom, but it is more likely that Jesus' speech is "contaminated" by authorial speech patterns.
>
> The difference between the idiom of the Johannine Jesus and the synoptic Jesus, on the one hand, and the similarity and language of the Johannine epistles, on the other hand, confirms that when Jesus, the literary character speaks, he speaks the language of the author and his narrator.[11]

Idiomatic diversity

If all of this is true, and it cannot be easily dismissed, then the search for distinctions between once and now are impossible. Pre- and post-resurrection, before and after incarnation, it is all the same. There is no point from which to conduct an adequate test. Nevertheless, when these boundaries are used as touchstones, a subtle Johannine version of the synoptic phenomenon does in fact emerge at the literary level that has escaped the notice of even the most thorough studies. It is important not to mis- or overstate the case. I will not attempt to join the debate about the Fourth Gospel's historical value any more than I did for the others. Nor do I wish to go beyond the evidence. One cannot find the massive and consistent patterns that inter-penetrate the synoptics. But there are enough of a significant kind to demonstrate that John's narrative has been stamped with a con-sciousness that could not be obscured even though the alternative portrayal of Jesus was done in so thoroughgoing a manner. As before, I shall focus upon the materials that betray John's theological colors most clearly: the Easter encounters of chapter 20, the Evangelist's self-conscious statement of purpose (v.31), and his most obvious explanations of events and utterances which without explanations might bring mystification or indifference even to the Christian reader.[12]

Post-resurrection encounters (20:8–29)

Mary Magdalene at the tomb (vv. 8–17)

As in the other gospels, the resurrection, judged by the disciples' reaction (or lack of it), seems an unexpected or misunderstood event. This is especially so in the Fourth Gospel where Jesus *never* speaks (even in indirect discourse) of his own resurrection with ἀνάστάσις, ἀνιστῆναι or ἐγείρειν, as he does in the synoptics. The closest he ever comes to broaching the subject is in the language of laying down his life and taking it up again (10:17–18). The vocabulary of exaltation, as others have frequently pointed out, need not include rising from the dead at all. It is only after the beloved disciple sees the empty tomb that he believes. And the *narrator* informs the reader that he had not known the Scripture that it was necessary for Jesus to rise from the dead (20:8–9).

One must not expect (on this thesis) that the transition from pre- to post-resurrection periods will have to be an abrupt one. John along with Matthew and Luke recounts that there was neither immediate recognition nor full-blown "Christian" confession after Easter upon encountering the risen Jesus. Weeping, Mary Magdalene sees the two angels dressed in white and seated at either end of the place where his body had lain (vv. 11–12). She explains her distress to them that someone has removed the body of τὸν κύριόν μου (v. 13). The fuller Johannine usage of this articular expression will be considered below. But it is wurth observing now that Mary, thinking the present Jesus *whom she sees* is the gardener, addresses him as κύριε, the merely honorific expression (vv. 14–15). When recognition does come (v. 16), it is as ῥαββουνί (which John conveniently translates as διδάσκαλε[!]). Of course, Thomas will make up for what some may regard as a rather flat "confession." (This appears to be the reason why D (it) has κύριε preceding διδάσκαλε.) And Thomas will call his Lord, ὁ θεός μου (v. 28). But Jesus charges Mary to announce to the disciples his return to his father and theirs, to θεόν μου and to their God (v. 17).

The commission (vv. 19–23)

On that first sabbath after the crucifixion, Jesus appears to the disciples who are hiding behind locked doors for fear of the Jews (v. 19). He pronounces his peace upon them, displaying the multiple wounds in hands and side (v. 20). The second bestowal of peace is followed by the Johannine commission.

"Just as the Father has sent me, so am I sending you" (v. 21)
Only once before does Jesus make this comparison between his mission (ἀπέσταλκέν με)[13] and theirs (πέμπω ὑμᾶς).[14] During the Prayer, he reviews what has been accomplished among them: "Just as you have sent me (ἀπέστειλας) into the world, so also have I sent them (ἀπέστειλα) into the world" (17:8). Yet there has been no sending earlier on, leading one to suspect that this comment anticipates 20:21. There had been a previous claim about sending (ἀποστέλλειν) the disciples to harvest whitened fields that others had sown (4:38). However, no report of such an event ever occurs. There is no mission. This must be the terminology appropriate to the subsequent era.

The assignment, before being specified further, is preceded by an act known as "the Johannine Pentecost".

"And when he had said this, he breathed and said to them, 'Receive the Holy Spirit'" (v. 22)

I need not solve the vexed questions here about the full meaning of this expression for John, the gospel tradition, and Acts.[15] All that needs saying for the thesis of this book is that the event and language are completely unanticipated by all that Jesus before the resurrection says about the Spirit. He will be sent by the Father (14:26) or by Jesus (14:16, 16:7) from the Father (15:26). Never is his *reception* by the disciples the focus. The event will occur in and because of his absence. Furthermore, the sense here seems to be the bestowal of a power or energy rather than the coming of an Advocate or Comforter.

Thus endowed, the disciples are entrusted with staggering authority.

"If you forgive anyone's sins, they stand forgiven" (v. 23)

Although at 1:29 John the Baptist had referred to Jesus as the Lamb of God that takes away the sin of the world, Jesus never pronounces forgiveness of sins. Nor is forgiveness ever connected with his death. Nor does it occur as part of the disciples' "mission," a mission which, though mentioned in passing, either never occurred (4:38) or was referred to proleptically (17:18).

Furthermore, the negative side of their role is also previously unexampled.

"If you retain [the sins] of any, they stand retained" (v. 23)

The two instances of κρατεῖν appear only here. Together with ἀφίεναι, they sound more like the Matthean binding (δέω) and loosing (λύειν) of 16:19 and 18:18 than anything Johannine. As it was in Matt. 28:18−20 and Luke 24:46−47, so also is it the case in John: nothing prior to this commission prepares us for the particulars of it. Even if one were to concede that the fact of the mission had been anticipated at 4:38 and 17:18, its precise nature becomes apparent only after the resurrection.

The confession (vv. 26−27)

Thomas had not been present during this first encounter with the risen Lord. At the news of what had occurred in his absence, the Doubter refuses to believe on anything less than empirical data. Eight days later, Jesus obliges him with such a tangible encounter. "The Twin" responds with a confession unique to the entire gospel tradition.

"My Lord and my God" (v. 28)

John's stated aim does not include getting his readers to believe that Jesus is Lord and God. No other NT writers have as their express goal to argue his deity, although many endeavor to encourage the confession that he is Lord. Yet, the Fourth Evangelist does not belong to this company. One might have expected as much, given Thomas' confession at 20:28 and the plethora of references to Jesus by the disciples after the resurrection in the absolute form,[16] ὁ κύριος. This datum is worth investigating further because no one in the narrative addresses him thus beforehand. It is a title at home exclusively in the post-Easter situation both of the disciples[17] and of the Evangelist as narrator, whose editorial comments are quite limited.

Jesus uses it in private with the disciples about his relation to them, drawing upon the analogy of how masters and slaves act towards each other (13:13, 14, 16; 15:15, 20). This is the *only* way that he employs the term. Neither the "higher-powered" eschatological sovereign of Matt. 7:21 (who still defers to his Father) nor David's Lord (who as God's right-hand man needs to have enemies subjected for him)[18] figures in the Fourth Gospel.

So far as the vocative is concerned, the "non-Christian" uses are instructive. While the Samaritan woman regards Jesus as "merely" a prophet, she calls him κύριε (4:19). So does the blind man *before* he believes in Jesus as the Son of Man (9:36) as well as after (v. 38). This range is reflected among the crowd[19] and the disciples (including intimates such as Mary and Martha).[20]

Only at 20:28 does anyone ever acclaim Jesus as God. The reading μονδγενὴς θεός at 1:18, although attested by P66 and P75, is too contested to be of any use.[21] Even if it were secure, however, there would be only these two statements in the Foreword and Afterword to go on. So far as the narrative is concerned, I shall later treat more fully the charge that Jesus made himself equal with God by calling him his own Father (5:17–18). In chapter 10, however, the charge of blasphemy becomes intensified. Although Jesus has averred the superiority of his Father (10:29), he nevertheless claims to be one with him (v. 30). This time, the attempted stoning proceeds from the inference of identification: σὺ ἄνθρωπος ὢν ποιεῖς σεαυτὸν θεόν (v. 34).[22]

Jesus, however, takes the tack of playing down the identity by appealing to the unbreakable witness of "their Law." Does not Scripture, the Word of God, itself report (Ps. 82:6) that others had been called gods (vv. 34–35)? Members of the divine council had been delegated various responsibilities. What if indeed he, as God's son, had been sent into the world on a special mission to do the works of God? Such correspondence between the activities of Father and Son must lead one to conclude that they abide one in the other (vv. 36–38).

So far as the ἐγώ εἰμι passages are concerned, J. A. T. Robinson notes that of the "absolute uses" most are simply establishing identification: "I am he" (including 4:26, 6:20; 9:9; 18:5–8).[23] C. K. Barrett, taking up the most difficult passages (8:24, 28, 58; 13:19), says of the latter ("Before Abraham was, I am") that "the main sense here is the continuous being of the Son – he exists before Abraham, now, and forever." The other passages, when examined in context, mean something far less than Jesus' taking up the divine name of the OT: "It is simply intolerable that Jesus should be made to say, 'I am God, the supreme God of the Old Testament, and being God I do as I am told.' Or, 'I am God, and I am here because someone sent me'."[24]

Thus, I conclude that, if Thomas registers the Evangelist's conviction that the risen Jesus is "Lord and God," he restrained himself from making these categories the routine expressions which Jesus used of himself or by which others referred to him before the resurrection.

The statement of purpose (20:30–31)

"These [signs] have been written"

For the author of the Fourth Gospel, the *report* of signs for subsequent generations will enable faith to be effected just as adequately as the original signs themselves. This conviction permeates the Gospel such that the characteristic Johannine "sign language" is noted by every interpreter. What generally escapes comment, however, is that it belongs to the narrator and the *dramatis personae*, not to Jesus by and large. Of the seventeen instances of σημεῖον (and the three uses of σημαίνειν), only two are spoken by Jesus, one of which seems somewhat negative: "unless you see signs and wonders, you will in no case believe" (4:48). The other expression illustrates both the intended effect and its failure to produce the correct response: "You seek me because you ate and were full, not because you saw signs" of something more profound (6:26). Overwhelmingly, it is John as narrator who interprets Jesus' activity[25] and death[26] with this term.[27]

Quite the opposite is the case with ἔργον and ἐργάζεσθαι. Of the thirty-five occurrences (twenty-seven and eight, respectively), only three can be attributed to John. And even these may belong to Jesus, depending on the speaker at 3:19–21. As many are used by various persons (6:28; 7:3; 10:33). Once again, such statistics are not being used to argue for historicity. They merely testify to the claim that there is an editorial language distinct from the narration *per se*, and the dividing line seems to be the resurrection.

"So that you might believe that Jesus is the Christ, the Son of God"

There is no need to delay the discussion by treating the textual issue at length. Whether one reads πιστεύσητε or πιστεύητε,[28] the object/subject of coming to faith or of ongoing belief is the same: that Jesus is the Christ, the Son of God.[29] Jesus is indeed the subject of believing both before and after the resurrection, making it appear that I cannot appeal to this category as a means of demonstrating that John maintained a distinction between his time and that of Jesus. One cannot ignore or qualify the abundant christocentricity of πιστεύειν in its various uses with εἰς, ἐν, and the direct object. The statistics are too incontestable to require comprehensive recitation or challenge. And there are two critical occasions where parallel πιστεύειν ὅτι constructions occur. Peter, "confessing" for the Twelve, exclaims ἡμεῖς πεπιστεύκαμεν καὶ ἐγνώκαμεν ὅτι σὺ εἶ ὁ υἱὸς τοῦ θεοῦ (6:69). Martha likewise acknowledges, ἐγὼ πεπίστευκα ὅτι σὺ εἶ ὁ υἱὸς τοῦ θεοῦ (11:27).

Furthermore, there is the phenomenon that John's Jesus, unlike his synoptic "alter ego," invites and instigates such response. To the Samaritan woman's conviction that the Messiah is coming to tell all, Jesus admits ἐγώ εἰμι ὁ λαλῶν σοι (64:25–26). Perhaps more startling is Jesus' interchange with the man cured of congenital blindness. Finding him, Jesus inquires, "Do you believe in the Son of Man?" Yes, were he to be identified. "You have indeed seen him and indeed he is the one speaking to you" (9:35–37). (Nowhere else does the Son of Man figure as the subject of believing.)

Nevertheless, it is the case that Jesus does not, strictly speaking, explicitly and regularly call for belief that he is the Son of God and Christ. The latter fails to appear on his lips. Barbara Bjelland has noted that the former occurs only once in public about his eschatological role: the dead, upon hearing the voice of the Son of God will live (5:25). The private use among his own is equally rare. At 11:4, Jesus assures Mary and Martha that Lazarus' illness would glorify the Son of God.[30] In this reserve, John joins the synoptists.

Furthermore, the theocentric exceptions to the general "rule" loom large. And their appearance at strategic moments in the narrative makes the point even more dramatically. Two instances warrant special attention. The first occurs in chapter 5, where Jesus comes under fire for healing a long-term paralytic on the sabbath (vv. 9–16). The Jews become even more enraged when Jesus justifies his action by claiming that he simply mirrored the action of God his Father (v. 17). They thus seek to execute him for committing two capital crimes according to the narrator: breaking the sabbath and making himself equal with God (v. 18). Jesus defends himself by appealing to the authority that he *derives* from being the Father's *obedient* Son (vv. 19–23; cf. v. 30). In keeping with this patricentricity, Jesus announces in solemn terms, "Amen, amen I say to you, whoever hears my word and believes *him that sent me* has eternal life and does not come into judgment, but has passed out of death into life" (v. 24).

The second instance is more striking still, both because of its strategic location in the narrative and for its absolute, unqualified language. For the better part of eleven chapters – half the book – and towards the close of his public ministry, Jesus calls for belief in himself. Chapter 11, recounting the raising of Lazarus from the tomb, is full of it (vv. 25–27). In chapter 12, Jesus enters Jerusalem "triumphantly" and engages in his final public interchange. John concludes this encounter with a summation of all that preceded: "although he had worked such signs before them all, they were not putting their trust in him" (οὐκ ἐπίστευον [or, ἐπίστευσαν] εἰς αὐτόν, v. 37). For the author, this response to Jesus fulfilled Isaiah's terrible prophecy (vv. 38–41). Nevertheless many of the Pharisees believed in him (ἐπίστευσαν εἰς αὐτόν); but, fearing expulsion from the synagogue and preferring human approbation to God's, they kept their allegiance private (vv. 42–43).

Given this context, then, v. 44 leaps out at one as an obvious anomaly. Jesus cries out, ὁ πιστεύων εἰς ἐμὲ οὐ πιστεύει εἰς ἐμὲ ἀλλὰ εἰς τὸν πέμψαντά με. The shift and its denial were intolerable for the translators of the New International Version. Governed by the doctrine of Scripture's inerrancy, they felt impelled to supply "only" after ἐμέ, although there is not the slightest textual warrant for it.[31] Here we have a statement of the kind that is more at home in the synoptic tradition where God is the subject of belief. In fact, Mark 9:37 provides an almost exact counterpart, although here spoken to the disciples in private. Receiving a child in Jesus' name amounts to receiving him. Yet "whoever receives me, does *not* receive me, but receives the one who sent me" (ὃς ἂν ἐμὲ δέχεται, οὐκ ἐμὲ δέχεται ἀλλὰ τὸν ἀποστείλαντά με).[32]

Are these two rare statements simply John's failure to remove synoptic-like theocentricity from the unbroken skein of a later age's unmitigated christocentricity? Or does the Evangelist highlight what he regularly and comprehensively asserts in various ways: that Jesus is *God's* ultimate revelation? At this point in his commentary, Hoskyns aptly observes, "Christian faith is not a cult of Jesus; it is faith in God."[33]

"And that by believing you might have life in his name"

Neither the expression "life in his name" nor the notion of believing in Jesus' name to achieve life can be found prior to 20:31. True, either Jesus' reply to Nicodemus or the narrator's rather direct address to the reader at 3:18 promises judgment, even now, to the one who has not believed in the name of God's only begotten Son. But this is at best exceptional and certainly not anything like a standard formulation. Only on two other occasions, both unmediated comments by the author, does πιστεύειν εἰς τὸ ὄνομα αὐτοῦ occur. According to the Prologue, one is given authority to become a child of God (1:12). At Passover in Jerusalem, many believed in his name, having observed the signs which Jesus did (2:23). Such belief, while correct, need not be complemented by the appropriate internal response.

Every time Jesus speaks of his earthly activity, it concerns something about the *Father's* name.[34] During that period, the disciples had not yet asked anything in Jesus' name (16:24). But *afterwards*, appealing to the Father in Jesus' name will bring a positive response.[35] In the new era, the disciples are to expect the Holy Spirit, whom the Father is to send in Jesus' name (14:26), and persecution will come because of it (15:20–21). As in the synoptics, the name of Jesus functions as a medium in his absence. Even then, however, Jesus promises to continue making the *Father's* name known to them (17:26). Thus, John himself has kept discrete the "naming of the name".[36] Christocentricity in the Prelude and Postlude enshrines a vigorous *patri*centricity.[37]

That there exists a relationship between the two will not be denied. Describing it has, of course, belonged to the tasks of interpreters ancient and modern.[38] To do so here would obscure the focused goal of the book in general and this chapter in particular. Whatever the proposal, it will have to take ˌinto account the maintenance, even by John, of a transition from one era to the next.[39] Such a shift transcends merely formal periodization of the kind usually recognized. And even where ideological contrasts are noted between the two times, they must be supplemented by the broader and deeper categories set forth here.

Before and after, outside and in

John's significant though not thoroughgoing distinction between before and after allows him to provide an insider's view on what from the outside would otherwise have seemed meaningless and inconsequential. With a frequency that has, for the most part, been overlooked by his interpreters, the Evangelist tells the reader what events and sayings *signified*.[40] Apparently, without his guidance, even a believer would be hard pressed to interpret them thus. Indeed, we are dependent on him to know that a particular comment or deed was a sign in the first place. Jesus' utterances and performances do not necessarily speak for or point beyond themselves. Were it not for John's "spiritual" interpretations, significant moments in this gospel would be as "somatic" as the others.[41] Small wonder, then, that one meets in the Fourth Gospel a narrator whose omniscience,[42] omnipresence, and intrusiveness exceed analogous phenomena in the synoptic tradition.

Thus the frequent appeal to John 3 cannot be regarded as if it were representative of the entire gospel. There, during the interchange with Nicodemus, the words of Jesus and those of the Evangelist begin to be indistinguishable. But this is the exception rather than the rule. Nothing like it happens again, notwithstanding the constant assertions of most critics. Although not frequent, the following represent the most obvious occasions where, despite the inside information provided by the Prologue, John intervenes to make certain that the reader will see what to unaided senses made little if any impact upon the original audience. Without his insight, even the benefit of living this side of Easter will not guarantee that the point will be taken.

The wedding at Cana (2:1–10)

The Evangelist goes to great lengths to relate how Jesus had miraculously extended the supply of wine. Oddly, the impact of the event upon the celebrants is nil, for no one knows about it except the disciples. It takes John (v. 11) to tell us that it was a sign (the first), though what is signified remains a mystery. At least in the synoptic parable about new wine requiring new wineskins, the message can be inferred with some caution. Not here. John maintains that the sign revealed Jesus' glory to the disciples. Yet how and what glory means are not disclosed. The disciples believe upon him, apparently as a result. But some of them had recognized him earlier as the Messiah (1:41) and the Son of God (v. 49). The latter confession, and the believing upon which it rested, resulted from Jesus' extraordinary farsightedness (v. 50).

The Temple cleansing (2:13–22)

In the wake of Jesus' disruptive action, the Jews quite understandably ask for a sign (v. 18). But he responds in "sign *language*" (v. 19) that has nothing obvious to do with the event: "destroy this temple and in three days I will raise it up." They take these remarks quite literally (v. 20), not knowing apart from the narrator's explanation that Jesus had spoken of his body (v. 21). Of course, the reader would have been in the dark, too, without the commentary. It took the disciples until the resurrection even to remember the remark and to believe both the Scripture and the word of Jesus, says John (v. 22).

The feeding of the five thousand (6:1–15)

John readily points out that the crowds drew the wrong conclusion from this sign. To avoid being made king by force (ἁρπάζειν αὐτὸν ἵνα ποιήσωσιν βασιλέα), Jesus withdraws to the mountain alone (vv. 14–15). Later in the chapter, during the Bread of Life discourse (vv. 25–59), he supplies the interpretation that should have been inferred. Unaided, the masses had sought Jesus, "not because you had seen signs, but because you had eaten the loaves and had your fill" (v. 26). When the people ask what sign he was doing (v. 30), Jesus appeals to manna, Moses, and himself (vv. 31–33). Without such amplification, neither the crowds nor the reader could see the relation of sign to signified and signifier.

Caiaphas' "prophecy" (11:47–52)

At a meeting of the Sanhedrin, distressed Pharisees report Jesus' success in attracting large numbers of believers through his signs (11:47–48). Caiaphas the High Priest attempts to calm their fears of a resulting Roman takeover (vv. 48–49) with the remark, "It is expedient for us that one man die on behalf of the people lest the entire nation perish" (v. 50). Alone, the comment stands as mere scapegoating. But with the benefit of eleven chapters, it ought by now to have been interpreted as ironic by the alert reader. Yet John will not risk his missing the point. The remark was not mere irony. It came from beyond Caiaphas as prophecy: τοῦτο δὲ ἀφ' ἑαυτοῦ οὐκ εἶπεν, ἀλλ' ... ἐπροφήτευσεν (v. 51). Apparently, neither he, nor they, nor the reader could know without interpretation from this side of the resurrection that he had spoken of Jesus' impending death for the people. Indeed, the divine revelation said even more than the High Priest's words allowed: the scattered children of God were to be gathered into one (v. 52).

The entry into Jerusalem (12:12–19)

After relating this event, with the multitude acclaiming Jesus as "the King of Israel" (v. 13; see v. 15), John adds these astonishing comments: "the disciples did not know these things at first." Only with Jesus' glorification did they remember that these events had even occurred (v. 16)! It is one thing to learn later that Zech. 9:9 had referred to this occasion. It is quite another to have forgotten about it altogether.

The Son of Man's "lifting up" (12:27–36)

In his final public appearance, Jesus speaks of the imminent judgment of the world, the casting out of Satan, his own ὕψωσις, and the consequent attraction of all people (vv. 31–32). Such a context would lead one to expect a triumphal exaltation. To forestall this natural interpretation, the Evangelist breaks into the narrative to explain that Jesus had spoken in sign language (σημαίνων) concerning his impending death (v. 33). Yes, he would be lifted up, but the ascent would be to another sort of throne.

Thus, when these few but significant moments in the gospel are given their due, one is bound to conclude with Carla Wall that John "is careful that the reader not assume more about the past than was true at that time.''[43] Northrop Frye's judgment, though covering the entire gospel, is particularly apt so far as these examples are concerned:

> The apostle feels that if we had been "there", we should have seen nothing, or seen something utterly commonplace, or missed the whole significance of what we did see. So he comes to us, with his ritual drama of a Messiah, presenting a speaking picture which has to be, as Paul says, spiritually discerned.[44]

Yes, the portrait requires spiritual discernment. But second sight is needed because of the Evangelist's scrupulous refusal to claim that the light had broken through the first time around and that anyone with eyes half open should have been able to see it.

Conclusions about John's βιβλίον

For one whose account of Jesus' life is so heavy with "the weight of glory,"[45] John nevertheless retained features in his gospel that resemble the sensibilities characteristic of the synoptics. In a way, this achievement is therefore more noteworthy because he combined a different agenda from theirs with an analogous *modus operandi*. Like them he worked with constraints that demarcated the great watershed of the resurrection. However one told the story of Jesus in the written gospel tradition, he was obliged to convey a sense of before and after idiomatically.

Such is the case with John both in the initial Easter encounters and throughout the preceding chapters at significant moments in the drama. The most lofty christological titles "Lord" and "God" appearing in a confession after the resurrection are not anachronistically forced upon the narrative beforehand. Other christologies and theologically significant terms bear different nuances before and after. Or they appear/disappear on one or the other side of the Boundary.

Because this phenomenon occurs throughout the gospels, one might think of it as a tradition or perhaps a genre in itself in a specialized sense. I am here referring to a deep and comprehensive mindset which controls and orders the telling. This outlook appears to be stamped upon each Evangelist's work in so profound a manner that it was not borrowed and passed on. Rather, the phenomenon of "the two times" as I have described it belonged so securely to the collective consciousness of the church that it left its imprint upon the Fourth Gospel.

6

SUMMARY AND IMPLICATIONS

It would not be an overstatement to say that, until this decade, critical study of the NT in general and of the gospels in particular has been dominated by historical concerns. Scholars have traced the "story" of manuscripts, words, sources, traditions, gospels, and hellenistic (including Jewish) religions. But only within the last ten or fifteen years have the texts *qua* texts been studied for the story *qua* story of Jesus. Formal scrutiny of the narrative has been aided by the presuppositions and methods of literary-critical study in general. Of course, depending on the variety of such examination, it too can become historical, especially when the effect of a text on the reader's/listener's history becomes the primary concern. Now, however, the subject stands in front of the literature rather than behind it.

Certainly, it would be a mistake to regard each of these separate tasks as isolated. Indeed, overlapping occurs among the various historical disciplines themselves and between historical and literary study. In the end, the question becomes one of emphasis. Where will one put the stress? What am I trying to do? Perhaps it is not presumptuous to suggest that my work can assist in the performance of several critical tasks. In particular, redaction and literary critics might benefit by being able to give a more precise account of how the past of Jesus has been represented in the gospels. (This has bearing on life-of-Jesus research, about which more will be said later.)

In the most prevalent mode of redaction criticism as described in chapter 1, the stress lies so heavily upon the *Sitz im Leben* (history) of the Evangelist, his readers, and opponents (each of whose concerns are allegedly mirrored in the narrative) that one rarely hears the question addressed, "What (precisely) is the nature, extent, and significance of the backward reference to the earthly Jesus?" A kindred query can be put to literary critics. Although the "narrative art" of the Evangelists has been explored so far as story, plot, character, and tone are concerned, writers on these subjects have not addressed the "pastness of the past" in the gospels in a thoroughgoing way. In the "fictive world" of the story, how do the characters speak? Do their voices differ from one another and from the narrator? Is there appropriate idiom and corresponding action, each suited to a sense of time? If so, how and to what extent? Ironically, the very forte of this discipline has not been applied to such matters. These concerns are germane whether or not the narrative bears any resemblance to "things as they really happened."

The data and observations that will help to supply answers to such questions were garnered through the application of the following principles of method. What the Evangelists believed this side of Easter were derived from the gospels themselves, principally the resurrection narratives and the editor's/narrator's telling of the story. As I could not otherwise justify invoking Paul's or James' point of view, so I did not employ the beliefs of a reconstructed Palestinian church or a hellenistic congregation to discern the meaning of terms and titles in the gospels.

Furthermore, I regarded Easter faith in its individuality. Since one allows that the significance of Jesus' death was viewed differently by the NT writers, so it must be with the resurrection. Its meaning and effect varied from author to author and from Evangelist to Evangelist. There is no monolithic Easter belief. One must be gospel-specific. Likewise, on analogy, I avoided importing external definitions of "kerygma," "gospel," and "faith." Nor did I hear them univocally from the inside. Finally, I strove for precision. "Kerygma," "gospel," and "faith" do not embrace the sum total of what each Evangelist believed. They have a limited, discrete connotation. When these principles were applied, the following results emerged.

The hardest available evidence from the gospels has confirmed the thesis that the Evangelists produced narratives about Jesus of Nazareth that were free of blatant attempts to infuse and overlay his story with their own later and developed estimates of his teaching, miracles, passion, and person. These Christian convictions appear in some kinds of private teaching given to disciples about the future, in the editorial framework, and especially at the end. Here, the main story line ends short of the gospel's finale. A significant change occurs. There is a "wrinkle in time"[1] that divides the narrative into before and after in a profound sense.

The theological *patois* of one era gives way to that of another. Jesus had proclaimed the Good News about God and his Government (Mark 1:14–15). Mark's Gospel is about Jesus Christ (1:1). In Matthew,

John the Baptist, Jesus, and the disciples had preached the same message: that the Kingdom of Heaven had drawn near (3:2; 4:17; 10:5). But after the resurrection, Jesus' disciples were to instruct the nations in the observance of his commandments (20:18–20). According to Luke, Jesus had announced the messianic task as the proclamation of release to captives (κηρύξαι αἰχμαλώτοις ἄφεσιν, 4:18). After Easter, he taught that the Christ was to suffer and that his disciples should proclaim forgiveness of sins to the nations (κηρυχθῆναι ... ἄφεσιν ἁμαρτιῶν, 24:46–47). Identified to his people as the Son of Man, he may now be known as Christ and Son of God. With a consistency that can be charted on virtually every page of text, the thought and idiom of his era are not reproduced in theirs. Or, more correctly, they do not retroject theirs into his. Such a claim, when carefully qualified, can even be made of John. At significant moments (5:24, 12:44), the most christocentric of Evangelists reveals a synoptic-like *theo*centricity that dominates the entire gospel.

The past and redaction

In view of the evidence provided by redaction critics in the years since World War II, who can deny that the Evangelists have, with various degrees of consistency, adapted tradition to conform to overall theological and compositional agendas? This has been achieved by the modification of common sources, the addition of special material, the displacement of tradition, and multiple reorganization of the whole. Evidence for this scattering, centrifugal impulse really cannot be controverted.

And yet, according to the preceding evidence, such tendentiousness has not affected the fundamental character of the story being related. Without denying that typical and characteristic language binds the various regions of each gospel together, the pre-resurrection narrative has not been homogenized with vocabulary contemporaneous to the Evangelists. Redaction did not obliterate theological idiom that divided the story of Jesus and the era of gospel writers into two periods.

The unified front presented by the synoptic gospels (supported in its own way by John) and their sources demonstrates a profound restraint, wide as well as deep, that prevented tendencies to modify the tradition from exceeding certain boundaries. Centripetal forces checked centrifugal ones. Adaptation did not obscure what had been adopted. As obvious as literary interdependence is theological interdependence: none of the Evangelists forgot that there was a fundamental difference between "the two times." Compared to this basic theme, other kinds of variations seem cosmetic.

Therefore, all extravagant assertions of how the gospel writers' faith led them to alter, add, remove, create, and arrange materials must be evaluated in view of the evidence. There are no serious grounds for believing that the Evangelists injected and combined their traditions with post-resurrection convictions to such an extent that their story was indistinguishable from Jesus' story.

The past and faith

If we allow the Evangelists to speak for themselves (i.e. confine ourselves to internal data rather than allow external definitions of what can or cannot be true), then certain common slogans need to be severely qualified or abandoned. Several are bound up together: the gospels are products of faith (or preaching), not history. Christians were not concerned about proclaiming the Jesus of history but the Christ of faith.

Besides begging for definitions that originate in the gospels themselves, these statements may not only be posing false alternatives; they also appear to allow no other set of alternatives. There is an intermediate category more appropriate to the phenomena that I have been describing. Before one speaks of faith and history, one must deal with the relation of faith to story or narrative. The issue is really quite separate. Whether or not the gospels bear the features of biography or history (however defined) must be determined by the application of external data.

In the meantime, there is no denying that these archaistic representations of Jesus were not inimical to the worship of him whom Christians were convinced was alive forevermore. The Risen Christ of faith may not be divorced from such accounts of the earthly Jesus. However we define the Evangelists' faith, we must acknowledge the role that such narratives play in its expression.

Unless one does so, rather anachronistic interpretations of the origins of the gospels may emerge. For example, W. Marxsen maintains that Mark sought to combat an historicistic reading of the gospels brought about by setting traditions alongside one another. With the allegedly paradoxical motif of the messianic secret, he undermined any possibility of reading them as an historically verifiable series of divine epiphanies.[2] But is not aversion to historicism possible only with the rise of modern historical science? And may the antithesis (faith vs. history) be the anachronistic projection of modern debates into the first century? The problem can be avoided entirely if one deals with the narrative *qua* narrative.

The past and the present

A corollary of the faith—history alternative emerges in this slogan: early Christians were not interested in what the earthly Jesus *said* but what the risen Christ *says*. This begs the question of the relation of the past to the present. Unless something is immediate and contemporary, it can have no meaning or relevance, according to this view. So, everything in the gospels must correspond directly to an issue being faced by the Evangelists' readers.

However, the data again bear eloquent testimony against such a one-to-one understanding of communication. For example, how could a Gentile reader of Mark's Gospel obey Jesus' command to the cured leper to get himself certified by a priest (1:44)? How could one eager to obey the Great Commission have complied with Jesus' prohibition against proclaiming the Kingdom of Heaven beyond Israel (10:5–6)? Such material is best regarded as "merely" informational. It provides the reader with a view of how it once was, how Jesus once operated and spoke.[3]

Such is the case with the "out-dated" christology, soteriology, view of the Spirit etc. that the Evangelists preserve with such fidelity in their narrative. If there is to be a contemporary point, it will have to be made obliquely and derivatively. Rather than conveying an immediate message to the reader in time (synchronically), the narrative provides it indirectly through time (diachronically) as the story of *Jesus*, first and foremost, moves from beginning to end.

And, because of the narrative's remoteness, it cannot function principally as a literary foil for the conflicts between opposing points of view in the gospel writers' congregations. (Once again the reminder must be given that I am not hereby arguing for historicity: remoteness does not necessarily mean accuracy.) Any tension that exists is not *primarily* between multiple post-Easter ideologies (christology, salvation, discipleship, etc.) but between pre-Easter ones (in the narrative world of the accounts) or between pre- and post-Easter issues.

The past and history

But how true to the facts are the gospel narratives? Could one regard them as historically reliable, at least in the context of the standards ancient historians might have applied? The question has, of course, been raised and answered before.[4] What makes it appropriate here is that the demonstrated restraint, the conservation of idiom, and the preservation of different theological categories reminds one of the criteria which the much-quoted Thucydides employed himself. Although usually cited in connection with speeches in Acts, they have a direct bearing on the gospels. In his *History of the Peloponnesian War*, Thucydides says:

> As to the speeches which were made either before or during the war, it was hard for me, and for others who reported them to me, to recollect the exact words. I have therefore put into the mouth of each speaker the *sentiments proper to the occasion*, expressed as I thought *he would be likely to express them*, while at the same time I endeavored, as nearly as I could, to give the general purport of what was actually said.[5]

However, the temptation to regard the gospels as providing *direct* access to Jesus as he was must be resisted. Unless the Evangelists can be shown to have striven for the ideal in Thucydides' final clause, we may only be left with historical or biographical fiction of a very high order rather than history *per se*. Here, too, the author strives for "an appropriate idiom and a sense of time." This is the point at which external data need to be applied to the sort of internal evidence which I have provided. Furthermore, the very phenomena that support the view of the Evangelists as conservers create their own set of problems which I shall discuss subsequently.

What, one may well ask, is the net gain of this study of narrative so far as the historical issue is concerned? At the very least, certain psychological, literary, and theological barriers ought to have been removed. One can no longer claim that the "faith perspective" of those who produced the gospels is inimical to the concern for Jesus' past. Any reluctance on the part of historians to pursue the point further and inquire about the accuracy of the gospel portraits cannot be justified so far as the narratives themselves are concerned.

And the professional historian is never ultimately daunted by tendentious material. The role of reconstruction often has only the flotsam and jetsam of human experience to work with. But documents such as the gospels, with the sort of features I have described, will at least not inhibit the task since their tendentiousness has been grossly overrated. More positively, we can say that the Evangelists' attitude towards and method of representing their Subject will itself become a substantial ingredient in the comprehensive case that an historian will have to make.

In advance of that effort, here are some points at which the gospels *already*, in their present state, conform to what has been derived through the application of that most severe of criteria for authenticity, the so-called "criterion of dissimilarity." Jesus' teaching was supremely theocentric, or more accurately, patricentric. He neither used "Lord," "Christ," or "Son of God" of himself nor did he allow others to do so or without substantially qualifying the expressions. Although he taught explicitly about God as Father, he never taught about himself as Son either directly or obliquely by parables.[6] Just the opposite is the case with the Kingdom of God, whose nature Jesus explicated by numerous modes and avenues. Although he saw his person and word as determinative for one's ultimate destiny (16:27//8:38//9:26), that relation is never called "faith" in the synoptics. And in John, where it appears in abundance, the nuances of its use require close scrutiny. Jesus did not make his death or universal forgiveness through it a part of his public teaching. They are rare enough even in private instruction of the disciples. Justification of sinners (Luke 18:14), forgiveness of sins (9:2//2:5//5:20), salvation (Luke 19:9), and eternal life (Luke 10:25–28) were bestowed *by his pronouncement*. Nor did Jesus teach the Jews that his mission and theirs was to mediate God's salvation to the Gentiles. (The most that can be said about the private teaching on these matters is that Jesus' death universalized what he had bestowed upon Israel during his life.)[7] True, Jesus assumed an authority that superseded anything that prophets and contemporary teachers had manifested. But this is something less than openly declaring himself to be him whom God, the demons, the Evangelists, and the reader know him to have been or become. And John, even more than the synoptists, stresses that Jesus' authority, though unprecedented, was nevertheless *derived* authority.

Such findings, corroborated by external data, indicate again how remarkably conservative the synoptic (and in their own way, Johannine) narratives are. And yet the conclusions drawn seem far from the portrait of Jesus that many conservatives tend to observe when reading them. Why might this be? One can only hazard some guesses. Standing within this tradition myself, I find that it is difficult to avoid the temptation to read the synoptic gospels without the Jesus of the Fourth Gospel or of the Ecumenical Creeds reverberating in one's awareness. Furthermore, I detect an inclination to read the texts flatly. In other words, little or no discrimination occurs, even among non-conservative specialists, between public and private teaching or between pre- and post-resurrection components of the story. Now, in making such distinction, I do not mean to imply that private instruction and post-resurrection teaching are necessarily less historical. I simply point out that there has been next to no recognition of the disjunction between them. One of the major challenges ahead for more traditional Christians consists in accounting for the hiatus between what Jesus tells the public and what he informs the disciples (and why).

Likewise, the great divide between pre- and post-resurrection thought and language will have to come under closer scrutiny by the historically disposed investigator. If the burden of all the Scriptures is that the Messiah should suffer and enter his glory (Luke 24:25–27, 45–46), why is this not the burden of Jesus' ministry, public and private, from beginning to end? And the concept of Jesus as teacher that emerges demands much more attention by those who would see him carefully preparing the disciples throughout. Can he really be appealed to as the "Model Teacher"? Given their obtuseness and their having to learn about a figure who fits none of the current messianic categories, one would have expected Jesus to remove any epistemic stupor well ahead of the resurrection. Yet only afterwards does the risen Lord "open their minds to understand the Scriptures" (Luke 24:45). Beforehand, they had even been *prevented* from getting the point of Jesus' teaching about his betrayal (9:45). While these instances help us to demonstrate a difference between before and after, they nevertheless pose difficult (though not necessarily insoluble) historical problems for the one who is otherwise disposed to trust the gospel narratives.

When the advantages and liabilities are added up, however, the net results of applying a version of the criterion of dissimilarity to whole gospels rather than to individual sayings amount to an exceedingly bountiful harvest. The Evangelists have demonstrated a high degree of narrative art that demands the attention of the literary critic, the professional historian, and the biblical theologian.

THE UNIFYING KERYGMA OF
THE NEW TESTAMENT

Introduction

Thesis

The purpose of this study is to offer evidence that, contrary to the prevailing view, there is a central, discrete, kerygmatic core that integrates the manifold plurality of the New Testament. Without denying the diversity that may be found therein, I hope to initiate a return to the largely neglected task of identifying the nature of its unity. My motivation to do so comes from the existence of data that suggest the need to fill a rather sizeable gap in the scenarios currently available for describing the character of early Christianity.

Earlier efforts

The static and kinetic inertia that has to be overcome is considerable, given the history of previous attempts to do so. Perhaps the most famous effort was conducted by C. H. Dodd just over half a century ago.[1] He identified a seven-point outline of primitive preaching by collecting fragments of tradition from Pauline literature[2] that corresponded in all but three items to the pattern of proclamation in the early sermons of Acts.[3] He then tried to show that, within the variety and development, this kerygmatic outline could be detected among the major representatives of the NT.[4] While many Anglo-American scholars initially responded favorably to Dodd's proposal, subsequent studies criticized what seemed to be an artificial harmonizing of Pauline material and an insufficiently critical reliance upon the speeches of Acts as accurate representations of apostolic preaching.[5]

The inability of Dodd's argument to elicit a sufficiently broad consensus was complemented by what appeared to be a more satisfying alternative. A quarter of a century earlier, W. Heitmüller set in motion the prevailing tendency to speak of the kerygma*ta* of the NT.[6] Its most comprehensive exposition lies in R. Bultmann's *Theology of the New Testament*, as anyone can readily see by comparing the table of contents with the major headings of Heitmüller's article.[7] Redaction criticism, with its avowed intent to determine the unique message(s) of each gospel,[8] belongs to this stream of thinking. And applying the term "kerygma" to the distinctive theme of a New (and even Old) Testament document can be seen in the series of articles that appeared in *Interpretation* during the 1960s.[9]

A current option

Perhaps the fullest flowering of this critical legacy is J. D. G. Dunn's *Unity and Diversity in the New Testament*.[10] Despite the promise of the title, the accent falls heavily on diversity. Yet Dunn tries to keep faith by setting forth, with proper qualifications, the "core kerygma." Its three components are "the proclamation of the risen, exalted Jesus," the "call for faith," and the "promise held out to faith" (i.e. the benefits that come when the proclamation is appropriated by faith in Christ).[11] Dunn then issues important disclaimers:

> This is the unity of the post-Easter kerygma. But beside it stands the considerable diversity of the different kerygmata. It must be clearly understood that the unified core kerygma outlined above is an abstraction. No NT writer proclaims this kerygma as such. No NT writer reduces the kerygma to this core. The basic kerygma in each of the cases examined above is larger than this core.[12]

Then comes a warning:

> We must therefore beware when we talk of "the NT kerygma." For if we mean the core kerygma, then we are talking about a kerygma which no evangelist in the NT actually preached. And if we mean one of the diverse kerygmata, then it is only one form of kerygma and not necessarily appropriate or acceptable to the different evangelists in the NT or their circumstances.[13]

Rather than a unifying statement or tradition, Dunn appeals to a supra-literary or trans-textual set of convictions. At another level, this time supremely christological, he asserts that unity lies in the spare but non-negotiable *"affirmation of the identity of the man Jesus with the risen Lord."*[14]

An alternative

While one cannot take lightly Professor Dunn's warning and the argument on which it rests, I must nevertheless beg to differ substantially. There is in fact evidence for a kerygma that is concrete, not abstract or reductionist, and wide-ranging enough to be regarded as a core running throughout the NT. Describing its components and setting forth the corroborating data will constitute the burden of what follows.

Procedure

But first a word needs to be said about procedure. In each of the representative works mentioned there is a common denominator, diverse though they are. The NT is not usually treated literarily and thus descriptively, but rather historically and reconstructively. In other words, the documents are mined for information about the evolution of Christian beliefs, either within a single stream or within manifold parallel streams, as even the title of Dodd's book illustrates.

This is an entirely legitimate enterprise; but it belongs really to the history of dogma from the earliest times to the alleged (and much-maligned) "early catholicism" of the sub-apostolic era. Although I hope that what follows will contribute to that discussion, my findings have emerged from a study of the NT *per se*, which is first and foremost a body of literature. Such textual examination has an integrity in its own right, so that it may be conducted separately from and indeed prior to the historical. Furthermore, one could argue that certain kinds of premature atomization of the text impede and obscure the historical task. Leaving the text too soon to write the church's history is as dangerous as writing the history of Jesus before doing a thorough literary analysis.[15]

The kerygma

Categories

The kerygmatic core here isolated contains six constant items, usually but not always introduced by a statement that what follows is kerygma, gospel, or message (λόγος) about:[16]

(1) God who
(2) sent (gospels) or raised
(3) Jesus.
(4) A response (receiving, repentance, faith)
(5) towards God
(6) brings benefits (variously described).

"Form"

That there is here a sort of "form" is suggested by the consistent occurrence of each of the six categories within the same context or passage. Thus, one need not harmonize them from various quarters of the same or other documents. This avoids the criticism leveled against Dodd. Furthermore, these same items persist throughout the NT (see below for the full extent). Yet they do not always appear in the same order. So there is a cohesiveness to the pattern without its being formulaic. And categories (4) and (6) show the greatest variability in content. (Of course, the fewer the components, the greater the consistency.) Such an informal formality suggests a stage prior to becoming tradition *per se*, rigidified and separable from its context. But my announced concern is not with the tradition history of this form. Rather, I mean to demonstrate its centrality and character further.

Scope

The persistence of this outline (if that is not too formal) is wide-ranging indeed. It may be found in every canonical unit (Gospels, Acts, Letters, and Revelation), literary genre (narrative, epistle, apocalypse), and "apostolic" tradition (synoptic, Johannine, Pauline [settled and disputed], and "Petrine"). Were we to add chronology to this predominantly literary spectrum, an analogous breadth could be delineated: from suspected pre-Pauline traditions (and earlier if the speeches in Acts were admitted) to the late Johannine material of gospel and Apocalypse (unless J. A. T. Robinson was right).[17]

Content

A separate point needs to be made concerning the content because it contravenes so much of the critically orthodox consensus about the substance of what the earliest Christians proclaimed and believed.

Items (1) and (5), which involve (2) and (4), call attention to the heavily *theo*logical component in the kerygma here identified. God invariably appears as the originator of the saving event and the recipient of Christian response. Furthermore, the content amounts to a *recital of divine activity* (narrative *in nuce*) rather than the *acclamation of christological status*. Much more of such theocentricity occurs in the NT; but I have deliberately confined myself to its presence in this kerygmatic form (and to the appearance of all six elements, even though more instances with fewer items could be adduced).

Disclaimers

The claim here is not that I have been the first to notice the theological dimension to kerygmatic statements. Rather, my point is that it is more extensive, more formal, and more significant than scholars have allowed. So, for example, Bultmann[18] and Kramer[19] cite kerygmata where God who raised Jesus is the focus of faith. But Bultmann sees them as reflecting a "dangerous" outlook that smacks more of Jewish sectarianism[20] than of essential Christianity. Only with Paul and John[21] does faith or belief shift focus from God's deed in Christ to that of effecting a relation with the person of Christ himself.[22] A more radical christocentricity among the earliest confessions is championed by O. Cullmann, who maintains vigorously that "faith in God is really a function of faith in Christ."[23] However, such value judgments and perhaps systematically inclined hermeneutics miss the point that the theocentricity persists amongst the very writers who have indeed moved Christian thinking in a more christological direction.

But using the language of early and late risks transgressing the territory of tradition history and the evolution of the Christian religion. Although it goes beyond my stated objectives to identify a literary phenomenon, I venture briefly to suggest that a case could be made for the primitive date of this kerygma if one is willing to acknowledge the contestable character of the following kinds of assertions: the briefest and most numerous form is the earliest,[24] acclamation or confession of Jesus' status preceded recital (which then becomes regarded as a secondary expansion)[25] and theological motifs signify missionary preaching to Gentiles.[26]

The data

Because my purpose is to show that the pattern in question occurs throughout the NT canon, I shall organize the evidence according to its major units. However, I have taken the liberty to re-arrange them so that the kerygma as proclaimed explicitly by the early church appears first. Such an order will also help the material to act as a foil for the gospels where, though the categories remain consistent, notice must be taken of how the differences in pre- and post-Easter settings affect the manner by which category (2) was expressed: the act of God in Christ. The greatest variation in content, though not in form, appears in the vocabulary (4) response to God and of (6) the forthcoming benefits.

Acts

While the historically conditioned debate about Luke's representation of the early church continues unabated, it need not deter the appeal to volume II of the *Doppelwerk* for the examples of a kerygma that permeated the rest of the NT. However one answers the historical question, it is noteworthy that instances of both Petrine and Pauline preaching substantiate the thesis in settings where Palestinian Jews, hellenistic Jews, and "devout proselytes" comprise the audience. In 5:30–32, the language of proclamation is that of bearing witness (μάρτυς, μαρτυρεῖν), although the relation of these terms to the announcement of Good News (εὐαγγελίζεσθαι) is clear (see 13:30–32). Before the Sanhedrin, Peter bears witness to (1) the God of their fathers who (2) raised and exalted (3) Jesus to give Israel (6) repentance and forgiveness of sins. The Holy Spirit, granted to those who (4) trust (πειθαρχεῖν) (5) God, also adds his testimony. Likewise Paul, in Pisidian Antioch, proclaims the Good News of (1) God's (2) raising (3) Jesus from the dead (13:30–34, 37). In him, there is (6) forgiveness of sins and justification (vv. 38–39). Those among the mixed audience who responded were (4) persuaded (πείθειν) to remain in the grace (5) of God (v. 43).

Another instance of the "form" in Acts lies in the fullest example of Paul's preaching to pagans (17:30–31). To the philosophers in Athens, he declares (καταγγέλλειν) the truth about the "Unknown God." After narrating the works of God in nature and in the human spirit (vv. 24–28), the Apostle voices God's command for people everywhere (4) to repent (that is to turn towards (5) God who had put it in their hearts (4) to seek him [v. 27]).²⁷ The motive is (6) to receive a favorable verdict at the impending judgment presided over by (3) a man whom (1) God had designated by (2) raising him from the dead (v. 31).

Letters: Pauline

Romans

Citing what many scholars believe to have been a widely known, commonly accepted tradition in Rom. 10:8−9, Paul maintains that the "word of faith" proclaimed (κηρύσσειν) is that if one confesses that Jesus is Lord and (4) believes in his heart that (1, 5) God (2) has raised (3) him from the dead, he (6) will be saved.²⁸ Were dating a primary concern, then one could argue for a pre-Pauline, early origin for the pattern, perhaps the most primitive version of it that I can cite, unless the passages in Acts qualify. But happily it does not belong to my task to demonstrate this.

2 Corinthians

Among the several letters written to Corinth, the outline appears in 5:19−20. The (3) Christ whom (1) God (2) raised (v. 15) is the agent of his (6) reconciling the world and the Corinthians to himself, not reckoning their transgressions against them (vv. 18−19). They should therefore respond appropriately to this imperative: (4) "be reconciled [5] to God" (v. 20). While the role of Christ in these statements is obvious, one cannot ignore their immediate, heavily theocentric setting and that of the nearer context (vv. 11−18).'

Galatians

The super-christocentricity of this letter might initially mask a version of the formula in 4:4−7. There, Paul narrates the gospel *in nuce*. "But when the time had fully come (1) God (2) sent forth (3) his Son ... (6) to redeem those under the law, so that we might receive adoption as children. And because you are children, God has sent forth the Spirit of his Son into our hearts, (4) crying [in faith and obedience] (5) 'Abba! Father!' So, (6) you are no longer a slave but a son: and if a son, then also an heir through God." Paul regards such intimacy as (4) "knowing (5) God," which one's former condition prohibited (vv. 8−9).

Ephesians

In confining oneself for the time being to a study of the literature of the NT, it is possible to proceed according to the canonical order without addressing the issue of authorship. Were this letter to be judged as post-Pauline, then there would be evidence for the pattern's wider scope, both in time and location. But this is an historical judgment and should therefore be reserved for separate consideration. In 2:4–10, "Paul" recites the loving intervention of (1) God among dead and disobedient persons, (2) raising them up (3) with Christ to a heavenly session. From this vantage point they (6) can glimpse and later experience the full measure of his grace (vv. 4–7). The appropriate response to this work (ποίημα) in Christ is (4) to walk in (5) God-initiated good works (ἔργοις ἀγαθοῖς, vv. 8–10).

Philippians

One might at first sight be tempted to exclude 2:5–11 because divine initiative seems displaced by Christ's and because no obvious expressions of (4) response (5) to God present themselves. However, a closer textual examination enables them to be excavated. (1) God (2) exalted (3) him to the heights and (6) gave him the name κύριος, which the universe will one day confess, *to the glory of God the Father* (vv. 9–11). This followed a life of (4) obedience as a man, even to the point of death on a cross (v. 8), an extension of his earlier self-effacing attitude towards God: (4) refusing to grasp at or jealously retain divine prerogatives (vv. 6–7). Emptying of self was his mode. And every element of the pattern, the same set of mind, is to be embraced by believers at Philippi (v. 5) as they conduct their life together on the basis of an other-oriented ethic (vv. 1–4).[29]

Colossians

However one assesses the authorship of Colossians, clearly the kerygma under examination occurs in this Pauline or Paulinist letter. (If the latter, then evidence for its wider scope is extended.) The vocabulary of the Christian gospel has a rather broad range to it. Paul refers to it as the Word of God that he was appointed to declare (1:25–27). Allied language about that role (announcing, convincing, teaching, v. 28) provides a more remote introduction than what we have been used to seeing for the content of the proclamation. The Colossians have been raised with Christ through (4) faith in the working (5) of God (1) who (2) raised (3) him from the dead (2:12). Furthermore, God has (6) enlivened them with Christ who were dead in trespasses which he pardoned (v. 13).

1 Thessalonians

Among the earliest of the universally acknowledged letters of Paul, 1 Thessalonians contains the elements within the thanksgiving of the introduction. The gospel (of God in 2:9) had come to these folk in power (1:5). They had responded by (4) believing in, turning towards, and serving (vv. 8–9) the (5) God (1) who had (2) raised (3) his son Jesus from the dead. He now (6) rescues them from the coming wrath (v. 10).

1 Timothy

Although not expressed crisply within the boundaries of a verse or two as is sometimes the case, the six members nevertheless appear in a sustained argument about sound teaching, the preservation of which is of great concern to the author (whose identity need not be considered at this point). The house of God, the church of the living God, is the pillar and bulwark of the truth (3:15). One example of this "doctrine" is the central confession which concludes with ἀνελήμφθη ἐν δόξῃ. Rendered in the active voice, the statement affirms that (1) God (2) "took up" (3) Jesus in glory (v. 16). However, this mystery of εὐσέβεια cannot merely be confessed. One must undergo training in (4:7–8). Such godliness promises value both in the present life and in that which is to come (v. 8). This is πιστὸς ὁ λόγος (v. 9).[30] In the meantime, toil and striving are motivated by (4) hope in (5) the living God who is (6) Savior of all (v. 10).

2 Timothy

Somewhat more concentrated is another instance of what the Pastor calls πιστὸς ὁ λόγος (2:11). He begins with the admonition to "remember (3) Christ Jesus (2) raised from the dead ... according to my gospel" (v. 8). As always, in the grammar of such passive expressions, the implicit subject is (1) God. Paul suffers and endures imprisonment for the elects' sake so that (6) they may obtain salvation in Christ Jesus (vv. 9–10). In view of such a legacy, Timothy must urgently (4) present himself to (5) God as a worthy workman (v. 15).

Titus

If another pastor besides Paul wrote Titus, then the persistence of this pattern in another and later tradition reinforces the point being made. At 3:4–8, the equivalent of the gospel (called the "word of faith," τὸ ῥῆμα τῆς πίστεως in Rom. 10:8) is "sound message" (or "aphorism"?): πιστὸς ὁ λόγος. This expression refers to the recital about (1) "God our Savior," whose redemptive acts effect (6) the washing of regeneration and the renewal of the Holy Spirit poured out richly (3) through Jesus Christ (whom God had (2) exalted, is the implication). With such a display of divine favor, Titus is to insist that those who (4) have trusted (5) God (οἱ πεπιστευκότες τῷ θεῷ) are to be mindful of doing good works.

Letters: Catholic

Hebrews

That the kerygma should appear in a work by an author so determined to get beyond the fundamentals of the faith (6:1–2) deserves our attention. But one needs to wait patiently for the full-membered form until chapter 13's doxology. Glory is ascribed to (1) the God of peace who (2) led out from the dead (3) Jesus, the great shepherd of the sheep (v. 20) through the blood of the (6) everlasting covenant. The author prays that God will make his readers perfect in every thing good (4) to do (5) his will (v. 21). Almost obscured by the language is the benefit: they belong to the shepherd's fold because the covenant has bonded them to him. And immediately prior to the benediction appear fuller expressions of response by those who confess God's name: they offer sacrifices of praise to him (v. 15). When God's people do good works and share resources, they offer pleasing sacrifices to him (v. 16). Categories (4) and (5) are well represented here.

1 Peter

While one might want to accuse Luke of artificially making Peter and Paul preach the same message in Acts 5 and 13, no such charge can be sustained here. Peter himself or a member of his "school" shares the sixfold kerygma with the historical Paul. The Good News announced to the readers (εὐαγγελίζεθαι in 1:25) recited (6) redemption through the precious blood of Christ, chosen (by God) before the foundation of the world (vv. 18–20), who enables Christians (4) to believe[31] (5) in God (1) who raised Jesus from the dead. Glory given to Jesus makes possible (4) faith and hope in (5) God (v. 21).

1 John

The first and lasting impression that this letter conveys is of the supreme christocentricity of its author. Such an impression is accurate. Yet, the God-oriented substratum of the appeal to the readers should not be overlooked. The sixfold pattern appears in 4:7–10. Most intriguingly, reference to Jesus' resurrection fails to occur (here, or anywhere). Instead, the accent falls heavily on God's *sending* him. This corresponds to the examples cited at John 5:24, 12:44, and to the gospel tradition generally. (See especially Mark 9:37.) John seeks to authenticate the claim (4) to know (5) the God of love (1) who (2) sent his (3) only son into the world (6) to save it and provide an atoning sacrifice for sins.

The apocalypse

A version of the kerygmatic pattern occurs here, too, but clothed in the symbolic garb of this genre. Although not called "gospel," the message comes by the way of a great sign appearing in heaven (12:1). But it is precisely through such "signing" that God has given his revelation to John (1:1) who bears witness to the word of God (v. 2). Once the magnificent woman's (3) son is born, he is (2) snatched away from the dragon's jaws (1) by God to his throne (12:5). Salvation comes to God's people in two phases. His forces under Michael expel the satan to earth where he can (6) no longer prosecute them before God (vv. 7–10). And the saints conquer the dragon through the death of the Lamb and the word of their own testimony even to death (v. 11). With so little time left, the ancient serpent then proceeds to make war with the rest of the woman's offspring who (4) keep the commands (5) of God (v. 17) and maintain the witness which Jesus gave (to God?).

The gospels

When C. H. Dodd appealed to the gospels, it was in their overall framework that he found the points reflecting that seven-member outline of the kerygma.[32] But the examples that I shall offer correspond to the more closely dissected, logion-like statements encountered so far. Moreover, so far as content is concerned, a difference appears in category (2), the action of God. Whereas the first Christians looked back mainly to his having been *raised* by God, Jesus in the following statements looks back to his having been *sent* by him (or else the sending envisions the entire mission).

Matthew

Matthew 10:40 illustrates the pattern well: "Whoever receives you receives me; and whoever receives me (4) receives (5) the one (1) who (2) sent (3) me." Unspecified but appropriate (6) "rewards" accrue as a result (vv. 41–42). The role of the disciples and of Jesus is to mediate God.[33]

Mark

It might seem that Mark 9:37 lacks category 6, the benefits or rewards that come from responding to God. Yet the language of "receiving" (δέχεσθαι) suggests that the very welcoming of him is itself also the "reward." Thus, "Whoever receives me does not receive me but [(4) receives (6)] the (5) one (1) who (2) sent (3) me." Furthermore, the primarily theocentric thrust of this statement is underscored by Jesus' removal of himself, a point unique among the synoptic Evangelists (cf. Matt. 18:5 and Luke 9:48; see John 12:44 below). It is the sort of comment that an historian might treasure. If Mark 9:37 cannot pass through the sieve of the so-called "criterion of dissimilarity," then what can?[34]

Luke

The breadth of Lucan usage (perhaps an instance of "theme and variations") becomes clear by its occurrence in Zechariah's prophecy (1:68–75). The old priest blesses (1) the Lord God of Israel for (2) "raising up (ἐγείρειν) ... (3) a horn of salvation" in the dynasty of David, his servant (v. 69).[35] This is viewed in nationalistic and ethnic terms: (6) salvation from Israel's enemies (v. 71). God's people are to (4) "serve (5) him in holiness and righteousness" during all of their days (vv. 74–75). The pattern that Luke represents in several instances of the Christian kerygma belongs in the anticipations of this saint as well.

John

A wholly analogous phenomenon occurs in the Fourth Gospel. At 20:31, the Evangelist clearly reveals his intent to elicit a certain response from his readers: engender or maintain faith in Jesus as the Christ and Son of God.[36] Yet within the narrative itself, there may be seen a more theocentric orientation. At 5:24, Jesus announces in public, "Whoever hears my word and (4) believes (5) him (1) who (2) sent (3) me (6) has eternal life." And, like Mark 9:37 is John 12:44. After eleven chapters of calling for belief in Jesus, John related that he cried out in public, "The one who believes in me does not believe in me but (4) [believes] in (5) him (1) who (2) sent (3) me." And the one who observes Jesus is rewarded with (6) the vision of God (v. 45; see 14:8–9). (Such a denial is not really out of keeping with other Johannine "subordinationism,"[37] but it is routinely overlooked in favor of the gospel's otherwise "high" christology and soteriology. One wonders if the comments about historicity in Mark 9:37 apply here, too.)

Summary and implications

I have presented evidence from nineteen of the twenty-seven books of the NT for the existence of a kerygmatic core whose six categories remain constant in all of the major representatives, genres, and traditions of the NT canon. It declares the Good News of God's sending or raising Jesus from the dead. By responding obediently to God, one receives the benefits stemming from this salvific event.[38]

In this spare statement (hardly more than a dozen words in many instances) lies the skeleton of early Christian convictions. Obviously, they believed much more, just as an archipelago of islands identifies the massive range of mountains below the surface. But here was the essence of the story whose highlights could be written on the fingertips of both hands. In future, more had to be said, but not less.

These data demonstrate that, amid the unquestionable pluralism of the NT, there lies a unifying, kerygmatic center. It is formal and specific rather than abstract and general, internal and native rather than external and artificial. Among the several trajectories along which *development* of thought can be discerned, there remains a complementary *stability*.

At the heart of this stabilizing core beats theology *per se*. God is the initiator of the redemptive act in Christ. And one's response is always to God. Of course, Christianity developed along christological lines. Who could or would deny it? But its theological moorings were never broken. One thing that these nineteen examples of the six-membered, theologically laden kerygma do is to alert one to the greater number of more fragmentary theological statements that exist in the NT. (In paleological sites, fragments of skeletons usually outnumber complete specimens.) An investigation like this suddenly opens one's eyes to data that have previously escaped notice. One might never have seen a Renault 4TL before. But buy one, and they appear everywhere (in better condition and no doubt at a third of the cost). Hoskyns' and Davey's comment on John 12:44 is entirely to the point here: "Christian faith is not a cult of Jesus."[39] God is the beginning and the end of the story.

The implications of this awareness for historical and biblical theology cannot be overestimated. What God was doing in Jesus and what he continued to do among his people should provide a more substantial avenue for comparing the kerygma of Jesus and that of the earliest Christians. His starkly theocentric proclamation (e.g. Mark 1:14–15) may not be as discontinuous with what Christians preached if God's deed and one's response to him are the common and prominent denominators. Consequently, Bultmann's famous slogan, "The proclaimer became the proclaimed,"[40] says both too little and too much if not sufficiently qualified by the sorts of data presented here. Unlike many of his less critical supporters, Bultmann did try in sixty pages to describe the transition.[41] But his observation that "He who formerly had been the *bearer* of the message was drawn into it and became its essential *content*"[42] tended to obscure the extensive historical development. Put the theocentric kerygma of Jesus and the christological thought of premier thinkers like Paul and John in a synopsis and there is bound to be a great gulf between them and the preaching of Jesus. But allow the kerygmatic core isolated here among the parallels and one can discern a theological bridge linking them. Finally, it is the doctrine of God in both his person and activity, that binds the Testaments together. The existence of this unifying kerygma legitimates the task of further defining the nature of biblical *theo*logy.

Excursus: Non-canonical literature[43]

Given the relatively high concentration of this pattern in the NT, it is surprising to note how comparatively rare its presence is in the sub-apostolic, apologetic, and apocryphal literatures of the next century. In the following examples, I shall be content simply to number the components in quoted material.

"I Clement"

"Let us consider, beloved, how the Master continually proves to us that there will be a future resurrection, of which (1) he has made the first-fruits, by (2) raising (3) the Lord Jesus Christ from the dead. (There then follows an appeal to the Phoenix as an image of life arising from death, XXV.) (6) In this hope then (Clement cites OT texts about the resurrection in XXVI:2–3) let our souls (4) be bound (5) to him who is faithful in his promises and righteous in his judgments" (XXVI:1).[44]

Polycarp, "To the Philippians"[45]

(Here, more than anywhere else, God and Jesus function jointly.) "Now may God and the Father of our Lord Jesus Christ, and the 'eternal Priest' himself, Jesus Christ, the Son of God, ... (6) give you lot and part with his saints, and to us with you, and to all under heaven who (4) shall believe in our Lord and God[46] Jesus Christ and (5) in his 'Father (1) who (2) raised (3) him from the dead'"(XII:2).

"The Epistle to Diognetus"[47]

"If you desire this faith, and receive first complete (4) knowledge of (5) the Father ... [The editor suspects a lacuna here]. For God loved mankind ..., to whom (1) he (2) sent (3) his only-begotten Son, to whom (6) he promised the kingdom in heaven, – and he will give it to them who loved him" (X:1–2).

Justin Martyr, "Dialogue with Trypho"[48]

"The remainder of the Psalm makes it manifest that he knew his (1) Father would grant to him all things which he asked, and would (2) raise (3) him from the dead; and that he urged all who (4) fear (5) God to (4) praise him [τὸν θεόν] because he (6) had compassion on all races of believing men, through the mystery of him who was crucified" (CVI).[49]

"The Acts of Paul and Thecla"[50]

"For this cause (1) God (2) sent (3) His own Son ... that men (6) may no longer be under judgment but (4) have faith and fear (5) of God, and knowledge of propriety, and love of truth" (3:17).

Conclusions

That the pattern identified in the NT continues to appear well into the second century is clear. But it is also obvious, judging by its infrequency, that there is a tapering off. Of course, the basic themes continue to be repeated in fragmentary form and elaborated upon. Yet they are not as concentrated in expression.[51] Thus, it seems that the phenomenon of a well-defined, circumscribed outline of Christians' fundamental story belongs primarily to the NT.[52]

The unifying kerygma of the New Testament

	GOSPELS			ACTS	
Matt. 10:40–41	Mark 9:37	Luke 1:68–75	John 5:24	5:30–32 (Peter–Jews)	17:27–31 (Paul–pagans)
(1) who	(1) who	(1) the Lord God	(1) who	(1) God	(1) God
(2) sent	(2) sent	(2) raised up	(2) sent	(2) raised	(2) raised
(3) me	(3) me	(3) horn	(3) me	(3) Jesus	(3) him
(4) receives	(4) receives	(4) serve	(4) believes	(4) trust	(4) turn to/ seek God
(5) him	(5) him not me	(5) him	(5) him	(5) God	(5) God
(6) rewards	(6) [receiving God]	(6) salvation from enemies	(6) eternal life	(6) repentance forgiveness	(6) positive judgment

LETTERS: Paul

Rom. 10:8–9	2 Cor. 5:19–20	Gal. 4:4–7	Eph. 2:4–10	Phil. 2:5–11
(1) God	(1) God	(1) God	(1) God	(1) God
(2) raised	(2) raised	(2) sent forth	(2) raised us up	(2) exalted
(3) Jesus	(3) Christ	(3) his son	(3) with Christ	(3) him
(4) believe that	(4) reconciled	(4) cry	(4) walk in	(4) not grasp/hold obedient
(5) God	(5) to God	(5) Abba Father	(5) God's good works	(5) equality with God [to God]
(6) be saved	(6) reconciled world	(6) to redeem	(6) salvation by grace	(6) named "Lord"

LETTERS: Paul

Col. 2:12–13 (see 1:25–28)	1 Thess. 1:5–10	1 Tim. 3:16, 4:7–8	2 Tim. 2:8–15	Titus 3:4–8
(1) God	(1) God	(1) God	(1) God	(1) God
(2) raised	(2) raised	(2) took up	(2) raised	(2) [exalted]
(3) Christ	(3) Jesus	(3) him	(3) Jesus Christ	(3) Jesus Christ
(4) faith in working	(4) believing in	(4) hope in	(4) present self	(4) trusted
(5) of God	(5) God	(5) living God	(5) to God	(5) God
(6) enlivened pardoned	(6) rescue from wrath	(6) salvation	(6) salvation	(6) regeneration renewal of Holy Spirit

LETTERS: Catholic

Heb. 13:20–21 (see vv.15–16)	1 Peter 1:18–21, 25	1 John 4:7–10	APOCALYPSE Rev. 12:1–11, 17 (see 1:1–2)
(1) God	(1) God	(1) who	(1) God
(2) led from dead	(2) raised	(2) sent	(2) caught up
(3) Jesus	(3) Jesus	(3) only son	(3) child
(4) to do confess	(4) believe hope	(4) to know	(4) keep commands
(5) God's will God's name	(5) in God	(5) God	(5) of God
a(6) covenant bond	a(6) redemption	a(6) salvation atoning sacrifice	a(6) no accusation defeat Satan

a Through Jesus' death

NOTES

1 Introduction: faith, kerygma, gospels

1 R. Morgan (with J. Barton), *Biblical Interpretation* (Oxford, University Press, 1988). See also A. E. Harvey (ed.), *Alternative Approaches to New Testament Study* (London, SPCK, 1985).

2 S. Neill and T. Wright, *The Interpretation of the New Testament 1861–1986* (Oxford, University Press, 1988), p. 403. G. N. Stanton advocates starting "with the top layer, with the gospels as we have them," in *The Gospels and Jesus* (Oxford, University Press, 1989), p. 152.

3 Neill and Wright, *Interpretation*, pp. 401–02.

4 L. Chouinard cites R. M. Frye in this connection in "Gospel christology: a study of methodology," *JSNT*, 30 (1987), 24. Although the likelihood is great that the original recipients of the gospels knew other oral and perhaps even written traditions, one must be constantly reminded that they did not examine them in the form of a *Synopsis Quattuor Evangeliorum*.

5 Tone is among the aspects of literary investigation that R. Alter lists, Chouinard, "Methodology," pp. 24–25.

6 Ibid., pp. 25, 30.

7 C. F. D. Moule, *The Phenomenon of the New Testament* (London, SCM, 1967), pp. 56–59.

8 Such would be the response of those who produced the series *Gospel Perspectives* (Sheffield, JSOT), ed. R. T. France and D. Wenham, vols. I–III (1980–83) and C. Blomberg and D. Wenham, vol. VI (1986). The arguments are marshaled comprehensively in C. Blomberg's *The Historical Reliability of the Gospels* (Downers Grove, IL, IVP, 1987). Two pioneer works, whose conclusions have yet to be fully appreciated, are T. W. Manson's *The Teaching of Jesus* (Cambridge, University Press, 1935) and J. A. Baird's *Audience Criticism and the Historical Jesus* (Philadelphia, Westminster, 1969). Both studies (the latter assisted by computer technology) attempt to relate theme to audience, suggesting that massive consistency points to historical reliability. Neither, however, endeavored to distinguish as I have between pre- and post-Easter vocabulary. All three agree that the Evangelists are attuned to context in its temporal, topical, and personal dimensions.

9 L. Chouinard cites remarks by R. Alter and J. J. Collins to this effect in "Methodology," pp. 24, 31.

10 S. D. Moore, "Doing gospel criticism as/with a 'reader'," *BTB*, 19 (1989), 85–93. One must be on guard to check cynicism among non-specialists who might feel that the lack of consensus after forty years of redaction-critical study will be mirrored among literary critics.

11 C. C. Black II, "The quest of Mark the redactor: why has it been pursued and what has it taught us?," *JSNT*, 33 (1988), 31. Of great importance for evaluating the course of Markan research is Black's major work, *The Disciples According to Mark. Markan Redaction in Current Debate*, JSNTSS 27 (Sheffield, JSOT, 1989).

12 Among those who have published major works with this openness are R. H. Gundry on Matthew, W. Lane and R. Pesch on Mark, I. H. Marshall on Luke, J. A. T. Robinson on John, and G. N. Stanton for the gospels in general (see bibliography). I have made the attempt on a smaller scale so that another dimension, the canonical, might be included. My question was, "What does one do, historically and theologically, with *two* redactional versions of the same tradition?" See "The parables of the great supper and the wedding feast: history, redaction and canon," *HBT*, 8 (1986), 1–26. Of course, there are many other redaction critics who, though they seldom if ever take up the historical task formally, are nevertheless open to its possibility and significance.

13 See the overview in J. D. Kingsbury, "Reflections on the 'reader' of Matthew's gospel," *NTS*, 34 (1988), 452–53. Kingsbury, the foremost American redaction critic of Matthew's Gospel, seems to have abandoned his career-long specialty and moved in the direction of literary criticism. Maintaining independence in the face of enormous pressures that belong to a "sociology of academic life" has to be encouraged. And one must be both sympathetic and supportive of those who, in the light of contrary argument and evidence, consider modifying the convictions of a lifetime. In the ecclesiastical realm, the ideal should be that truth is the best apologetic. As one can offer only attempts at the ideal, s/he must be particularly diffident about the significance of one's contribution to the enterprise.

14 G. Bornkamm, "The stilling of the storm in Matthew," in *Tradition and Interpretation in Matthew*, ed. G. Bornkamm, G. Barth, and H. J. Held (London, SCM, 1963), pp. 52–53.

15 Recently Morna Hooker has argued that πίστις χριστοῦ refers to one's faith(fulness) towards the Christ whose faith(fulness) towards God brought about the participatory experience of ἐν χριστῷ. Her SNTS Presidential Address appeared as "ΠΙΣΤΙΣ ΧΡΙΣΤΟΥ," *NTS*, 35 (1989), 321–42.

16 R. Bultmann, *Theology of the New Testament* (New York, Scribners, 1951), pp. 34, 92.

17 By "after the resurrection," I mean in the resurrection narratives. At Matthew 18:6, Jesus does, in private with his disciples, refer to

children or immature followers who "believe in me." This is the single exception to the rule in the entire synoptic tradition.

18 R. Bultmann, "πίστις and πιστεύω in Paul," *TDNT*, ed. G. Kittel and G. Friedrich, vol. VI (Grand Rapids, Eerdmans, 1968), p. 217. Faith of this kind is "believing acceptance of that which the kerygma claims" and "the way of salvation ordained by God and opened up in Christ." D. Hay argues that πίστις can be rendered "objective ground for subjective faith" in certain contexts. See "Pistis as 'ground for faith' in hellenized Judaism and Paul," *JBL*, 108 (1989), 465.

19 Bultmann, *Theology*, pp. 37, 43, 80–81, 83–89.

20 Ibid., pp. 34, 91.

21 Ibid., p. 89.

22 A. E. Harvey, *Jesus and the Constraints of History* (Philadelphia, Westminster, 1982), pp. 159–63.

23 Bultmann, *Theology*, p. 33.

24 Ibid.

25 Ibid.

26 Ibid., p. 34.

27 See E. E. Lemcio, "The unifying kerygma of the New Testament," *JSNT*, 33 (1988), 3–17. See esp. p. 17 and n. 37 (in the present book, p. 127). A sequel with the same title in the same journal (38 [1990], 3–11) identifies nine more instances, bringing the total to nineteen of the twenty-seven documents, a clear majority. Sometimes confusion about the meaning of κήρυγμα stems from a lack of precision in the absence of clear and agreed-upon criteria. The point is well illustrated in the opening sentence of R. E. Brown's "The kerygma of the gospel according to John," *Int*, 21 (1967), 387: "'Kerygma,' despite the frequency of its use in modern biblical studies, remains, for this writer at least, a term with many meanings: and so it is perhaps best to state at the beginning of this paper that the kerygma of the Fourth Gospel is here understood to be its central salvific message." However, to avoid idiosyncratic and arbitrary definitions, one ought to appeal to those statements actually designated "kerygma" and "gospel" by the NT writers themselves. This was my approach in "Unifying kerygma."

28 C. F. D. Moule has supported the suggestion that the opening phrase "is the sort of heading that any scribe might supply, if presented with only a mutilated exemplar to copy": *The Birth of the New Testament*, 3rd edn (San Francisco, Harper & Row, 1982), p. 131, n. 1. However, in the absence of any textual evidence, it must remain a matter of speculation.

29 See the recent examination of W. D. Davies and D. C. Allison, Jr., *A Critical and Exegetical Commentary on the Gospel According to Saint Matthew*, ICC (Edinburgh, T. & T. Clark, 1988), vol. I, pp. 149–55.

30 H. Koester, "From the kerygma-gospel to written gospels," *NTS*, 35 (1989), 381.

31 Ibid.

32 Ibid., p. 380.
33 J. D. Kingsbury, if I understand him correctly, tries to make a case that the last two statements, ostensibly by Jesus, are references by Matthew to his own gospel. Besides assuming that Jesus could not have forecast the dissemination of the gospel that he himself preached, it also assumes that Matthew conceived of his own work as a gospel, a notion for which there is no direct or even indirect evidence. See *Matthew: Structure, Christology, Kingdom* (Philadelphia, Fortress, 1975), pp. 130–31.
34 Ibid., p. 367. It is more common to refer to this as one of the "speeches" of Acts. G. N. Stanton's analysis is relevant to what follows, although he attempts to discern pre-Lucan influences among the differences whereas my observations regard them as evidence of language suited to the three periods narrated. See *Jesus of Nazareth in New Testament Preaching*, SNTSMS 27 (Cambridge, University Press, 1974), pp. 78–79, esp. 80–81, 84–85, and n. 3.
35 The most recent, comprehensive expression of this view may be found in J. D. G. Dunn, *Unity and Diversity in the New Testament* (Philadelphia, Westminster, 1977).
36 H. Koester and J. M. Robinson have contributed most to the systematic exposition of this account of early Christian tradition-history in *Trajectories Through Early Christianity* (Philadelphia, Fortress, 1971).
37 T. J. Weeden has given this scenario its definitive treatment in *Mark – Traditions in Conflict* (Philadelphia, Fortress, 1971).
38 Does the penchant for seeing controversy behind variety stem from the legacy of F. C. Baur? See the sketch of his career and influence in Neill and Wright, *Interpretation*, pp. 23–26.
39 N. Perrin, *What is Redaction Criticism?* (Philadelphia, Fortress, 1970), pp. 41–42. Bornkamm, "Stilling," did not espouse this in so vigorous and comprehensive a manner forty years ago. Nevertheless, there lies a mildly controversial tone in his analysis. Matthew's quarrel seems to be with his main source. Mark's account is more realistic and "novelistic" (p. 54). Jesus functions as "the great miracle worker." "Pious motives are pushed into the background." The "straightforward miracle story ... has no kind of pious sound; it runs quite profanely" (p. 53). In Matthew's hands, Mark's story is transformed into a "kerygmatic paradigm of the danger and glory of discipleship" (p. 57). Jesus "subdues the demonic powers and brings the βασιλεία of God"; but he is introduced as "the Son of Man who has not [*sic*] where to lay his head" (ibid.). The fearful, faith-deficient disciples whom Matthew calls οἱ ἄνθρωποι "are obviously [!] intended to represent the men who are encountered by the story through preaching" (p. 56).
40 Lemcio, "Unifying kerygma," pp. 6–7.
41 M. Kähler, *The So-called Historical Jesus and the Historic Biblical Christ*, ed. C. Braaten (Philadelphia, Fortress, 1964), p. 81.
42 Ibid., p. 83. Better known is Kähler's oft-quoted description of the gospels as "passion narratives with extended introductions" (p. 80

n. 11). Although regarded as apt by virtually everyone, I believe that it has skewed the discussion literarily and theologically. In admitted overstatement ("To state the matter somewhat provocatively"), Kähler complained that something so *theologically* weighty was being minimized by historians whose biographies of Jesus devoted a mere 20 percent of text to the PN (by the way, the proportion in Mark). So, he maximized it by calling the preceding stories "introductions", although Kähler had to acknowledge their substantial presence with the word "extended." The PN is significant, but its theological and literary importance will have to be re-assessed free of Kähler's dictum and in the context of Greco-Roman biography (of which more will be said below). For now, I shall simply note the observation of D. Aune that "The focus on the death of Jesus which characterizes all of the Gospels ... is a theme characteristic of a development in Greco-Roman biography of the first century A.D.." See Aune's contribution to a volume edited by him: "Greco-Roman biography," in *Greco-Roman Literature and the New Testament*, SBLSBS 21 (Atlanta, Scholars, 1988), p. 123. E. Best also sees the problem with Kähler's dictum in *Mark: the Gospel as Story* (Edinburgh, T. & T. Clark, 1983), p. 136.

43 G. Bornkamm, *Jesus of Nazareth* (New York, Harper & Row, 1960), p. 25.

44 Kähler, *So-called Historical Jesus*, p. 83.

45 W. Wrede, *Das Messiasgeheimnis in den Evangelien* (Göttingen, Vandenhoeck and Ruprecht, 1901), pp. 209–36.

46 Ibid., p. 5. For this criticism, see W. C. Robinson, Jr., "The quest for Wrede's secret Messiah," *Int*, 27 (1973), 10.

47 For an overview of the line of interpretation stressing polemics, see the "Introduction" by W. Telford in the volume that he has edited: *The Interpretation of Mark* (London, SPCK, 1985), pp. 19, 24–26.

48 Is there a trace of the Hegelian thesis, antithesis, synthesis rubric in this model?

49 See C. Tuckett's "Introduction" to the volume which he has edited: *The Messianic Secret* (Philadelphia, Fortress, 1983), pp. 10–19.

50 Telford, *Interpretation of Mark*, p. 27.

51 Morgan, *Biblical Interpretation*, p. 212.

52 Perrin, *Redaction Criticism?*, p. 42.

53 Bornkamm, "Stilling," p. 55.

54 Ibid., p. 55, n. 37.

55 This is A. E. Harvey's expression from the book cited in n. 22 above.

56 D. E. Aune, *The New Testament in its Literary Environment* (Philadelphia, Westminster, 1987), p. 23.

57 Ibid., p. 22.

58 Ibid., p. 29.

59 Ibid., p. 31.

60 Ibid., p. 46.

61 Ibid., pp. 91–92. The same is true of Josephus (p. 106).

62 Ibid., p. 91.

63 Ibid., p. 60. On the larger question Aune makes the critical point

that "To claim that the Evangelists wrote biography with historical intentions ... does not guarantee that they preserved a single historical fact" (p. 65).

64 U.Luz attempts to give each its due in "The disciples in the Gospel according to Matthew," *The Interpretation of Matthew*, ed. G. N. Stanton (London, SPCK, 1983), pp. 98–128. He expects that careful exegesis will be adequate to the task. But it is clear from G. Strecker's contribution in the same volume how one's broader construct of Christianity influences the outcome of close textual study (pp. 69–70 and my discussion in ch. 3).

65 Aune, *Literary Environment*, p. 61.

66 Ibid., p. 60. Best, *Story*, p. 136 also does not take into account the full phrase, "believe in the gospel [of the Kingdom of God]" as having no NT parallel. One cannot isolate individual words and assign them absolutely to a particular *Sitz im Leben*.

67 Ibid., p. 126.

68 Moule, *Birth*, p. 4.

69 Ibid., p. 10.

70 Ibid., p. 4.

71 F. Martin (ed.), *Narrative Parallels to the New Testament*, SBLRBS 22 (Atlanta, Scholars, 1988), 23.

72 P. L. Shuler, *A Genre for the Gospels. The Biographical Character of Matthew* (Philadelphia, Fortress, 1982), p. 109. I owe this citation to Martin, *Narrative Parallels*, p. 24.

73 Martin, *Narrative Parallels*, p. 24.

2 Mark

I should like to thank Dr. Russell Morton, a former student, for reading and responding to an earlier draft of this chapter.

1 C. F. D. Moule, *The Phenomenon of the New Testament*, SBT, 2nd ser. 1 (London, SCM, 1967), pp. 100–14. Reprinted from *New Testament Essays: Studies in Memory of T. W. Manson*, ed. A. J. B. Higgins (Manchester, University Press, 1959), pp. 165–79. Pagination in the following notes is from the former work.

2 Ibid., pp. 102, 105, 113.

3 Ibid., pp. 102, 106, 110, 113–14.

4 Ibid., p. 109.

5 Ibid., pp. 108, 110–12.

6 Ibid., p. 111.

7 Ibid., pp. 106–10.

8 Ibid., pp. 107–08.

9 More than a decade later, however, his position began to be cited by such scholars as J. Roloff, *Das Kerygma und der irdische Jesus* (Göttingen, Vandenhoeck and Ruprecht, 1970), pp. 44–45. More recently, R. Pesch, in his massive, multi-critical study, has not only noted Professor Moule's essay (vol. I, p. 63) but has also himself come to similar conclusions. He insists that, in contrast to the other synoptists, Mark's literary and theological achievements have been

overrated (pp. 15, 54). The gospel would have been useful for missionary and catechetical work (pp. 53, 63, 74, 106). Furthermore, "Das Evangelium ist indirekt Predigt, direkt Geschichtserzählung–nicht umgekehrt" (p. 51). See *Das Markusevangelium*, HTK 2 (Freiburg–Basle–Vienna, Herder, vol. I, 1976. vol. II, 1977). See also vol. I, pp. 25, 148, 277–81 and vol. II, pp. 36–47.

10 See Pesch, *Markusevangelium*, vol. I, p. 13 n. 3 for those who advocate a more eastern provenance.

11 See p. 26 and nn. 50–51 for the fuller discussion.

12 Moule, *Phenomenon*, pp. 56–59.

13 Chief among such interpreters is T. J. Weeden, *Mark – Traditions in Conflict* (Philadelphia, Fortress, 1971). H. C. Kee, using other methods, sees the church's situation differently from Weeden and those who share his view. Cf. *Community of the New Age: Studies in Mark's Gospel* (Philadelphia, Westminster, 1977).

14 *Das Messiasgeheimnis in den Evangelien* (Göttingen, Vandenhoeck and Ruprecht, 1901), pp. 5–6. Cf. pp. 209–36. W. C. Robinson, Jr., offers a penetrating critique on this point in "The quest for Wrede's secret messiah," *Int*, 27 (1973), 10, 15.

15 Such a reversal of the usual order would put criticism at all levels on a more secure footing. Only when the most tangible data are controlled and their character understood may one with integrity and some degree of confidence proceed to the lesser – or unknown – terrority behind the text. Recently, D. Rhoads and D. Michie have been the first to respond comprehensively to the challenge posed a decade or so ago by that quintessential redaction critic, Norman Perrin, that New Testament scholars acquire and apply the techniques of literary criticism from experts in the discipline. See their *Mark as Story: An Introduction to the Narrative of a Gospel* (Philadelphia, Fortress, 1982). Although my work was done independently of them and on a much-reduced scale, I applaud their efforts and hope that our conclusions are mutually informative. The most crucial difference between us lies in my attempt to elucidate the narrative's attention to "before" and "after."

16 Subsequently, I shall commit myself to one of the ten interpretations of Ἀρχή discussed by C. E. B. Cranfield in *The Gospel According to Saint Mark* (Cambridge, University Press, 1959), pp. 3–35. He also marshals weighty arguments favoring the inclusion of υἱὸς θεοῦ, even though Χ Θ 28 255 1555* sy[pal] geo[l] arm (some MSS.) and substantial patristic references omit them (p. 38). Since the evidence is controverted, I have avoided making a case on it.

17 G. Strecker, "Literarkritische Überlegungen zum εὐαγγέλιον – Begriff im Markusevangelium," in *Neues Testament und Geschichte*, ed. H. Baltensweiler and Bo Reicke (Tübingen, Mohr [Siebeck], 1972), p. 92 and n. 9.

18 Authorities are divided over the meaning of χριστοῦ, some regarding it as a proper name, others as a title.

19 The tendency to identify τὸ εὐαγγέλιον τοῦ θεοῦ at 14c with

monotheistic, hellenistic missionary preaching as evidenced at Rom.
1:1 simply ignores the statement in v. 3 that it concerns "his Son
Jesus Christ our Lord," christology which never appears in Mark's
narrative on Jesus' lips as a self-reference. The Evangelist here
summarizes the content of Jesus' message, not his own or that of
other Christians.

20 J. M. Robinson has provided the full argument in *The Problem of
History in Mark* (London, SCM, 1957), pp. 23, 24, 32.

21 The written narrative about the earthly Jesus is regarded primarily
as a vehicle for the words and deeds of the risen Christ. See n. 64
below for a sample provided by Marxsen himself.

22 W. Marxsen, *Mark the Evangelist. Studies in the Redaction
History of the Gospel* (Nashville, Abingdon, 1969), pp. 131–38.

23 The only christological expression which Jesus will own throughout
the course of the narrative is "The Son of Man," which never occurs
in confessions, acclamations, or ascriptions.

24 Subsequently, I shall examine the usage of πιστεύειν and the
christological issues surrounding the messianic secret more fully.

25 P⁴⁶ D 28 700 *al* omit ἐμοῦ καὶ from ἕνεκεν ἐμοῦ καὶ τοῦ
εὐαγγελίου in 8:35.

26 Unless I have misunderstood him, R. Pesch in *Markusevangelium*,
vol. 1, seems sometimes to hold this (p. 76 n. 6) and sometimes not
(p. 106). Cf. the same apparent ambivalence in his contribution to
a collection of essays edited by him: *Das Markus-Evangelium*
(Darmstadt, Wissenschaftliche Buchgesellschaft, 1979), pp. 337 and
341–42.

27 The textual witnesses are divided, the *lectio plenior* which includes
εἰς ἐμέ being supported by three different text families: the Alex-
andrian (including B), Western (it^{aur,c,f,e,q,} etc.) and Caesarean
(f^1, f^{13}). This should caution one against rejecting the longer
reading merely as a scribal attempt at assimilation to Matt.
18:6. Mary Ann Beavis does not pay sufficient attention in the
text of her article to the "objects" of faith. And the diagram
does not help to sort out how faith in God and Jesus (never in
the absolute sense) may be understood. Is it believing in Jesus'
power to heal, or believing that God can heal (through Jesus),
or believing in God and Jesus? See "Mark's teaching on faith,"
BTB, 16 (1986), 139–42. As we saw, post-resurrection relations
to Jesus are described as not being ashamed of his person and
word (8:38) and receiving him (yet not him, but God, 9:37).
C. D. Marshall has studied this theme comprehensively, concluding
that "faith is believing confidence in Jesus inasmuch as he concretely
manifests the saving action of God." Nevertheless this falls
short of "believing in Jesus," an expression that does not really
have a home in the synoptic gospels. It will be useful to study
faith in connection with other terms that express relation to
Jesus, especially the language of "receiving." See *Faith as a
Theme in Mark's Narrative*, SNTSMS 64 (Cambridge, University
Press, 1989), p. 231.

28 J. M. Robinson, *Problem*, pp. 74–75, comes close to this conclusion in his analysis, citing M. Werner's distinction between Mark's view and Paul's concept of "faith" in Christ," p. 75 n. 2.

29 His view has been expressed recently in "The portrayal of the life of faith in the Gospel of Mark," *Int*, 22 (1978), 387–99.

30 The soteriology expressed by λύτρον ἀντὶ πολλῶν is found only here, in the exact Matthean parallel and in a "hellenized" form in 1 Tim. 2:5–6, which speaks of the one mediator between God and men, ἄνθρωπος χριστὸς 'Ἰησοῦς, ὁ δὸς ἑαυτὸν ἀντίλυτρον ὑπὲρ πάντων.

31 Pesch, *Markusevangelium*, vol. II, pp. 358–59 approves of E. Best's observation that *"my* blood of the Covenant" implies a new covenant. By appealing to targumic interpretations of Exod. 24:7–8, Pesch argues that the covenant bond comes into being by atonement through the forgiveness of sins.

32 Although the statement here is not connected with any title, Jesus in v. 21 pronounced woe upon the man, present at the meal, by whom the Son of Man was about to be betrayed.

33 This position will be evaluated more fully under "Implications" below.

34 All evidence that ὅτι χριστοῦ ἐστε is a conjecture has been removed from the latest Nestle-Aland apparatus (26th edition). In the 25th, Schmiedel's reconstruction was still noted. A fuller account of the textual data appears in the earlier edition of K. Aland's *Synopsis Quattuor Evangeliorum*, 9th edn, Stuttgart, Württembergische Bibelanstalt, 1976), p. 248. W has χριστός; but ℵ* has ἐμόν, neither of which fits the sense or grammar of ἐστε.

35 While the weightiest manuscripts read 'Εγώ εἰμι, there is not inconsiderable support for σὺ εἶπας ὅτι: Θ φ *f*¹³ 565 700 *pc*; Or.

36 There is no need to suppress the demons following their address at 5:7 because the setting is private: among the tombs with only Jesus and his disciples present. No injunction is required following 14:61 because Caiaphas merely inquires about Jesus' being the Son of the Blessed One; he, of course, does not regard him as such.

37 Greek grammar ("Colwell's Rule") permits, but does not demand, the article to be supplied. See C. F. D. Moule, *An Idiom-Book of New Testament Greek*, 2nd edn (Cambridge, University Press, 1963), pp. 115–16.

38 Moule observed long ago that "half its content was already a thing of the past and half was – at any rate in the eyes of the early church – yet in the future." Consequently, "It is more appropriate to the past and future; but not to the present." So long as the church was in a *Zwischenzeit*, between Jesus' going and coming, the term had little or no relevance. "Far more relevant is the term Lord, which with its associations with Ps. cx, exactly fits the heavenly session. Ps. cx is, accordingly, one of the most frequent of all testimonia." See "The influence of circumstances on the use of christological terms," *JTS*, 10 (1959), 257–58.

39 See n. 37, above.

40 Nowhere is the political aspect of χριστός more evident than at 15:32 where Jesus is mockingly addressed as "the Christ, the King of Israel." Five times previously in this chapter, throughout the course of the Roman trial and its aftermath, he had been referred to as "the King of the Jews" (vv. 2, 9, 12, 18, 26).

41 Such discrete usage should prevent one from confusing these categories or from subsuming all under the general (and misleading) heading of "messianic."

42 Κύριος occurs in Mark fourteen times. Eight of these refer to God by various persons: one by the Evangelist (1:3), another by the crowd (11:9), and six by Jesus (5:19; 13:20. See the four instances where he quotes the OT: 12:11, 29—30, 36. Only the Gentile woman uses it of Jesus, where it may well be honorific, and in any case uttered privately, 7:28). Jesus will refer to earthly lords in 12:9 and 13:35 and to the Messiah at 12:37 (though here certainly being superior to David is not necessarily suggesting equality with God). Finally, 2:28 says less than a first glance reveals: "The Son of Man is Lord even of the Sabbath" (2:20). The presence of καί here (absent in Matthew and Luke) suggests something less than a full-fledged divine equivalent. If κύριος = God, then he would *certainly* be Lord of the seventh day. Only someone with lesser, disputed, or unknown authority would say "even." The matter becomes somewhat less debatable if one avoids importing into Mark's gospel the convictions of Christians in other circles ('Ιησοῦς Κύριος). Mark 1:1 does not describe his work as the beginning of the Good News about the Lord Jesus Christ (the Son of God). J. D. Kingsbury in *The Christology of Mark's Gospel* (Philadelphia, Fortress, 1983) regards this among "several designations that either play only a minor christological role or are without titular significance" (p. 53). The term is dealt with in a medium-size paragraph (p. 54). See the fuller treatment of κύριος in ch. 3 and Kingsbury's estimation of it in Matthew.

43 Curiously, R. Tannehill virtually ignores "the Son of Man" category in his essay, "The Gospel of Mark as narrative christology," *Semeia*, 16 (1979), 57—59.

44 See E. Lohmeyer, *Das Evangelium des Markus*, 15th edn (Göttingen, Vandenhoeck and Ruprecht, 1959) and Marxsen, *Mark*.

45 G. Bornkamm, *Jesus of Nazareth* (New York, Harper & Row, 1960), p. 25. W. Marxsen, *Introduction to the New Testament* (Philadelphia, Fortress, 1968), p. 143.

46 See W. C. Robinson, Jr., "Quest," n. 15 above and J. Roloff, "Das Markusevangelium als Geschichtsdarstellung," *EvTh*, 27 (1969), 73—74 n. 2.

47 G. Strecker describes Mark's Gospel as *"Botschaft als Bericht"* in "Zur Messiasgeheimnistheorie im Markusevangelium," *SE*, ed. F. L. Cross, *TU* 88 (Berlin, Akademie-Verlag, 1964), vol. III, p. 104.

48 For a fuller account of this position, see ch. 1.

49 H. Koester and J. M. Robinson (among others) have asserted, without sufficient argument or data, that collections of wisdom sayings, miracle stories, etc., defined in an exclusive and comprehensive way

the christology or kerygma of each group which transmitted them. See *Trajectories Through Early Christianity* (Philadelphia, Fortress, 1971). Note the tendency to equate terms such as "kerygma," "symbol," "creed," and "belief" on pp. 50, 68, 211–29.

50 Ibid., pp. 48–49. Cf. pp. 227–30.

51 H. Conzelmann, *An Outline of the Theology of the New Testament* (London, SCM, 1968), p. 139.

52 H. Conzelmann, "Jesus Christus," *RGG*, vol. III (Tübingen, Mohr [Siebeck], 1959), p. 633 and *Outline*, pp. 138–39.

53 H. Conzelmann, "Present and future in the synoptic tradition," *JTC*, 5 (1968), 42. Cf. "Gegenwart und Zukunft in der synoptischen Tradition," *ZTK*, 54 (1957), 294.

54 Conzelmann, *Outline*, p. 143.

55 A. Ambrozic, in his desire to invest the secret with contemporary, kerygmatic relevance, "transcategorizes" the temporal εἰ μὴ ὅταν ... ἀναστῇ into a conditional statement. See *The Hidden Kingdom* (Washington, DC, CBA, 1972), p. 38.

56 Conzelmann, *Outline*, p. 143.

57 Roloff, "Markusevangelium," pp. 90–93 and Strecker, "Messias-geheimnistheorie," pp. 97–100, 102 have argued this point convincingly.

58 While it is true that the disciples did not understand what Jesus' reference to "rising from the dead" meant (9:10), there is no suggestion that they *could* not have understood. Throughout, Jesus' attitude implies the opposite. Furthermore, nowhere in the gospels is the resurrection *eo ipso* an epistemological turning point for them. Some special act of the risen Jesus is required. In Acts, Pentecost turns the disciples' understanding around.

59 So far as W. Marxsen is concerned (see *Introduction*, pp. 137, 144, and n. 46 above), it is just such a level of temporality which gave Mark pause. By means of the messianic secret, he intended to combat an historicism which emerged when traditions set beside one another implied a series of historically verifiable epiphanies. This suggested that salvation had occurred in a past event rather than in the present through the kerygma. But Marxsen's opinion becomes subject to J. Roloff's observation that such interpretation amounts to a retrojection of modern hermeneutical concerns into the first century (Roloff, "Markusevangelium," p. 77). And it seems to deny that salvation did in some real sense occur in the past.

60 J. B. Tyson, "The blindness of the disciples in Mark," *JBL*, 80 (1961), 261–68.

61 So far as I can determine, it was J. Schreiber who first proposed that Mark criticized miracle traditions, infused with θεῖος ἀνήρ christology, by means of a *theologia crucis*. See "Die Christologie des Markusevangeliums," *ZTK*, 58 (1961), 158–59. Weeden has given the thesis its most systematic and thoroughgoing expression (see n. 14, above). In recent years, however, the position is being abandoned or heavily qualified. C. R. Holladay finds no real antecedents to the motif in the religio-historical milieu by which it

allegedly entered the Christian tradition, hellenistic Judaism. See *Theios Aner in Hellenistic Judaism: a Critique of the Use of the Category in New Testament Christology* (Missoula, MT, Scholars, 1977).

62 W. Kelber denies that Mark intended to make his narrative the means by which the risen Jesus directly addressed the reader. Such re-presentation by itinerant prophets through oral traditions allegedly produced a crisis of faith during the first Jewish War with Rome when Jesus' real absence became all too obvious. In the move from orality to textuality, the Evangelist's narrative distanced the reader from Jesus' past and his future parousia. While one may disagree with Kelber's speculations, one cannot help but notice the rather striking departure from the more usual redaction-critical stance. See "Mark and oral tradition," *Semeia*, 16 (1979), 7−55, esp. 40−46.

63 Perhaps the most explicit illustration of this appears in W. Marxsen's paradoxical summary of the kerygma of Mark's passion narrative which he equates with that of the gospel: "The Risen Lord (the glorified One, the Son of Man, the Son of God) goes to his Cross. This makes it quite clear that the story is not meant to be read as the account of an historical sequence of events." See *Introduction*, pp. 132, 137.

64 O. Cullmann has put the matter in more general, yet succinct, terms. "Sonship is essentially characterized not by the gift of a particular power, nor by a substantial relationship with God by virtue of divine conception; but by the idea of *election* to participation in divine work through the execution of a particular commission, and by the idea of strict obedience to the God who elects." See *The Christology of the New Testament* (London, SCM, 1959), p. 275.

65 Jer. 5:6−7; Hos. 6 and 9; Mal. 1:6, 2:10, 3:17. I employed the same bi-polar model to interpret an aspect of the disciples' misunderstanding and disobedience in "External evidence for the structure and function of Mark iv. 1−20, vii. 14−23 and viii. 14−21," *JTS*, 29 (1978), 323−38.

66 See the much-neglected but important study by J. Bowker, "The Son of Man," *JTS*, 28 (1977), 19−48.

67 Moule has contributed significantly to the interpretation of this passage and its use in the NT. See *The Origin of Christology* (Cambridge, University Press, 1977), pp. 11−22

68 Rhoads and Michie, in *Mark as Story*, p. 101, use similar categories in their literary-critical analysis of character: what one is and what s/he does.

69 H. E. Tödt, *The Son of Man in the Synoptic Tradition* (Philadelphia, Westminster, 1965), p. 191.

70 C. E. B. Cranfield, *The Gospel According to Saint Mark* (Cambridge, University Press, 1959), pp. 280−81.

71 R. Barbour shows a refreshing sensitivity to these christological distinctions in "Gethsemane in the tradition of the passion,"

NTS, 16 (1970), 236, 242, 247. See his penetrating theological discussion on pp. 242—51.

72 J. L. Clark, "A re-examination of the problem of the Messianic secret and its relationship to the synoptic Son of Man sayings" (New Haven, Yale University, 1962), p. 116. This dissertation has been published recently, but the monograph is unavailable to me. Although they have not argued the point thus, Moule and Morna Hooker also see the Marcan Son of Man as a symbol for obedience. See his *Origin*, pp. 14, 27 and her *The Son of Man in Mark* (London, SPCK, 1967), pp. 190—93.

73 Others, of course, have argued for Mark's intent to distinguish between the past of *Jesus* and the Evangelist's circumstances, e.g. Roloff, "Markusevangelium," pp. 73—93, esp. 90—93; Siegfried Schulz, *Die Stunde der Botschaft* (Hamburg, Furche-Verlag, 1967), p. 39; Strecker, "Messiasgeheimnistheorie," pp. 87—104, esp. 97—104. But the issue is not simply a matter of "onceness" which can be conveyed with the past tense of verbs. Rather, the distinctions revolve around theological and christological issues.

74 Kelber, "Mark and oral tradition," p. 16 regards the Evangelist's "total written story as the beginning of the gospel" whose ending lies in one's personal "actualization." Would such an estimate of Mark's work put it in the same category as Luke's διήγησις (1:1) or Matthew's βίβλος γενέσεως (1:1)?

75 See n. 49.

76 R. Bultmann, *Theology of the New Testament* (New York, Scribner's, 1951), vol. I, p. 33.

77 E.g. Acts 2:36, Rom. 10:9—10, 1 Cor. 15:3—5. Cf. John 5:24, 12:44; 1 Thess. 2:2, 8—9, 3:2; 1 Pet. 1:21. See also the appendix in this book.

78 The analysis above showed that "following" principally described the disciples' response to Jesus during his lifetime (although nothing prevents it from having a secondary and extended meaning later). But in his absence everyone could receive a child in his name and so "receive" Christ and God. What relates the two times is the movement from the temporal and particular to the eternal and universal (not philosophically understood). "Forgiveness" and non-eschatological uses of "salvation" (healing) are limited prior to the cross to acts done on occasion for persons mainly within Judaism. But Jesus' death effects both release and covenant bonding for the many (Gentiles). Once again, limits of time, space, and now nationality become transcended; soteriology is deepened.

79 E.g. J. Meagher, "Die Form- und Redactionsungeschickliche [*sic*] Methoden: the principle of clumsiness and the Gospel of Mark," *JAAR*, 43 (1975), 459. This thesis has been expanded in *Clumsy Construction in Mark's Gospel. A Critique of Form- and Redaktionsgeschichte*, TST 3 (Toronto, Edwin Mellen, 1979). See n. 10 above (Pesch). E. Best attributes this lack of tidiness to a profound respect for the traditions he received: "Redaction critics argue that Mark was a genuine author and not a scissors-and-paste

editor. This requires more careful definition. In the way in which he has placed the tradition in his total context supplying audience, place, time, and sequence and in the summaries he has written he has been quite obviously creative. But in the way in which he has preserved the material which existed before him he has been conservative. Perhaps we should not think of an author but of an artist creating a collage. Mark appears to have had a positive respect for the material which he used; this is not to say that he was attempting to write "history," or that he possessed a journalist's ideal – facts are sacred, comment is free – or that he was positively attempting to preserve for the future what lay before him." See "Mark's preservation of the tradition," *The Interpretation of Mark*, ed. W. Telford (Philadelphia, Fortress, 1985), p. 128.

80 See N. Peterson, *Literary Criticism for New Testament Critics* (Philadelphia, Fortress, 1978), pp. 78–80. In a helpful treatment of the relation between past, present, and future, the author concludes that Mark rooted his message about Jesus in narrative form (rather than epistle or apocalypse) because his opponents had taken this approach. The Evangelist endeavored to provide a truer account of the circumstances (p. 80). If this was indeed the case, then choosing between the two versions would depend upon establishing the veracity of one or the other.

3 Matthew

1 J. D. Kingsbury, "Reflections on the 'reader' of Matthew's gospel," *NTS*, 34 (1988), 445–46, 453–54.

2 G. Strecker, "The concept of history in Matthew," in *The Interpretation of Matthew*, ed. G. N. Stanton (Philadelphia, Fortress, 1983), pp. 69–70. Strecker argues that the Evangelist sees salvation "history unfolding in three epochs" (preparation, focus in Jesus, extension in the church, pp. 73–74), but he does not stress that each of these has its own idiom of expression. Strecker hints at such distinction-keeping when he says, "In the redactional context, Matthew has not attempted to establish baptism as a sacramental occurrence, *nor does the baptismal formula quoted in triad form in 28:19 have any support in the redactional material*" (my italics; p. 78). But Strecker does not suggest why this is so. A similar observation can be made about U. Luz's helpful essay in the same collection. He means to identify both historical and contemporizing ("transparent") features in Matthew's view of discipleship. But there is little effort to distinguish then and now on the basis of a different idiom. See "The disciples in the Gospel according to Matthew," pp. 98–128.

3 The most comprehensive, recent analyses of the pericope are by B. J. Hubbard, *The Matthean Redaction of a Primitive Apostolic Commissioning: An Exegesis of Matthew 28:16–20*, SBLDS 19, (Missoula, MT, Scholars, 1974) and Jane Schaberg, *The Father, the Son and the Holy Spirit. The Triadic Phrase in Matthew 28:19b*,

SSBLDS 61 (Chico, CA, Scholars, 1982). Despite much intensive scrutiny, they tend to exploit similarities and differences in order to make judgments about tradition and redaction rather than to determine any narrative role that they might have. Neither discriminates between language before and after Easter. An analogous problem appears in J. D. Kingsbury's most recent work, *Matthew as Story* (Philadelphia, Fortress, 1986). Despite the attention to various levels of narration and audience, there is no attention to the "pastness" of the story which such distinctions allow one to give. Furthermore, most of what Kingsbury says about the narrative is not particularly Matthean. It is also true of Mark and Luke. Oddly, he does not acknowledge for the reader the vast stretches of the Matthean story line that all three Evangelists share.

4 This rendering of אנש בר (υἱὸς ἀνθρώπου) has been persuasively argued by Bowker, "The Son of Man," pp. 19–48.

5 C. F. D. Moule has been the most vigorous advocate of this interpretation. He uses it as the basis for Jesus' appropriation of the expression. See *Origin*, pp. 11–22.

6 For an analysis of this passage, see R. E. Brown's commentary *The Gospel According to John*, AB 29A (New York, Doubleday, 1970), vol. II, pp. 1,023, 1,038–39.

7 One of the few scholars to give this phenomenon its due is C. F. D. Moule in "The intention of the evangelists," in *New Testament Essays: Studies in Memory of T. W. Manson*, ed. A. J. B. Higgins, (Manchester, University Press, 1959), pp. 165–79 and reprinted in *The Phenomenon of the New Testament* (London, SCM, 1967), pp. 100–14.

8 3:11, 16//1:8//3:16, 22; 4:1//1:12//4:1; 10:20//13:11//12:12; 12:31–32//3:29//12:10.

9 See 22:43 at Mark 12:36. References to conception by the Spirit, not strictly from Q, are to be found at 1:18, 20//1:35. Jesus' casting out demons by the "Spirit of God" (12:28) is an expression one would have thought more appropriate to Luke who has "finger of God" (11:20).

10 See the insightful discussion by my colleague, R. W. Wall, "'The finger of God': Deuteronomy 9.10 and Luke 11.20," *NTS*, 33 (January 1987), 144–50.

11 For the usage of τηρεῖν, ἐντέλλεσθαι and ἐντολή, see 19:17//Mark 10:3; 15:3//Mark 7:8; 17:19//Mark 9:9 (Jesus orders silence about the transfiguration); 22:36 (Mark 12:28; Matt. 22:38, 40 heighten the significance of the twin commands of the law to love God and neighbor).

12 A. Schweitzer, *The Quest of the Historical Jesus* (London, Adam and Charles Black, 1911), pp. 357–61.

13 3:17//1:11//3:22; 4:3, 6//Luke 4:3, 9; 8:29//5:7//8:28; 11:27// Luke 10:22; 17:5//9:35; 21:37//12:6//20:13; 24:36//Mark 13:32; 26:63//14:61//22:70; 27:54//Mark 15:39.

14 John A. T. Robinson credits J. Jeremias with this observation in *The Priority of John*, ed. J. F. Coakley (London, SCM, 1985),

p. 360. The linguistic argument can be found in Jeremias' *New Testament Theology I: The Proclamation of Jesus* (London, SCM, 1971), p. 59.

15 For a more comprehensive treatment of these questions, see my study, "Supper and wedding," pp. 1–26.

16 See Blomberg, *Historical Reliability* pp. 51–2.

17 It is otherwise with the name "Jesus" by which Mary's son is to be known, since he is to save his people from their sins (1:21). And the name by which Isaiah's prophecy is to be fulfilled (i.e. Emmanuel) seems to define by its proximity (v. 23) the means of that salvation: to mediate the presence of God. Yet "Emmanuel" never occurs again. The focus remains upon Jesus' name throughout. To receive a child or assemble in Jesus' name is to receive him and experience his presence (18:5, 20). Leaving all on account of his name brings rewards in the present age and eternal life at the end (19:29).

18 Matthew does not retain Mark's ἀββὰ ὁ πατήρ (14:36) at 26:39 (πάτερ μου//22:42, πάτερ). R. H. Gundry observes that "whatever individualism may characterize the use of אַבָּא in those NT passages where it is transliterated, the plural of the first person pronoun throughout the Lord's Prayer makes 'Father' a communal address (even when unaccompanied by 'Our' as in Luke)." See *Matthew. A Commentary on his Literary and Theological Art* (Grand Rapids, MI, Eerdmans, 1982), p. 105.

19 Bornkamm, "Stilling," pp. 52–7.

20 J. D. Kingsbury, "The title 'Kyrios' in Matthew's Gospel," *JBL*, 94 (1975), 246.

21 Bornkamm, "End-expectation and church in Matthew" (in the volume cited in n 19 above), pp. 41–43.

22 1:20, 22, 24; 2:13, 15, 19; 3:3; 27:10; 28:2.

23 D. A. Carson, "Christological ambiguities in the Gospel of Matthew," *Christ the Lord. Studies in Christology Presented to Donald Guthrie*, ed. H. H. Rowden (Leicester, IVP, 1982), p. 109. Carson contends that Matthew does portray Jesus as divine. But this occurs implicitly rather than through the use of christological titles (pp. 109–10).

24 B and א are divided over ἔρημος, but the latter is joined by P[77] in support of it. And Matthew immediately follows the lament with the Olivet Discourse and its prediction of Jerusalem's tragic fate. See the same theme in 23:5–6.

25 Luke places the saying at 13:35, well in advance of the Temple cleansing, thereby historicizing the event.

26 Kingsbury, "Kyrios," p. 248 sees its purpose as attributing "divine authority to Jesus in his capacity as 'the Christ', 'Son of God', or 'Son of Man'." Somewhat more diffidently, "it basically refers beyond itself to some other, more definite title" (p. 255).

27 8:20//9:58, 11:19//7:34, 12:32//12:10.

28 9:6//2:10//5:24, 12:8//2:28//6:5, 26:64//14:62//22:69.

29 16:27–28//8:38, 9:1//9:26–27; 17:22//9:31//9:44; 20:18//10:33// 18:31; 26:24//14:21//22:22.

30 17:9//9:9, 20:28//10:45, 26:45//14:41.
31 The single exception (eschatological) is 24:30//13:26//21:27.
32 16:20//8:30//9:21, 24: 5//13:5//21:8.
33 16:16//8:29//9:20, 22:42//12:35//20:41, 26:63//14:61//22:67. See 24:24//Mark 13:22.
34 D.A Carson comes to similar conclusions in "Christological ambiguities," pp. 102–03. This is a fine survey and corrective to much of current discussion about Matthean christology.
35 Luke has this saying at the end of Jesus' encounter with Zacchaeus (19:10).
36 The only other christological association occurs at 12:31, 32 in a secondary and negative sense: while blasphemy against the Son of Man can be forgiven (cf. Luke 12:10), that against the Holy Spirit cannot (3:29//12:10).
37 Wrede, *Messiasgeheimnis*.
38 For a collection of essays that among them survey the high points of this effort, see *The Messianic Secret*, ed. C. Tuckett, (Philadelphia, Fortress, 1983).
39 U. Luz, "Das Geheimnismotiv und die markinische Christologie," *ZNW*, 56 (1965), 9–30. See n. 39 and J. D. G. Dunn, "The messianic secret in Mark," *TynBul*, 21 (1970), 92–117 and C. F. D. Moule, "On defining the messianic secret in Mark," *Jesus und Paulus: Festschrift für Werner Georg Kümmel zum 70. Geburtstag*, ed. E. E. Ellis and E. Grässer (Göttingen, Vandenhoeck and Ruprecht, 1975), pp. 239–52 and W. C. Robinson, Jr., "Quest," pp. 10–30. (These titles offer samples of attempts to challenge the notion of a unitary and unified secrecy phenomenon.)
40 S. Brown, "The Secret of the Kingdom of God (Mark 4:11)," *JBL*, 92 (1973), 60–74.
41 Triple tradition (9:2//2:5//5:20; 9:22//5:34//8:48; 9:28–29// 10:52//18:42; 21:25//11:31//20:5), Q (8:10//7:10), Matt.// Mark// (21:21–22//11:22–24; 24:23//13:21). The same restraint occurs in those instances where the Evangelist adds to the parallel: 8:13, 15:28, 14:46.
42 9:9//2:14//5:27–28; 8:19, 22//9:57, 61; 10:38//14:27; 4:19– 20//1:17–18. So G. Kittel in *TDNT* (Grand Rapids, MI, Eerdmans, 1964), vol. I, p. 214, though he makes the claim for the historical Jesus.
43 Such a point tends to be missed in redaction-critical studies like those of Hubbard's and Schaberg's (n. 1), who regard these as Christian responses (see ch. 1).
44 It may not be necessary, then, to make even the cautious allowances for Matthew's exceptional use that Moule does in his excursus on the subject, *Origin*, pp. 177–78.
45 See Weeden, *Traditions in Conflict*. Weeden asserts that the disciples (foils for Mark's theological opponents) reject Jesus, who in turn rejects them. But this extreme position cannot make sense of the angel's reminder to the women at the tomb that the disciples and Peter are to see the risen Lord in Galilee (16:7). Luz, "Disciples,"

pp. 101–02 (see n. 2 above) takes a position similar to mine. He further claims that Matthew consistently makes the disciples able to understand (p. 102). But the motive is as much christological as anything else: "So Jesus is shown here as a good teacher who successfully gives the disciples full instructions about everything. They do not understand of their own accord" (p. 103). Luz seems, however, to have overlooked the texts discussed above.

46 Luz, ibid., seems to blur the distinction between Peter and the other disciples who together with him are transparent figures (p. 115), types who show what Christians should and should not be (p. 108). If so, then why is the authority promised to Peter in 16:19 to be extended to the entire community on a separate occasion (18:18–19)? Apparently, his experience could be misinterpreted as a unique one.

47 Kingsbury, *Matthew*, is not justified in observing that the Jewish crowds are " 'without faith' in him" (p. 24). No one, including the disciples, relates to Jesus by believing in him. (See my earlier remarks on this terminology.)

48 F. F. Bruce, *Tradition: Old and New* (Grand Rapids, MI, Zondervan, 1970), pp. 50–1.

49 The directives of vv. 7–8 do retain their distinctives over against 28:19–20. While he is with them, the disciples are to continue Jesus' ministry to Israel (9:59) in a theocentric proclamation and by mighty works of healing. After the resurrection, Jesus gives them a christocentric didache and a "Trinitarian" cultic agenda for the world.

50 F. W. Beare, "The mission of the disciples and the mission charge: Matthew 10 and parallels," *JBL*, 99 (1970), 2. Luz, "Disciples," attempts to identify historical and contemporizing features in the First Evangelist's view of discipleship. But he makes little effort to distinguish between then and now on the basis of a different idiom. Nor does his analysis of μαθητής and μαθητεύω (p. 109) take into account that, though Jesus made disciples before the resurrection, they did not.

51 R. E. Morosco, "Redaction criticism and the evangelical: Matthew 10 a test case," *JETS*, 22 (1979), 329. Luz, "Disciples," p. 100 observes that "the disciples are not sent out during the lifetime of Jesus: they have only got their instructions." Consequently, at the narrative level the awkwardness is reduced.

52 R. T. France cautions against an unhistorical reading of this passage, i.e., seeing the instances of ἐκκλησία as anachronistic. "But this is to read all the later connotations of *ekklēsia* ('church') into a word which in terms of its Old Testament background (where LXX used it to translate Heb. *qāhāl*, one of the regular terms for the 'congregation' or 'community' of God's people) would be completely appropriate to describe the 'Messianic community' of the disciples of Jesus. Indeed, 'a Messiah without a Messianic Community would have been unthinkable to any Jew' (AB, p. 195)." "What is striking is not so much the idea of 'building a community,' but the boldness of Jesus' description of it as *my* community rather than God's."

See *The Gospel According to Matthew* (Grand Rapids, MI, Eerdmans, 1985), p. 255.
53 Bornkamm, "End-expectation," p. 39.
54 Ibid.

4 Luke

1 C. F. D. Moule, "The christology of Acts," *Studies in Luke–Acts*, ed. L. E. Keck and J. L. Martyn (New York, Abingdon, 1966), pp. 162–63 where a similar point is differently made.
2 R. J. Dillon, *From Eye-Witnesses to Ministers of the Word* (Rome, Pontifical Biblical Institute, 1978), p. 129.
3 Ibid., p. 130. Dillon's study shares the same approach as Hubbard's and Schaberg's on Matthew. The redaction-critical penchant for finding connections throughout a gospel tends to ignore the discontinuities. Of course, searches for the latter run the opposite risk. R. Tannehill's work, while full of fine observations about the total achievement of the Third Evangelist, tends either to minimize differences or to by-pass their significance. See, for example, *The Narrative Unity of Luke–Acts* (Philadelphia, Fortress, 1986), pp. 200, 284, 295–96.
4 I. H. Marshall acknowledges the particular point without making the more comprehensive one: "what was said earlier about the Son of man is now predicated of the Messiah. Thereby the identification of the Son of man in Jesus' teaching with the Messiah in the church's teaching is established." See *The Gospel of Luke*, NIGTC (Grand Rapids, MI, Eerdmans, 1978), p. 905.
5 See C. H. Talbert for the view that Luke's altering the order of the second and third temptations enables him to refer the reader to Gen. 3 and conclude that Jesus as second Adam succeeded where the first Son of God (3:38) failed: *Literary Patterns, Theological Themes and the Genre of Luke–Acts*, SBLMS 20 (Missoula, MT, Scholars, 1974), p. 47.
6 E. Lövestam, *Son and Saviour: A Study of Acts 13:32–37: with an Appendix: "Son of God" in the Synoptic Gospels* (Lund, Gleerup, 1961), p. 104 n. 2.
7 F. Danker, who serves the reader a rich feast of classical allusions pertaining to Luke's Gospel, notes that the centurion's verdict "echoes what the Hellenistic world values most, namely excellence of the highest order, featuring especially magnanimity and integrity, the marks of a truly great benefactor." See his subtle and elegant study, *Luke*, 2nd edn (Philadelphia, Fortress, 1987), p. 106. Luke's skill could net both kinds of readers: the hellenistic Jew familiar with the Wisdom of Solomon and the pagan not acquainted with Jewish literature.
8 Moule, "Christology," pp. 160–61. The exclusion of honorific address, κύριε, is as appropriate here as it was for Mark and Matthew.
9 Although he makes some of these distinctions, J. Fitzmyer's failure

to recognize the greater complexity of Luke's usage leads him to make the common claim that "Luke has time and again retrojected this title into the phase of Jesus' earthly ministry." Has Luke thereby been extremely careless when he reports Peter's assertion that God made Jesus Lord in the resurrection (Acts 2:36)? See *The Gospel According to Luke I–IX*, vol. I, AB 28 (Garden City, NY, Doubleday, 1981), pp. 202–03.

10 κατὰ τὸν νόμον Μωϋσέως (2:22), οἱ προφῆται (16:16, 29, 31), ἐν βιβλίῳ ψαλμῶν (20:42), Μωϋσῆς καὶ οἱ προφῆται (16:29, 31).

11 All nine instances of πίστις also follow the pattern established for Mark and Matthew earlier. The eleven examples of πιστεύω conform to the general pattern, no matter what the source or setting. Never is Jesus himself explicitly the subject of faith. Furthermore, as in the other synoptists, "receiving" language characterizes the post-Easter relation to Jesus rather than "believing" or "following."

12 Such distinctions tend to counter the claim of J. Fitzmyer that the Lucan presentation of Jesus and his preaching "obviously reflects an early Christian understanding of the kerygma in which the herald is already being presented as the one heralded. Luke, in making use of this in the programmatic Nazareth synagogue scene, may be retrojecting back into the ministry and preaching of Jesus a developed understanding of him." See *Luke I–IX*, pp. 153–54.

13 E. E. Ellis, in my view, overstates the point (with most commentators): "The post-resurrection mission is still the mission of Jesus (Ac. 1:1, 'began'; 9:4). In it the same message is proclaimed and the Spirit and the 'name' of Jesus still have the same function. Cf. 4:18; 10:21; Ac. 1:8; 3:16; ...." See *The Gospel of Luke*, NCBC (Grand Rapids, MI, Eerdmans, 1974), p. 15. The "name" of Jesus and endowment with the Spirit are discussed below.

14 It may well be correct to say that Jesus' fellowship at table with sinners implies forgiveness; but that only proves the point. One must infer for the ministry what became only explicit later.

15 A summary of the event, the content of their preaching, the healing ministry, impediments to be avoided, establishing a "base of operation," responses to rejection, a report of their return.

16 Although occasionally the Kingdom of God is the subject of preaching in Acts, it is never that God's Rule has drawn near.

17 F. W. Beare, *The Earliest Records of Jesus* (New York, Abingdon, 1962), p. 156. Beare notes A. Farrer's observation that Luke found typology in Numbers where Moses chose Twelve to represent the Twelve Tribes (1:4–6) and Seventy of the Elders to share his responsibility (ch. 11).

18 E. Schweizer tends to "spiritualize" these statements. Regarding "salvation from our enemies" (v. 71), he says that "Luke probably has in mind temptations." He acknowledges that "[74] The ultimate purpose of God's salvation presupposes deliverance from the enemy [75] but is in fact undisturbed worship": *The Good News According to Luke* (Atlanta, John Knox, 1984), p. 43. Yet, the point is that such worship depends upon political liberation. This calls to mind

God's demand of Pharaoh, "Let my son go so that he may serve me ..." (Exod. 4:23). Schweizer does acknowledge such a level of meaning but apparently ascribes it to a previous tradent, "a Jewish Christian" (p. 44).

19 H. Conzelmann, famous for his theory about Luke's periodizing the ministries of Jesus and the church, acknowledges this disparity: "The introductory chapters of the Gospel present a special problem. It is strange that the characteristic features they contain do not occur again either in the Gospel or in Acts." See *The Theology of St. Luke* (London, Faber, 1960), p. 172.

20 When these distinctions are not observed, then such overstatements become possible: "the infancy narrative sounds initially many of the motifs to be orchestrated later on in the Gospel and Acts. Many of the chords of the Lucan composition are first struck in it: for instance, John as the precursor of Jesus, Jesus as the Savior, Messiah, and Lord." See Fitzmyer, *Luke I–IX*, p. 163. Yet little if anything of what these saints sing has to do with the life of Jesus as Luke recounts it. John the Baptist's query in Q (11:3//7:19–20) fits the situation exactly. Nothing that he knew, whether by Scripture, the expectation of his parents and kin, or direct revelation, had prepared him for what Jesus was doing – or not doing.

21 T. Issachar 5:2, T. Dan 5:3.

22 Mark and Luke report the success of the "free-lance" exorcist using Jesus' name (9:38–40//9:49–50).

23 Fitzmyer, *Luke I–IX*, p. 224, puts it this way: "He has, by all that he was and did, cancelled the debt of guilt incurred by their evil conduct." G. Caird has described the connection another way: "the death of Christ was only the inevitable outcome of the life he had lived. If at the end *he was reckoned with transgressors* (22:37), it was because he had always chosen to be numbered with them. This was the price of friendship with tax gatherers and sinners." See *Saint Luke* (Philadelphia, Westminster, 1963), p. 39. Seeing Jesus' entire life as redemptive has now become a "commonplace" view according to E. Richard in "Luke – writer, theologian, historian: research and orientation of the 1970's," *BTB*, 13 (1983), 6.

24 Modern students of *narrative* are more inclined to see the use of titles as being true to *character* than are redaction critics, who see them as true to the alleged *reader's* interests. See the helpful, but not comprehensive, study by J. M. Dawsey, "What's in a name? Characterization in Luke," *BTB*, 16 (1986), 146. I mention Acts here only because of the tendency to claim parallel themes for the two volumes.

25 For a fuller treatment of this point, see my study, "Supper and wedding," pp. 8–9, 13–15.

26 J. Jervell, although making a different point, notes the different treatment: "In Luke 9:51ff. the Samaritans reject Jesus because of his connections with Jerusalem." See *Luke and the People of God* (Minneapolis, Augsburg, 1972), p. 126.

27 Conzelmann, *Theology*, p. 179 n. 2 acknowledges that the two epochs of salvation are distinguished by different manifestations and roles attributed to the Spirit.

28 A careless reading of Marshall, *Luke*, p. 909 might lead one to infer that διιστῆναι is the means by which "Luke often describes the departure of supernatural visitors." The conclusion could be drawn that Jesus' divinity is suggested by the use here of a quasi-technical term.

29 Fitzmyer, *Luke I–IX*, pp. 827–28.

30 In Acts 1:9–11 the range of vocabulary also includes ἐπήρθη, ὑπέλαβεν, and πορευομένου.

31 The pattern reminds one of Phil. 2:11 where the confession of Jesus as "Lord" is to the glory of *God the Father*.

32 B. M. Metzger, *A Textual Commentary on the Greek New Testament*, 3rd edn (New York, United Bible Societies, 1971), pp. 189–91 for a full discussion of the variants.

33 It is not necessary to settle the debate as to whether αὐτόπται and ὑπρέται are synonyms or references to separate groups. The main point is that the former term shares with ἐνώπιον in John a root that pertains to vision: -ωπ- and -οπ-. Both refer to persons with first-hand acquaintance.

34 Although they cannot be part of the main argument, the linguistic phenomena of Acts corroborate this contention. Some of the Prologue's language occurs in volume II. Of Apollos, Luke says that "he had been instructed [κατηχηένος] in the way of the Lord and with zealous spirit spoke and taught accurately [ἀκριβῶς] the things concerning Jesus, although he knew only John's baptism" (18:25). It was up to Prisca and Aquila to set forth the way of God more accurately (ἀκριβέστερον, v. 26). (Might the description of Apollos provide clues about Theophilus, both in what each possessed and lacked?) Felix himself wanted more precise knowledge about the Way (24:22). Πρᾶγμα shows up only here and at Acts 5:4 (in the singular). Ἐπιγινώσκω will appear six more times in the gospel, all in the narrator's comments but none with the sense of deepening previous understanding (1:22; 5:22; 7:37; 23:7; 24:16, 31). The same is true of thirteen instances in Acts, although 24:8, 11 and 25:10 belong to the narrative. Ἀσφαλεία and its cognates will surface again only in Acts, three times with γινώσκω (2:36; 21:34; 22:30) and once with γράφω (25:26, in Festus' conundrum of what to say to Caesar about Paul).

35 N. Q. King, "The 'universalism' of the third gospel," in *SE*, ed. K. Aland, F. L. Cross, J. Daniélou, H. Riesenfeld, and W. C. van Unnik, TU 73/18 (Berlin, Akademie-Verlag, 1959), pp. 204–5.

36 See the discussion in ch. 1.

37 J. Drury, *Tradition and Design in Luke's Gospel* (Atlanta, John Knox, 1977), p. 13. The author goes on to say, "He has the historian's nose. Above all he shows the need of a community for strong, historical roots, how a talented writer went about providing them, and the problems which such an achievement solves and raises."

38 In treating the phases of Luke's salvation-historical schema, Fitzmyer acknowledges the Evangelist's dividing it into periods that nonetheless maintain a high level of continuity: "What Jesus proclaimed about himself and the kingdom is now continued in the apostolic kerygma and in Luke's own kerygma." See *Luke I–IX*, pp. 181–87, esp. 186. While acknowledging the temporal demarcation, Fitzmyer takes no notice of the kind of ideological and terminological distinctives that I have identified between the phases of Jesus' career and Luke's narrating of them.

39 J. M. Dawsey, *The Lukan Voice. Confusion and Irony in the Gospel of Luke* (Atlanta, Mercer, 1986) applies well-known studies of Lucan language to categories commonly employed by literary critics. Supplementing them with his own analyses, he claims to be able to distinguish the language and style of speech assigned to Jesus, various characters, and the Narrator himself, who is yet different from Luke the Author/Evangelist (pp. 157–83, 13–16). Dawsey concludes that Luke thereby created a narrative full of irony wherein the narrator's exalted prose (e.g. in the Prologue) and glorified *christ*ology contrast sharply with the peasant dialect and reversal *theo*logy of the earthly Jesus (pp. 143–56). Although much of Dawsey's work is congenial to mine, I feel that his case could have been made stronger by a more comprehensive coverage of theologically significant terms. Furthermore, I do not believe that the evidence marshaled necessarily leads to his ironic reading of the Third Gospel.

5 John

1 The expression, used in an entirely different context, comes from C. S. Lewis, *That Hideous Strength* (New York, Macmillan, 1965), p. 228.

2 Only once does πιστεύειν εἰς occur in the synoptics (Matt. 18:6) and there with the pronoun ἐμέ rather than a title. Even in John, "believing in the Son of Man" remains confined to this instance.

3 See the Introduction (ch. 1), pp. 11–16, for fuller arguments.

4 Although this sort of christology, soteriology, and response occurs in many separate statements throughout, all three converge in such notable places as ch. 4 (the encounter in Samaria) and ch. 6 (the Bread from Heaven discourse). Jesus, who reveals himself as the Messiah (4:26), will supply water that keeps on springing up for eternal life (v. 14). Many Samaritans believe and come to know that he is indeed the Saviour of the World (v. 42). Two chapters later, when his scandalous talk produces a great division and departure even among the disciples (6:66), Peter speaking for the Twelve says, "Lord, to whom shall we go? You have the words of eternal life. And we have believed and come to know that you are the Holy One of God" (vv. 68–69).

5 John's manner elsewhere is also evangelistic; that is, he will not allow a point to be missed or misconstrued. He is always at the ear or

behind the elbow lest one veer too far to the left or right. And while the other gospel writers take their liberties as omniscient narrators determined to ensure understanding, John makes them appear altogether diffident.

6 On "the many" who believed in Jesus, see 2:23; 4:39, 41; 7:31; 8:30; 10:42; 11:45; 12:11, 42.

7 The use of John 3:16 in evangelistic efforts often obscures the point when the theme of forgiveness of sins through Jesus' death is read into the passage. It is the one who trusts Jesus as God's supreme revelation who has eternal life and avoids perdition.

8 Thus, what characterizes the response of disciples after Easter is not saving faith but fuller understanding. The revelation itself was adequate enough. But their perception lacked clarity and depth. This deficiency was to be overcome by the Spirit of *Truth* who would aid memory, increase knowledge, and bring about authentic interpretation.

9 Perhaps the best known recent attempt is that by R. T. Fortna, *The Gospel of Signs: A Reconstruction of the Narrative Source Underlying the Fourth Gospel*, SNTSMS 11 (Cambridge, University Press, 1970).

10 D. A. Carson, "Current source criticism of the Fourth Gospel: some methodological questions," *JBL*, 97 (1978), 411–29.

11 R. A. Culpepper, *The Anatomy of the Fourth Gospel. A Study in Literary Design* (Philadelphia, Fortress, 1983), pp. 40–41.

12 G. N. Stanton has called my attention to X. Léon-Dufour who has noted the "two-timed" nature of the Johannine narrative. His examples are fewer and other than mine (the post-Easter accounts do not play a role for him); and he suggests a different motive than I do. By stressing the function of symbols as joining agents, Léon-Dufour claims that the author of the Fourth Gospel meant to connect the reader's post-resurrection revelation of Jesus with the revelation that occurred during his life (not as historically reconstructed, however). Each era has its characteristic vocabulary and meaning. Where we differ most is on the nature of this variation. He sees it as a Johannine hermeneutical device. I regard it as co-extensive with phenomena occurring in the synoptics and attribute it to a narrative function. This is not to deny that Johannine symbolism works in the manner that Léon-Dufour has suggested. I simply claim that John joins the other gospels in distinguishing narrative time in this way. See "Towards a symbolic reading of the Fourth Gospel," *NTS*, 27 (1980), 439–56.

13 Of the twenty-seven prior occurrences of this verb, six involve human senders and two refer to Jesus' action (discussed in this paragraph). The large majority ascribe the initiative to God.

14 Human senders account for only one of the thirty-one instances of this verb (1:22). Jesus speaks of a time when the one whom he sends will be the means of mediating both himself and God (13:20). Otherwise, it is God's action in Jesus.

15 See R. E. Brown's judicious discussion of the range of interpretation in *The Gospel According to John*, AB 29A (New York, Doubleday, 1970), pp. 1,023, 1,036–9.
16 20:2, 13, 18, 25, 28; 21:7. At 20:2 and 13, Mary Magdalene calls him "the Lord", and "my Lord" *believing him to be dead.* Thus, the title *need* not have any direct Easter connections.
17 6:23; 11:2; 12:38 (of God); 20:13; 21:7, 12.
18 22:41–46//12:35–7//20:41–44.
19 4:11, 15, 49; 5:7; 6:34; 11:34; 12:21 (the Greeks to Philipp).
20 6:68; 11:3, 12, 21, 27, 32, 39; 13:6, 9, 25, 36; 14:5, 8, 22; 20:15 (Mary Magdalene to the "Gardener"); 21:15, 16, 17, 20, 21. Barbara Bjelland observes that when the disciples inform Jesus (κύριε) of the obvious (that Lazarus, if asleep, will recover), they do not predicate omniscience of him (11:12). See "John's Portrait of Jesus," an unpublished research paper (Seattle, WA, Seattle Pacific University, Dec. 5, 1986), p. 4.
21 On the division of opinion, see B. M. Metzger, *A Textual Commentary on the Greek New Testament* (London, United Bible Societies, 1971), p. 198.
22 P⁶⁶ does make the identification even stronger with τὸν θεόν, but that very fact suggests scribal interference.
23 J. A. T. Robinson, *The Priority of John*, ed. J. F. Coakley (London, SCM, 1985), pp. 386–87.
24 C. K. Barrett, "'The Father is greater than I.' John 14.28. Subordinationist christology in the New Testament," *Essays on John* (Philadelphia, Westminster, 1982), pp. 11–12. The essay was originally published in *Neues Testament und Kirche, für Rudolf Schnackenburg*, ed. J. Gnilka (Freiburg, 1974), pp. 144–59.
25 2:11, 23; 4:54; 6:2, 14; 10:41; 12:18; 12:37; 20:30.
26 12:33; 18:32. It is Peter's death to which Jesus, according to John, speaks in 21:19.
27 Various persons or groups use σημεῖα to refer to Jesus' deeds: 2:18; 3:2; 6:30; 7:31; 9:16; 11:47.
28 See the rationale given by B. M. Metzger for representing both readings in the UBS text by enclosing σ within square brackets: *Textual Commentary*, p. 256.
29 For a stimulating treatment of text, tense and "christology," see D. A. Carson's study, "The purpose of the Fourth Gospel: John 20:31 reconsidered," *JBL*, 106 (1987), 639–51.
30 Bjelland, "John's portrait," pp. 7–8.
31 A member of the overseeing committee of fifteen editors told me that they deliberately tried to mitigate the possibility of a reader seeing this as a contradiction.
32 Were establishing historical probability the concern of my study, then it would be possible to argue that both John 12:44 and Mark 9:37 could pass through the sieve of the "criterion of dissimilarity."
33 E. C. Hoskyns, *The Fourth Gospel*, ed. F. N. Davey (London, Faber, 1940), p. 430.
34 5:43; 10:25; 12:28; 17:6, 11, 12, 26.

35 14:13, 14; 15:16; 16:26.
36 Three of the twenty-five instances refer to the names of people (1:6; 3:1; 18:10). One of the rest concerns the name of sheep (10:3). The people hail Jesus as coming in the name of the Lord (God) at 12:13.
37 Barrett puts the matter this way, "There could hardly be a more christocentric writer than John, yet his very Christocentricity is theocentric." See "Subordinationist christology", p. 32.
38 See the discussion surrounding Barrett's succinct summation, "Jesus is central, yet he is not final" in "Christocentric or theocentric? Observations on the theological method of the Fourth Gospel," most recently reprinted in *Essays on John* (Philadelphia, Westminster, 1982), p. 8. The essay originally appeared in *La Notion biblique de Dieu: Le Dieu de la Bible et le Dieu des philosophes*, ed. J. Coppens, BETL 41 (Louvain, University, 1976), pp. 361–76.
39 Barrett, "Subordinationist christology," p. 32 claims that "from one point of view the aim of the book is that men may believe that Jesus is the Christ, the Son of God (20:31); yet it is a profounder truth that the aim of the actions the book describes is that men may worship the Father in Spirit and in truth (4:21, 23)." But the issue is more than a matter of depth. There is a dynamic, linear movement of thinking and action in and through time.
40 D. Seeley called my attention to this in a paper read to the Northwest Regional Meeting of the Society of Biblical Literature in Spokane, WA, on April 16, 1988. However, he made an entirely different application of the phenomenon. If I understood him correctly, the separate, fuller explanation of an event or saying corresponds to the Word's/Son's role in exegeting the Father whom no one has ever seen.
41 Clement of Alexandria's distinctions are thereby even less satisfactory than usual. In fact, the fuller statement aggravates the difficulty. Writing the "spiritual gospel" was not simply John's choice; it was inspired by the Spirit: πνεύματι θεοφορηθέντα ποιῆσαι εὐαγγέλιον. Clement's comments were recorded in Eusebius' *Ecclesiastical History* IV.14.5–7. The text quoted from appears in H. Merkel's *Die Pluralität der Evangelien als theologisches und exegetisches Problem in der Alten Kirche*, TC 3 (Bern, Peter Lang, 1978), p. 16.
42 6:64; 13:28. See Culpepper, *Anatomy*, pp. 21–26.
43 Carla Wall, "John's stereoscopic view," an unpublished research paper (Seattle, Seattle Pacific University, 1988). Mrs. Wall argues for a much more elaborate and subtle occurrence of this first- and second-sight phenomenon. But I have chosen to confine myself to the most obvious examples in a manner which accords with the method of the preceding chapters. Nevertheless, her argument warrants more careful attention, and I have benefitted from it immensely.
44 N. Frye, "The critical path; an essay on the social context of literary criticism," *In Search of Literary Theory*, ed. M. W. Bloomfield (Ithaca, NY, Cornell University Press, 1972), pp. 146–47. This essay, unavailable to me, was quoted in Culpepper, *Anatomy*, p. 28.

45 I have borrowed this expression from the title of a collection of sermons and talks by C. S. Lewis. However, I have been unable to find more details from current bibliographical resources.

6 Summary and implications

1 This expression comes from the book by M. L'Engle, *A Wrinkle in Time* (New York, Dell, 1973).
2 W. Marxsen, *Introduction to the New Testament* (Philadelphia, Fortress, 1968), pp. 137, 144.
3 Luz, "Disciples," p. 106.
4 G. N. Stanton, *Jesus of Nazareth in New Testament Preaching* (Cambridge, University Press, 1974), pp. 117–36.
5 *History*, I.22.1. The italics are mine, while the translation is Benjamin Jowett's: *Thucydides* (Oxford, Clarendon, 1881), vol. I, p. 15.
6 See chs. 2 and 3.
7 Matt. 20:28//Mark 10:45; Matt. 26:28//Mark 14:24.

Appendix   The unifying kerygma of the New Testament

Combined here are two articles which I wrote originally for *JSNT*: "The unifying kerygma of the New Testament," 33 (1988), 3–17 and "The unifying kerygma of the New Testament (II)," 38 (1990), 3–11.

1 C. H. Dodd, *The Apostolic Preaching and Its Developments* (London, Hodder and Stoughton, 1936).
2 Ibid., pp. 9–28.
3 Ibid., pp. 29–64, esp. 47–51.
4 Ibid., pp. 77–129 (gospels), pp. 133–77 (Paul and John).
5 R. C. Worley, *Preaching and Teaching in the Earliest Church* (Philadelphia, Westminster, 1967), pp. 27–86. See also the briefer and once sarcastic recital by J. I. H. McDonald in *Kerygma and Didache: The Articulation and Structure of the Earliest Christian Message*, SNTSMS 37 (Cambridge, University Press, 1980), pp. 1–11. The author attributes the initial popularity of Dodd's proposal of a relatively fixed kerygmatic pattern as evidence of a flaw in character: "Such widespread acceptance of a hypothesis that was by no means exhaustively argued suggests that it spoke to some psychological need on the part of the English-speaking theological public" (p. 3). Would such an unfair and unscholarly attitude enable one to recognize and then appropriate contrary evidence?
6 W. Heitmüller, "Zum Problem Paulus and Jesus," *ZNW*, 13 (1912), 320–37.
7 R. Bultmann, *Theology*, vol. I, pp. vii–viii and vol. II, pp. v–vi.
8 J. Rohde, *Rediscovering the Teaching of the Evangelists* (London, SCM, 1968).
9 M. Barth, "The kerygma of Galatians," *Int*, 21 (1967), 131–46; M. Rissi, "The kerygma of the Revelation to John," *Int*, 22

(1968), 3–17; F.F. Bruce, "The kerygma of Hebrews," *Int*, 23 (1969), 3–19.

10 J.D.G. Dunn, *Unity and Diversity in the New Testament* (Philadelphia, Westminster, 1977).

11 Ibid., p. 30.

12 Ibid.

13 Ibid., pp. 30–31.

14 Ibid., pp. 227–28. See also pp. 367–71.

15 The discipline of NT theology has been plagued by a failure to resolve this dilemma, which W. Wrede posed in its sharpest terms nearly a century ago: one must either *describe* the theology *of* the canonical text or *reconstruct* the history (religion) of earliest Christianity *from* the text (and relevant extra-canonical literature). Initial probings suggest that what I have posited for the literature can be demonstrated for the history, too.

16 Such conveniently specific language helps to avoid idiosyncratic, arbitrary, and therefore uncontrolled definition by allowing the authors of the NT themselves to define terms. It also ought to help minimize confusion with terms like "confession" and "creed." But the distinction ought not to be pressed absolutely. One believes and confesses what has been preached.

17 J.A.T. Robinson, *Redating the New Testament* (London, SCM, 1976) and *The Priority of John*, ed. J.F. Coakley (London, SCM, 1985).

18 Bultmann, *Theology*, p. 34.

19 W. Kramer, *Christ, Lord, Son of God* (London, SCM, 1966), pp. 26, 33, 35.

20 Bultmann, *Theology*, pp. 34–37.

21 Ibid., vol. I, p. 300; vol. II, p. 75. See p. 10 above and n. 15.

22 Ibid., pp. 91–92.

23 O. Cullmann, *The Earliest Christian Confessions* (London, Lutterworth, 1944), p. 39.

24 Ibid., p. 36. Cullmann once allows an exception that is fatal to his point: bi-partite expressions (those mentioning God and Christ) are as old as the ones containing only a christological reference.

25 V. Neufeld, *The Earliest Christian Confessions* (Leiden, Brill, 1963), pp. 67, 126. That confession occurs subsequent to and as a condensation of earlier, fuller statements is supported by the NT itself in the near context of an oft-cited text (Rom. 10:10, 14): confession comes after believing, hearing, and preaching.

26 Kramer, *Christ*, p. 46. The point is not that Jews would not need to have God identified for them as Gentiles might. At stake is not the identity of God, but that the God of Abraham, Isaac, and Jacob is the one who raised Jesus. Thus, the theological element seems quite at home in a Jewish environment.

27 B.M. Metzger shows how τὸν θεόν in v. 27 explains the alternatives. See *Textual Commentary*, pp. 456–57.

28 Another example, not explicitly identified as kerygma, occurs in a critical argument of Paul's at Rom. 4:24: "God will (6) credit

righteousness to us (4) who believe (5) in him (1) who (2) raised (3) Jesus from the dead.'' In the next verse, the Apostle again links justification with the resurrection but precedes it by connecting forgiveness of sins with Christ's death. This instance provides a good example of where it would be hazardous to conclude that, because the content of (6) varies (salvation and crediting righteousness), we are faced with two different kerygmata.

29 If this passage reflects a hymn known to Paul and his congregation, then there is evidence for a pre- and extra-Pauline origin for the pattern. Such a traditio-historical consideration will be developed in a subsequent study.

30 See the detailed notes by C. F. D. Moule under Excursus III, "ΠΙΣΤΟΣ Ο ΛΟΓΟΣ,'' in *Birth*, pp. 283–84.

31 The primary textual variants in v. 21, πιστεύοντας or πιστούς, do not affect the point. Their object is the same: εἰς θεόν.

32 Dodd, *Apostolic Preaching*, pp. 104–105 (summarily) and 106–29 (more fully).

33 See the statements lacking (6) at Luke 9:48 and 10:16 (expressed negatively) and John 13:20. Matthew has an exclusively christological saying at 18:5.

34 For a thorough evaluation of this and other standards, see R. H. Stein's, "The 'criteria' for authenticity,'' in *Gospel Perspectives*, vol. 1, pp. 225–63.

35 On the lips of this Jewish saint, a specific messianic designation or direct reference to Jesus would not be appropriate. However, the ultimate significance would not have been missed by the reader familiar with the OT. J. Fitzmyer notes that ἐγείρειν "is used of God's providential summoning into existence favored or anointed instruments of salvation for his people (see Judg. 2:16, 18; 3:9, 15; cf. Acts 13:22). In any case, 'horn of salvation' must be understood here as a title for an agent of God's salvation in David's house, i.e., in a loose sense a messianic title.'' See *Luke I–IX*, p. 383.

36 The textual variants here do not alter the fact that in this editorial comment the thrust is christological.

37 For a summary of this theme with representative bibliography, see J. A. T. Robinson, *Priority*, pp. 349–52.

38 Only in four of the nineteen examples of the kerygma do the writers connect the benefits of God's action with the death of Jesus (1 Pet. 1:18–20; Heb. 13:20; 1 John 4:10; Rev. 12:11). Otherwise, they spring from the resurrection, or in one case from the present work of Christ (1 Thess. 1:10). Historical theologians sometimes use such differences to determine the relative age or ideological contexts of the various expressions.

39 E. C. Hoskyns, *The Fourth Gospel*, ed. F. N. Davey (London, Faber, 1947), p. 430.

40 Bultmann, *Theology*, p. 33.

41 Ibid., pp. 33–92. See ch. 1 above for a fuller discussion.

42 Ibid., p. 33.

43 I should like to acknowledge that, under my direction, two graduate students in the M.A. program at Seattle Pacific University located these examples: Carla Wall (*I Clement*; Polycarp, *To the Philippians*, *The Epistle to Diognetus*, Justin Martyr, *Dialogue with Trypho*) and John Groce (*The Epistle to Diognetus*, *The Acts of Paul and Thecla*). They read in translation all of the Apostolic Fathers, the Ignatian correspondence, Justin's *Apology*, and the NT Apocrypha. It remained for me to confirm their findings in the Greek text and the Latin of Polycarp's *Letter* at ch. XII. However, Justin's *Dialogue* at ch. CXVI and *The Acts of Paul and Thecla* were available to me only in translation. The full references appear below.

44 K. Lake (transl.), *The Apostolic Fathers*, LCL I (Cambridge, MA, Harvard, 1959), pp. 51, 55. The interruption of chs. XXV–XXVI may disqualify this passage, even though XXIV–XXVII are bound by a sustained argument. At LXIV.1, Clement refers to God's choosing Jesus (ὁ ἐκλεξάμενος) rather than his raising him: "Now may (1) God, the all-seeing, and the master of spirits, and the Lord of all flesh, who (2) chose out (3) the Lord Jesus Christ and us through him (6) for a 'peculiar people,' give unto every soul that is called by his glorious and holy name, faith, fear, peace, patience and long-suffering, self-control, purity, sobriety, (4) that they may be well-pleasing (5) to his name" (ibid., pp. 119, 121). Both references to "name" are ambiguous. If they mean "Jesus," then, of course, this example cannot be used, either.

45 Ibid., p. 299.

46 Ibid., p. 298, where the editor notes that *et deum* is absent from some manuscripts. Perhaps, then (on text-critical grounds), it should appear in the apparatus. Although not a difficult reading, it is the more full or specific theologically.

47 Ibid., II, p. 371.

48 J. Donaldson and A. Roberts (eds.), *Ante-Nicene Christian Library* (Edinburgh, T. & T. Clark (1867), vol. II, p. 232. The only Greek text (for CVI) available to me appears, quite fortuitously, in K. Aland's *Synopsis Quattuor Evangeliorum*, 3rd edn (Stuttgart, Württembergische Bibelanstalt, 1965), p. 532.

49 There is another passage (CXVI) where category 2 refers to Jesus' being sent rather than raised (as is the case in the gospel tradition, Galatians, and 1 John): "And though the devil is ever at hand to resist us, and anxious to seduce all to himself, yet the Angel of God, i.e. the Power of (1) God (2) sent to us through (3) Jesus Christ, rebukes him and he departs from us ...; even so we, who through the name of Jesus have (4) believed as one man (5) in God the Maker of all, (6) have been stripped, through the name of His first-begotten Son, of the filthy garments, i.e. of our sins" (Ibid., p. 257).

50 E. Hennecke and W. Schneemelcher, *New Testament Apocrypha* (Philadelphia, Westminster, 1965), vol. II, p. 357.

51 The uncertainty of 1 Clement's contributions reduces to four the number of non-canonical instances of the pattern.

52 Would it be too bold to suggest that this reflects the canon *behind* the canon — that apostolic *verbal* witness to which documents had to conform if they were to belong to the *written* canon?

BIBLIOGRAPHY OF WORKS CITED

Aland, Kurt (ed.). *Synopsis Quattuor Evangeliorum*, 3rd edn, Stuttgart, Württembergische Bibelanstalt, 1965; 9th edn, 1976; 10th edn, 1978

Alter, Robert. *The Art of Biblical Narrative*, New York, Basic Books, 1981

Ambrozic, Aloysius. *The Hidden Kingdom*, Washington, DC, CBA, 1972

Aune, David E. *The New Testament in its Literary Environment*, Philadelphia, Westminster, 1987

"Greco-Roman biography," in *Greco-Roman Literature and the New Testament*, ed. D. Aune, SBLSBS 21, Atlanta, Scholars, 1988, pp. 107–26

Baird, J. Arthur. *Audience Criticism and the Historical Jesus*. Philadelphia, Westminster, 1969

Barbour, Robin. "Gethsemane in the tradition of the passion," *NTS*, 16 (1970), 231–51

Barrett, Charles K. "Christocentric or theocentric? Observations on the theological method of the Fourth Gospel," in *Essays on John*, Philadelphia, Westminster, 1982, pp. 1–18. Originally in *La Notion biblique de Dieu: Le Dieu de la Bible et le Dieu des philosophes*, ed. J. Coppens, BETL 41, Louvain, University, 1976, pp. 361–76

"'The Father is greater than I.' John 14.28. Subordinationist christology in the New Testament," in *Essays on John*, Philadelphia, Westminster, 1982, pp. 19–36. Originally published in *Neues Testament und Kirche, für Rudolf Schnackenburg*, ed. J. Gnilka, Freiburg, Herder, 1974, pp. 144–59

Barth, Markus. "The kerygma of Galatians," *Int*, 21 (1967), pp. 131–46

Beare, Francis W. *The Earliest Records of Jesus*, New York, Abingdon, 1962

"The mission of the disciples and the mission charge: Matthew 10 and parallels," *JBL*, 99 (1970), 1–13

Best, Ernest. *Mark: the Gospel as Story*, Edinburgh, T. & T. Clark, 1983

"Mark's preservation of the tradition," *The Interpretation of Mark*, ed. William Telford, Philadelphia, Fortress, 1985, pp. 119–33

Bjelland, Barbara, "John's portrait of Jesus," unpublished research paper, Seattle, WA, Seattle Pacific University, Dec. 5, 1986

Black, C. Clifton II. "The quest of Mark the redactor: why has it been pursued, and what has it taught us?", *JSNT*, 33 (1988), 19–33

The Disciples According to Mark. Markan Redaction in Current Debate, JSNTSS 27, Sheffield, *JSOT*, 1989

Blomberg, Craig. *The Historical Reliability of the Gospels*, Downers Grove, IL, IVP, 1987

Bornkamm, Günther. *Jesus of Nazareth*, New York, Harper & Row, 1960

"End-expectation and church in Matthew," in *Tradition and Interpretation in Matthew*, ed. G. Bornkamm, G. Barth, and H. J. Held, London, SCM, 1963, pp. 15–51

"The stilling of the storm in Matthew," in *Tradition and Interpretation in Matthew*, ed. G. Bornkamm, G. Barth, and H. J. Held, London, SCM, 1963, pp. 52–57

Bowker, John. "The Son of Man," *JTS*, 28 (1977), 19–48

Brown, Raymond E. *The Gospel According to John*, AB 29A, New York, Doubleday, 1970

"The kerygma of the gospel according to John," *Int*, 21 (1967), 387–400, reprinted in *New Testament Studies*, ed. Richard Batey, London, SCM, 1970, pp. 210–25

Brown, Schuyler. "The secret of the kingdom of God (Mark 4:11)," *JBL*, 92 (1973), 60–74

Bruce, Frederick F. "The kerygma of Hebrews," *Int*, 23 (1969), 3–19

Tradition: Old and New, Grand Rapids, MI, Zondervan, 1970

Bultmann, Rudolf. *Theology of the New Testament*, vol. I, New York, Scribner's, 1951

"πίστις and πιστεύω in Paul," in *TDNT*, ed. Gerhard Kittel and Gerhard Friedrich, Grand Rapids, Eerdmans, 1968, vol. VI, pp. 217–22

Caird, George B. *Saint Luke*, Philadelphia, Westminster, 1963

Carson, Donald "Current source criticism of the Fourth Gospel: some methodological questions," *JBL*, 97 (1978), 411–29

"Christological ambiguities in the gospel of Matthew," *Christ the Lord. Studies in Christology presented to Donald Guthrie*, ed. H. H. Rowden, Leicester, IVP, 1982, pp. 97–114

"The purpose of the Fourth Gospel: John 20:31 reconsidered," *JBL*, 106 (1987), 639–51

Chouinard, Larry. "Gospel christology: a study of methodology," *JSNT*, 30 (1987), 21–37

Conzelmann, Hans. "Jesus Christus," *RGG*, vol. III, Tübingen, Mohr (Siebeck), 1959, 619–53

The Theology of St. Luke, London, Faber, 1960

"Present and future in the synoptic tradition," *JTC*, 5 (1968), 26–44. Originally "Gegenwart und Zukunft in der synoptischen Tradition," *ZTK*, 54 (1957), 277–96

An Outline of the Theology of the New Testament, London, SCM, 1968

Cranfield, Charles E. B. *The Gospel According to Saint Mark*, Cambridge, University Press, 1959

Cullmann, Oscar. *The Christology of the New Testament*, London, SCM, 1959

The Earliest Christian Confessions, London, Lutterworth, 1944

Culpepper, R. Alan. *The Anatomy of the Fourth Gospel. A Study in Literary Design*, Philadelphia, Fortress, 1983

Danker, Frederick. *Luke*, 2nd edn, Philadelphia, Fortress, 1987

Davies, William D. and Allison, Dale C., Jr. *A Critical and Exegetical Commentary on the Gospel According to Saint Mark*, ICC, vol.I, Edinburgh, T. & T. Clark, 1988

Dawsey, James M. *The Lukan Voice. Confusion and Irony in the Gospel of Luke*, Macon, GA, Mercer, 1986

"What's in a name? Characterization in Luke," *BTB*, 16 (1986), 143–47

Dillon, Richard J. *From Eye-Witnesses to Ministers of the Word*, Rome, Pontifical Biblical Institute, 1978

Dodd, Charles Harold. *The Apostolic Preaching and Its Developments*, London, Hodder & Stoughton, 1936

Donaldson, James and Roberts, Alexander. *Ante-Nicene Christian Library*, Edinburgh, T. & T. Clark, 1867, vol. II.

Drury, John. *Tradition and Design in Luke's Gospel*, Atlanta, John Knox, 1977

Dunn, James D. G. "The messianic secret in Mark," *TynBul*, 21 (1970), 92–117

Unity and Diversity in the New Testament, Philadelphia, Westminster, 1977

Ellis, E. Earle. *The Gospel of Luke*, NCBC, Grand Rapids, Michigan, Eerdmans, 1974

Fitzmyer, Joseph. *The Gospel According to Luke I–IX*, AB 28, Garden City, NY, Doubleday, 1981

Fortna, Robert. *The Gospel of Signs: A Reconstruction of the Narrative Source Underlying the Fourth Gospel*, SNTSMS 11, Cambridge, University Press, 1970

The Fourth Gospel and its Predecessor, Philadelphia, Fortress, 1988

France, Richard T. *The Gospel According to Matthew*, Grand Rapids, MI, Eerdmans, 1985

France, Richard T. and Wenham, David (eds.). *Gospel Perspectives*, Sheffield, JSOT, 1980–83

Frye, Northrop. "The critical path: an essay on the social context of literary criticism," *In Search of Literary Theory*, ed. M. W. Bloomfield, Ithaca, NY, Cornell University Press, 1972, pp. 91–194

Gundry, Robert H. *Matthew. A Commentary on His Literary and Theological Art*, Grand Rapids, MI, Eerdmans, 1982

Harvey, Antony E. *Jesus and the Constraints of History*, Philadelphia, Westminster, 1982

(ed.). *Alternative Approaches to New Testament Study*, London, SPCK, 1985

Hay, David M. "Pistis as 'ground for faith' in hellenized Judaism and Paul," *JBL*, 108 (1989), 461–76

Heitmüller, Wilhelm, "Zum Problem Paulus und Jesus," *ZNW*, 13 (1912), 320–37

Hennecke, Edgar and Schneemelcher, Wilhelm. *New Testament Apocrypha*, vol. II, Philadelphia, Westminster, 1965

Holladay, Carl R. *Theios Aner in Hellenistic Judaism: a Critique of the Use of the Category in New Testament Christology*, Missoula, MT, Scholars, 1977

Hooker, Morna D. *The Son of Man in Mark*, London, SPCK, 1967

"ΠΙΣΤΙΣ ΧΡΙΣΤΟΥ," *NTS*, 35 (1989), 321–42

Hoskyns, Edwyn C. *The Fourth Gospel*, ed. F. Noel Davey, London, Faber, 1947

Hubbard, Benjamin J. *The Matthean Redaction of a Primitive Apostolic Commissioning. An Exegesis of Matthew 28:16–20*, SBLDS 19, Missoula, MT, Scholars, 1974

Jeremias, Joachim. *New Testament Theology I: The Proclamation of Jesus*, London, SCM, 1971

Jervell, Jacob. *Luke and the People of God*, Minneapolis, Augsburg, 1972

Jowett, Benjamin. *Thucydides*, vol. I, Oxford, Clarendon, 1881

Kähler, Martin. *The So-called Historical Jesus and the Historic Biblical Christ*, ed. C. Braaten, Philadelphia, Fortress, 1964; first published as *Der sogennante historische Jesus und der geschichtliche, biblische Christus*, 2nd edn, Leipzig, A. Deichert, 1986

Kee, Howard C. *Community of the New Age: Studies in Mark's Gospel*, Philadelphia, Westminster, 1977

Kelber, Werner. "Mark and oral tradition," *Semeia*, 16 (1979), 7–55

King, Neill Q. "The 'universalism' of the third gospel", *SE*, ed. K. Aland, F. L. Cross, J. Danielou, H. Riesenfeld, and W. C. van Unnik, *TU* 73/18, Berlin, Akademie-Verlag, 1959, pp. 204–05

Kingsbury, Jack D. *Matthew: Structure, Christology, Kingdom*, Philadelphia, Fortress, 1975
"The title 'Kyrios' in Matthew's Gospel," *JBL*, 94 (1975), 246–55
The Christology of Mark's Gospel, Philadelphia, Fortress, 1983
Matthew as Story, Philadelphia, Fortress, 1986
"Reflections on 'the reader' of Matthew's Gospel," *NTS*, 34 (1988), 442–60

Kittel, Gerhard. *TDNT*, vol. I, Grand Rapids, MI, Eerdmans, 1964

Koester, Helmut. "From the kerygma-gospel to written gospels," *NTS*, 35 (1989), 361–81

Koester, Helmut and Robinson, James M. *Trajectories Through Early Christianity*, Philadelphia, Fortress, 1971

Kramer, Werner. *Christ, Lord, Son of God*, London, SCM, 1966

Lake, Kirsopp (transl.). *The Apostolic Fathers*, LCL I, Cambridge, MA, Harvard University Press, 1959

Lane, William. *The Gospel According to Mark*, NICNT, Grand Rapids, MI, Eerdmans, 1974

Lemcio, Eugene E. "External evidence for the structure and function of Mark iv. 1–20, vii. 14–23 and viii. 14–21," *JTS*, 29 (1978), 323–38
"The intention of the evangelist Mark," *NTS*, 32 (1986), 187–206
"The parables of the great supper and the wedding feast: history, redaction and canon," *HBT*, 8 (1986), 1–26
"The unifying kerygma of the New Testament," *JSNT*, 33 (1988), 3–17
"The unifying kerygma of the New Testament (II)," *JSNT*, 38 (1990), 3–11

L'Engle, Madeleine. *A Wrinkle in Time*. New York, Dell, 1973

Léon-Dufour, Xavier. "Toward a symbolic reading of the Fourth Gospel," *NTS*, 27 (1980), 439–56

Lewis, Clive S. *That Hideous Strength*, New York, Macmillan, 1965

Lohmeyer, E. *Das Evangelium des Markus*, 15th edn, Göttingen, Vandenhoeck and Ruprecht, 1959

Lövestam, Evald. *Son and Saviour: A Study of Acts 13:32–37: With an appendix: "Son of God" in the Synoptic Gospels*, Lund, Gleerup, 1961

Luz, Ulrich. "Das Geheimnismotiv und die markinische Christologie," *ZNW*, 56 (1965), 9–30

"The disciples in the Gospel According to Matthew," *The Interpretation of Matthew*, ed. Graham Stanton, Philadelphia, Fortress, 1983, pp. 98–128

McDonald, James I. H. *Kerygma and Didache: The Articulation and Structure of the Earliest Christian Message*, SNTSMS 37, Cambridge, University Press, 1980

Manson, Thomas W. *The Teaching of Jesus*, Cambridge, University Press, 1935

Marshall, Christopher D. *Faith as a Theme in Mark's Narrative*, SNTSMS 64, Cambridge, University Press, 1989

Marshall, I. Howard. *Luke: Historian and Theologian*, Grand Rapids, MI, Zondervan, 1970

The Gospel of Luke, NIGTC, Grand Rapids, MI, Eerdmans, 1978

Martin, Francis (ed.). *Narrative Parallels to the New Testament*, SBLRBS 22, Atlanta, Scholars, 1988

Marxsen, Willi. *Introduction to the New Testament*, Philadelphia, Fortress, 1968

Mark the Evangelist. Studies in the Redaction History of the Gospel, Nashville, Abingdon, 1969

Meagher, John. "Die Form- und Redaktionsungeschickliche [sic] Methoden: the principle of clumsiness and the gospel of Mark," *JAAR*, 43 (1975), 459

Clumsy Construction in Mark's Gospel. A Critique of Form- and Redaktionsgeschichte, TST 3, Toronto, Edwin Mellen, 1979

Merkel, Helmut. *Die Pluralität der Evangelien als theologisches und exegetisches Problem in der Alten Kirche*, TC 3, Bern, Peter Lang, 1978

Metzger, Bruce M. *A Textual Commentary on the Greek New Testament*, New York, United Bible Societies, 1971

Moore, Stephen D. "Doing gospel criticism as/with a 'reader'," *BTB*, 19 (1989), 85–93

Morgan, Robert (with John Barton). *Biblical Interpretation*, Oxford, University Press, 1988

Morosco, Robert E. "Redaction criticism and the evangelical: Matthew 10 a test case," *JETS*, 22 (1979), 323–31

Moule, Charles Francis Digby. "The influence of circumstances on the use of christological terms," *JTS*, 10 (1959), 247–63

An Idiom-Book of New Testament Greek, 2nd edn, Cambridge, University Press, 1963

"The christology of Acts," *Studies in Luke–Acts*, ed. L. E. Keck and J. L. Martyn, New York, Abingdon, 1966, pp. 159–85

"The intention of the evangelists," in *The Phenomenon of the New*

Testament, SBT, 2nd ser. 1, London, SCM, 1967. Reprinted from *New Testament Essays: Studies in Memory of T. W. Manson*, ed. A. J. B. Higgins, Manchester, University Press, 1959, pp. 165–79

"On defining the messianic secret in Mark," *Jesus and Paulus: Festschrift für Werner Georg Kümmel zum 70. Geburtstag*, ed. E. E. Ellis and E. Grässer, Göttingen, Vandenhoeck and Ruprecht, 1975, pp. 239–52

The Origin of Christology, Cambridge, University Press, 1977

The Birth of the New Testament, 3rd edn, San Francisco, Harper & Row, 1982

Neill, Stephen and Wright, Tom. *The Interpretation of the New Testament 1861–1986*, Oxford, University Press, 1988

Nestle, Erwin and Aland, Kurt (eds.). *Novum Testamentum Graece*, 26th edn, Stuttgart, Deutsche Bibelstiftung, 1979

Neufeld, Vernon. *The Earliest Christian Confessions*, Leiden, Brill, 1963

Perrin, Norman. *What is Redaction Criticism?*, Philadelphia, Fortress, 1970

Pesch, Rudolf. *Das Markusevangelium*, 2 vols., *HTK* 2, Freiburg, Herder, 1976

(ed.) *Das Markus-Evangelium*, Darmstadt, Wissenschaftliche Buchgesellschaft, 1979

Peterson, Norman. *Literary Criticism for New Testament Critics*, Philadelphia, Fortress, 1978

Rhoads, David and Michie, Donald. *Mark as Story: An Introduction to the Narrative of a Gospel*, Philadelphia, Fortress, 1982

Richard, Earl. "Luke – writer, theologian, historian: research and orientation of the 1970's," *BTB*, 13 (1983), 3–15

Rissi, Mathias. "The kerygma of the Revelation to John," *Int*, 22 (1968), 3–17

Robinson, James M. *The Problem of History in Mark*, London, SCM, 1957

Robinson, John A. T. *Redating the New Testament*, London, SCM, 1976

The Priority of John, ed. J. F. Coakley, London, SCM, 1985

Robinson, William C., Jr. "The quest for Wrede's secret messiah," *Int*, 27 (1973), 10–30

Rohde, Joachim. *Rediscovering the Teaching of the Evangelists*, London, SCM, 1968

Roloff, Jürgen. "Das Markusevangelium als Geschichtsdarstellung,"*EvTh*, 27 (1969), 73–93

Das Kerygma und der irdische Jesus, Göttingen, Vandenhoeck and Ruprecht, 1970

Schaberg, Jane. *The Father, the Son and the Holy Spirit. The Triadic Phrase in Matthew 28:19b*, SBLDS 61, Chico, CA, Scholars, 1982

Schreiber, Johannes. "Die Christologie des Markusevangeliums," *ZTK*, 58 (1961), 154–183

Schulz, Siegfried. *Die Stunde der Botschaft*, Hamburg, Furche, 1967

Schweitzer, Albert. *The Quest of the Historical Jesus*, London, Adam and Charles Black, 1911

Schweizer, Eduard. "The portrayal of faith in the gospel of Mark," *Int*, 22 (1978), 387–99

The Good News According to Luke, Atlanta, John Knox, 1984

Shuler, Philip L. *A Genre for the Gospels. The Biographical Character of Matthew*, Philadelphia, Fortress, 1982
Stanton, Graham N. *The Gospels and Jesus*, Oxford, University Press, 1989
  Jesus of Nazareth in New Testament Preaching, Cambridge, University Press, 1974
Stein, Robert H. "The 'criteria' for authenticity," *Gospel Perspectives*, ed. R. T. France and D. Wenham, vol. I, Sheffield, JSOT, 1980, pp. 225–63
Strecker, Georg. "Zur Messiasgeheimnis im Markusevangelium," *SE* 3, TU 88 (1964), 87–104
  "Literarkritische Überlegungen zum εὐαγγέλιον-Begriff im Markusevangelium," Neues Testament und Geschichte, ed. H. Baltensweiler and Bo Reicke, Tübingen, Mohr (Siebeck), 1972
  "The concept of history in Matthew," in *The Interpretation of Matthew*, ed. G. N. Stanton, London, SPCK, 1983
Talbert, Charles H. *Literary Patterns, Theological Themes and the Genre of Luke–Acts*, SBLMS 20, Missoula, Scholars, 1974
Tannehill, Robert. "The gospel of Mark as narrative christology," *Semeia*, 16 (1979), 57–95
  The Narrative Unity of Luke–Acts, Philadelphia, Fortress, 1986
Telford, W. (ed.) *The Interpretation of Mark*, London, SPCK, 1985
Tödt, Heinz, *The Son of Man in the Synoptic Tradition*, Philadelphia, Westminster, 1965
Tuckett, Christopher (ed.). *The Messianic Secret*, Philadelphia, Fortress, 1983
Tyson, John B. "The blindness of the disciples in Mark," *JBL*, 80 (1961), 261–68
Wall, Carla. "John's Stereoscopic View," unpublished research paper, Seattle, WA, Seattle Pacific University, 1988
Wall, Robert W. "'The finger of God': Deuteronomy 9.10 and Luke 11.20," *NTS*, 33 (1987), 144–50
Weeden, Theodore J. *Mark – Traditions in Conflict*, Philadelphia, Fortress, 1971
Worley, Robert C. *Preaching and Teaching in the Earliest Church*, Philadelphia, Westminster 1967
Wrede, William. *Das Messiasgeheimnis in den Evangelien*, Göttingen, Vandenhoeck and Ruprecht, 1901

INDEX OF BIBLICAL REFERENCES

Ancient Christian Writings

INDEX OF MODERN AUTHORS

INDEX OF SUBJECTS